Frederick Denison Maurice

Christmas Day and other sermons

Frederick Denison Maurice

Christmas Day and other sermons

ISBN/EAN: 9783743349384

Manufactured in Europe, USA, Canada, Australia, Japa

Cover: Foto ©Lupo / pixelio.de

Manufactured and distributed by brebook publishing software (www.brebook.com)

Frederick Denison Maurice

Christmas Day and other sermons

CHRISTMAS DAY
AND OTHER
SERMONS

CHRISTMAS DAY

AND OTHER

SERMONS

BY

FREDERICK DENISON MAURICE, M.A.

CHAPLAIN OF GUY'S HOSPITAL, AND
PROFESSOR OF ENGLISH LITERATURE IN KING'S COLLEGE, LONDON

London

MACMILLAN AND CO.

AND NEW YORK

1892

The Right of Translation is reserved

First Edition, published elsewhere, 1843.
Second Edition, 1892.

TO

BENJAMIN HARRISON, Esq.,

TREASURER OF GUY'S HOSPITAL,

THESE SERMONS,

PREACHED FOR THE MOST PART TO THE PATIENTS

OF AN INSTITUTION

OVER WHICH HE HAS WATCHED

WITH UNCEASING DILIGENCE AND AFFECTION

FOR MORE THAN FIFTY YEARS,

ARE INSCRIBED,

WITH EVERY SENTIMENT OF RESPECT AND GRATITUDE,

BY HIS

OBLIGED SERVANT,

THE AUTHOR.

PREFACE.

It may seem unsuitable to connect the thought of the great Christian Festival with discourses preached to sick and dying people. The first Sermon in this volume will explain why I do not feel the force of this objection. But if it be a valid one, it applies to all; for in all I have spoken to the inmates of the Hospital as if they were interested in every blessing which Christmas-day proclaims to mankind. The title has not been chosen, because I desire to impart to the reader a festal tone of feeling, which certainly is in no wise characteristic of the preacher, but rather to signify that the highest gifts of God, like the days that testify of them, are common gifts which we must be content to enjoy as members of one body with the most ignorant and wretched, if we would enjoy them at all.

Guy's Hospital,
December 15.

CONTENTS.

SERMON I.

CHRISTMAS DAY . . . . PAGE 1

The Word was made flesh and dwelt among us, and we beheld His glory, the glory as of the only begotten of the Father, full of grace and truth.—*John* i. 14.

SERMON II.

THE UNBELIEF OF THE GALATIANS 17

For ye are all the children of God, by faith in Christ Jesus.—*Galatians* iii. 26.

SERMON III.

WHO DID SIN; THIS MAN OR HIS PARENTS? . . 31

And as Jesus passed by he saw a man which was blind from his birth. And his disciples asked him, saying, Master, who did sin, this man or his parents, that he was born blind? Jesus answered, Neither did this man sin nor his parents, but that the works of God should be made manifest in him.—*John* ix. 1, 2, 3.

SERMON IV.

THE FLESH AND THE SPIRIT 46

PAGE

Brethren, we are debtors, not to the flesh, to live after the flesh. For if ye live after the flesh, ye shall die: but if ye through the Spirit do mortify the deeds of the body, ye shall live. For as many as are led by the Spirit of God, they are the sons of God. For ye have not received the Spirit of bondage again to fear; but ye have received the Spirit of adoption, whereby we cry, Abba, Father. The Spirit itself beareth witness with our spirit, that we are the children of God: and if children, then heirs; heirs of God, and joint-heirs with Christ.—*Romans* viii. 12-17.

SERMON V.

THE FOOLS AND THE WISE 56

See then that ye walk circumspectly, not as fools, but as wise, redeeming the time, because the days are evil.—*Ephesians* v. 15, 16.

SERMON VI.

THE KINGDOM WHICH CANNOT BE MOVED 65

Wherefore we receiving a kingdom which cannot be moved, let us have grace whereby we may serve God acceptably with reverence and godly fear; for our God is a consuming fire.—*Hebrews* xii. 28, 29.

SERMON VII.

THE RACE AND THE PRIZE 82

Know ye not that they which run in a race run all, but one receiveth the prize? So run, that ye may obtain. And every man that striveth for the mastery is temperate in all things. Now they do it to obtain a corruptible crown; but we an incorruptible.

I therefore so run, not as uncertainly; so fight I, not as one that beateth the air.

But I keep under my body, and bring it into subjection: lest that by any means, when I have preached to others, I myself should be a castaway.—1 *Corinthians* ix. 24–27.

SERMON VIII.

THE PERFECT SACRIFICE 95

For if the blood of bulls and goats, and the ashes of an heifer sprinkling the unclean, sanctifieth to the purifying of the flesh, how much more shall the blood of Christ, who through the eternal Spirit offered himself without spot to God, purge your conscience from dead works to serve the living God?—*Hebrews* ix. 13, 14.

SERMON IX.

THE SICK MAN'S PRAYER 105

O Lord, I am oppressed, undertake for me.—*Isaiah* xxviii. 14.

SERMON X.

THE CHRISTIAN COVENANT THE GROUND OF NATIONAL EDUCATION 114

Only take heed to thyself, and keep thy soul diligently, lest thou forget the things which thine eyes have seen, and lest they depart from thy heart all the days of thy life; but teach them thy sons, and thy sons' sons. Specially the day that thou stoodest before the Lord thy God in Horeb, when the Lord said unto me, Gather me the people together, and I will make them hear my words, that they may learn to fear me all the days that they shall live upon the earth, and that they may teach their children.—*Deuteronomy* iv. 9, 10.

SERMON XI.

CHRIST IN THE WILDERNESS 131

Then was Jesus led up of the Spirit into the Wilderness, to be tempted of the devil.—*Matthew* iv. 1.

SERMON XII.

COMMAND THESE STONES TO BE MADE BREAD . . . 142

And when the tempter came to him, he said, If thou be the Son of God, command that these stones be made bread.—*Matthew* iv. 3.

SERMON XIII.

CAST THYSELF DOWN FROM HENCE 157

Then the devil taketh him up into the holy city, and setteth him upon a pinnacle of the Temple, and saith unto him, If thou be the Son of God, cast thyself down; for it is written, He shall give his angels charge concerning thee, and in their hands they shall bear thee up, lest at any time thou dash thy foot against a stone.—*Matthew* iv. 5, 6.

SERMON XIV.

THE KINGDOMS OF THE WORLD AND THEIR GLORY . . . 170

Again, the devil taketh him up into an exceeding high mountain, and sheweth him all the kingdoms of the world, and the glory of them; and saith unto him, All these things will I give thee, if thou wilt fall down and worship me. Then saith Jesus unto him, Get thee behind me, Satan; for it is written, Thou shalt worship the Lord thy God, and him only shalt thou serve.—*Matthew* vi. 8, 9.

SERMON XV.

THE ALABASTER BOX OF OINTMENT 184

Now when Jesus was in Bethany, in the house of Simon the leper, there came unto him a woman having an alabaster box of very precious ointment, and poured it on his head, as he sat at meat. But when his disciples saw it, they had indignation, saying, To what purpose is this waste? for this ointment might have been sold for much, and given to the poor. When Jesus understood it, he said unto them, Why trouble ye the woman? for she hath wrought a good work upon me, for ye have the poor always with you; but me ye have not always. For in that she hath poured this ointment on my body, she did it for my burial. Verily, I say unto you, Wheresoever this Gospel shall be preached in the whole world, there shall also this, that this woman hath done, be told for a memorial of her.—*Matthew* xxvi. 6-13.

SERMON XVI.

THE PRINCE OF SUFFERERS 196

Then came Jesus forth, wearing the crown of thorns, and the purple robe. And Pilate said unto them, Behold the man!—*John* xix. 5.

SERMON XVII.

THE UNIVERSAL PRAYER 208

For there is one God, and one Mediator between God and man, the man Christ Jesus, who gave himself a ransom for all, to be testified in due time.—1 *Timothy* ii. 5, 6.

SERMON XVIII.

THE RESURRECTION OF THE SPIRIT 218

Therefore we are buried with Him by baptism unto death, that, like as Christ was raised up from the dead by the glory of the Father, we also should walk in newness of life.—*Romans* vi. 4.

SERMON XIX.

THE RESURRECTION OF THE BODY 226

O death, where is thy sting? O grave, where is thy victory? The sting of death is sin; and the strength of sin is the law. But thanks be unto God, which giveth us the victory through our Lord Jesus Christ.— 1 *Corinthians* xv. 55-57.

SERMON XX.

THE RESPONSIBILITIES OF MEDICAL STUDENTS 235

Now there are diversities of gifts, but the same Spirit. And there are differences of administrations, but the same Lord. And there are diversities of operations, but it is the same God which worketh all in all.— 1 *Corinthians* xii. 4-6.

SERMON XXI.

HUMAN SORROW THE BEST EVIDENCE OF CHRISTIANITY . . 266

Surely he hath borne our griefs and carried our sorrows.— *Isaiah* liii. 4.

SERMON XXII.

THE TRUE REST AND HOPE OF MAN 290

I am the resurrection and the life; he that believeth in me, though he were dead, yet shall he live, and whosoever liveth and believeth in me shall never die. Believest thou this?—*John* xi. 25, 26.

SERMON XXIII.

THE INVISIBLE GUIDE 312

> I will inform thee, and teach thee in the way wherein thou shalt go; I will guide thee with mine eye. Be ye not like to horse and mule, which have no understanding: which must be held in with bit and bridle, lest they fall upon thee.—*Psalm* xxxii. 9, 10.

SERMON XXIV.

THE FEAST OF PENTECOST 324

> If ye love me, keep my commandments; and I will pray the Father, and he shall give you another Comforter, that he may abide with you for ever, even the Spirit of truth.—*John* xiv. 15, 16.

SERMON XXV.

STRENGTH IN WEAKNESS 335

> My strength is made perfect in weakness.—2 *Corinthians* xii. 9.

SERMON XXVI.

THE MUSTARD TREE 347

> Another parable put he forth unto them, saying, The kingdom of heaven is like unto a grain of mustard seed, which a man took and sowed in his field: which indeed is the least of all seeds; but when it is grown, it is the greatest among herbs, and becometh a tree, so that the birds of the air lodge in the branches of it.—*Matthew* xiii. 31, 32.

SERMON XXVII.

THE PRINCIPLES AND METHOD OF CHRISTIAN CIVILIZATION . 362

> Let every soul be subject to the higher powers; for there is no power but of God, and the powers that be are ordained of God.—*Romans*, xiii. 1.

SERMON XXVIII.

THE HINDRANCE TO CHRISTIAN MISSIONS 376

> There is one body and one Spirit, even as ye are called in one hope of your calling; one Lord, one Faith, one Baptism, one God and Father of all, who is above all, and through all, and in you all.—*Ephesians* iv. 4-6.

SERMON XXIX.

DEATH AND LIFE 392

> For if we believe that Jesus died and rose again, even so them also which sleep in Jesus will God bring with Him.—1 *Thessalonians* iv. 14.

CHRISTMAS DAY

AND OTHER SERMONS

SERMON I.

CHRISTMAS DAY.

(Preached at Guy's Hospital.—Christmas Day, 1839.)

The Word was made flesh and dwelt among us, and we beheld His glory, the glory as of the only begotten of the Father, full of grace and truth.—St. John i. 14.

My Brethren,—You that are here to-day, have come together from various places. Many of you do not know each other now, scarcely any of you knew each other a few weeks ago. You have been brought up in different families, perhaps many miles, or hundreds of miles apart. You have had different joys, and different sorrows. Each of you has some ache or sickness of his own. Each of you knows a whole world of things about himself, and knows very little about his neighbours. And yet I can wish you all a happy Christmas to-day. And I know that the words belong to one of you as much as to another. To you that were born here in London, and to him that was born (if there be such a one) over the sea; to you who have a wife and children, and to you who have none; to healthy men, and sick men, be their sickness what it may. It is strange that it should be so; but you know that so it is. These same words 'A happy Christmas to you!' have been spoken this morning by people who never heard of us. The like of them have been spoken in other languages. They have been spoken now for nearly eighteen hundred years. The persons who heard them through all that time, and in all those places, understood that they were addressed to themselves.

It is a pleasant thought, this, that we are not shut up, each in his own narrow circle; that people have some common thing to be glad about, if it were but for a little while; for one day in the whole year. And yet, I think, there would be a sadness in that thought too. It would be sad to feel "We have been brethren in joy for a few hours, but it could not last. In a little time the flood of our private feelings, and sorrows, and sins, broke in upon us, and we were divided and solitary again." It would be better, would it not, if this joy, in which we are all sharers, was one which had something to do with each of us, one which each of us, in his private chamber, had been crying after; something that would give another meaning to our own pleasures, and that would take the sting out of our pains. Then that common day of happiness would be one which we might remember, it would not be a day of twenty-four hours, but a day to last for ever.

Let us see whether Christmas day be such a day as this. You are told what it means in the verse I have just read, "And the Word was made flesh, and dwelt among us; and we beheld his glory, the glory as of the only begotten of the Father, full of grace and truth." These words explain Christmas to us; the Church uses them for that end. But the words themselves are most wonderful—who shall interpret *them*? Perhaps you may say, 'The chapter which you read to us from the desk interprets them. That tells us when and how the Word was made flesh.' You would say rightly; but still that answer would not be enough. It is true that the event which that chapter speaks of, is the event which the text speaks of. But what did that event mean? What does St. John mean when he says THE WORD was made flesh? We turn back a few verses, and we find him saying, "In the beginning was the WORD, and the Word was with God, and the Word was God. The same was in the beginning with God. All things were made by Him, and without Him was not anything made that was made. In Him was life, and the life was the light of men. And the light shineth in the darkness, and the darkness comprehended it not." 'What,' you will exclaim, 'and do such words as these make Christmas day clearer to us? Surely they speak of things almost too deep for an angel to think of. Can you suppose that they will help us poor and ignorant men to understand anything? Christmas day we have kept for many years; old men and children, young men and maidens, have kept it. Must we go back to the beginning of the world before we can learn how to keep it rightly?'

Yes! brethren, I believe that you must give heed to these words if you would know what Christmas day is, or what any day of your lives is, or what you yourselves are, or why you have come into this world, and what you have to do in it. But I believe, also, that they are not hard words; not words which poor and ignorant need turn away from. I am sure they are meant especially for those who find that the things which are told them in books puzzle them very much, and that they cannot make out the sense of what is told them from pulpits; for men who have a livelihood to get by the sweat of their brows; for men whose bodies and minds are wasted by disease. I say this confidently, and I think when you have considered what it is that perplexes you in books and in sermons, you will agree with me. Is it not the *words* you read and hear in them? They float about you; they tell you of something that you are sure you want to know, but you cannot see them or handle them, and the things you can see and handle, do not tell you what they signify. Whence do they come? Who has given them to you? Who has taught you to utter them? St. John reveals the secret. He speaks to us of THE WORD. Of One from whom all words have come; of One in whom the very life and sense of them dwells. " In him," he says, " was life," and not only this, but " the life was the light of men." All the light or intelligence that has ever been in any man's mind, has come from him, has been communicated by him. All those thoughts and questionings with us which words try to explain, are awakened by him. It is he who leads each man to ask, " What am I? Whither am I going? What is it to be a man?' It is he who gives the answer. But this is not enough. We are living in the midst of a strange world; we have eyes and ears to take in the sights and sounds of it; but we do not know what all these sights and sounds have to do with us; what use we are to make of them;

whether they are our masters or our servants. "All things," says St. John, "were made by him, and without him was not anything made that was made." What clear bright sunbeams are these! It seems as if they caught light from the very source of light. This world, that is so beautiful when we look at it, and yet seems so confused when we think about it, was made by him who is the Lord of men; by that Word who inspires their thoughts, who gives them language. Out of him came the light that makes each thing distinct from the other, and the life that brings all things into one. He is the maker of the world, and the interpreter of it.

This is strange and amazing; but it is not all. You are confused about yourselves, and your own lives, and you are confused about the world that surrounds you. But is there no other thought more confusing and overwhelming still? Is there not a whisper in your hearts about One who is higher than yourselves; and higher than the world; about One who is all Powerful and all Right; One who cannot look upon any evil thing, or be satisfied with anything that is less good and holy than himself? Is there no whisper about God? Hear once again: "In the beginning was the Word, and the Word was with God, and the Word was God. The same was in the beginning with God." He then who made the worlds, he who is the light of men, was with God before all things were. He knew the absolute and awful Being whom our lips tremble to speak of; He held converse with Him; He delighted in Him. Yea, he *was* God. This unseen Teacher of men, this source of our light and our life, was perfectly one with Him whom no man hath seen or can see; the brightness of his glory, the express image of his person.

Brethren, am I speaking of things too deep and fearful for men to utter? I should think so indeed, if St. John had not uttered them, and if the Church had not bidden me set them before you to-day. The more deep and awful they seem to you and to me, the better it is for us. Let us pray God that every day we may grow into the feeling which Moses had when he drew nigh to the bush, and was commanded to put his shoes from off his feet, because the place whereon he stood was holy ground. But we shall not have this feeling unless we do approach when God speaks to us and bids us approach him. The coward has no reverence; only a vague dread of something that he thinks will do him harm. If we would tremble with a real holy fear, we must come into the light, and see everything as it stands out beautifully and gloriously, not stay in the darkness, where there are nothing but dim shadows and spectres which frighten us, and which we wish to fly from. St. John warns us of this. After he has spoken of him who is the light of man, he says, "And the light shineth in the darkness, and the darkness comprehended it not." This light is with us, about us, at every hour and moment. It comes to us, and brings a thousand things back to us that we thought were gone for ever—words that were spoken to people who have left the world; acts that no human eye saw; thoughts that passed in the depths of our own souls. You know—you that have been on sick beds—that what I say is true; you know that all these have visited you as you lay at night, longing for sleep and not finding it. And have you not also felt this? 'Now, even now there is an evil near me, clinging to me, that I cannot get rid of: it is part of my own self; if it dies, I must die.' And then how dark the future has looked to you. You have said to yourselves, 'It *may* be better, the light may break in upon it:' you could not wholly lose that hope. But it has grown dimmer and dimmer, and you have feared that the time to come would be darker and more miserable than the time gone by, and you could see no end of it. Here, brethren, is the Light shining in the darkness. Some one there is who has power to recall those things that you thought had perished, to set them clearly and fully before you. Some one there is who is admonishing you of your state now. Some one there is who can enable you to look onward. And, oh! brethren, have you not oftentimes felt, 'He who has *this* power, has another too. He might deliver me out of this evil, even of that past evil which seems to possess me. He might give me a new life in the midst of this death. If I could see and know him, and converse with him, I believe that he would; for he must be good, else why does the evil in me so struggle with him, why does he condemn it?' "The light shineth in the darkness, and the darkness has not comprehended it." It tries to inclose it, and quench it; but in vain. The light is there still, and by it we know what the darkness is.

I have spoken to you in this way, because I know that you have all hearts and consciences, which testify of the presence of Him whom these verses declare to us. I hope that some of you have more than this; but my message is to all, and what I am saying now is true, not only about you who are here, but about all men who have ever been in the world.

"He hath ordered the times before appointed (saith St. Paul), and the bounds of men's habitation, that they should seek the Lord, if haply they might feel after him, and find him." That is to say, God hath placed one man in this period, one man in that; one man in this country, one man in that; but in every age and in every country, He has been, by some means or other, stirring men up to feel his presence, and to inquire after him. And therefore men have said, 'Where is he, and how can we know him? Where does that Word dwell who is speaking to me inwardly, and making me feel that he is my Lord, and that I ought to serve him? Where is he? Is he in the air, or in the clouds; is he in the ocean when it rages against me, or in the woods through which the wind is roaring at night? Who can declare him to me?' This was the question which men were asking of each other; and now they seemed to find him here, now there; now in animals more mean than themselves, which did them good or harm; now in the beautiful lights of heaven, now in the creatures of their own race, who had lived on the earth and left it. Still they sought him, and dreamed of him; but could not discover him. He must be like themselves, they said, and yet he must be most different. He must hate their evil, and yet they wanted one who could sympathise in it. He must bring them together, and keep them as one, and yet each man seemed to need a separate God for himself, to enter into his miseries. Yet all this while "He was not far from every one of them, for in Him," says St. Paul again, "we live, and move, and have our being." Though it seemed as if the thought of his presence confounded them, and made them wretched; yet from that presence came all their light, and their freedom, and their hope. In spite of all disappointments, they could not but believe that he would make himself known, and that their blindness should not hinder them from beholding Him.

"The Word was made flesh and dwelt among us." This is St. John's declaration. He does not invent a great many arguments to prove it; he simply says, 'So it was.' This poor fisherman, who was once upon a time sitting in his father's ship on the lake of Galilee, mending his nets,—this man who was infinitely humbler and less self-conceited now than he was then, says out boldly and without hesitation, 'This everlasting Word, in whom was life, and whose life was the light of men, this Word who was with God and was God, was made flesh and dwelt among us; He whom all nations and kindreds and people have been longing to see, He whom they have been worshipping in the sun and the moon and the stars; He whom their consciences have been confessing and witnessing of, He has actually shewn himself to us; He has been born into the world in a little village in our country; He has grown up among us, we have seen Him, heard Him, handled Him; He has walked about with us, we have had the most intimate converse with Him; we are sure that He was a real man, that He was in all outward respects like us, speaking with a human voice, sensible of bodily fatigue, enduring bodily pain; we are certain that He had all the feelings and sympathies of a man; we are certain that He had friends, that He sorrowed with them and for them, that He cared for little children; in everything He was human.'

"And yet (he adds) we beheld his glory—the glory as of the only begotten of the Father." We are sure that in this man—this poor man, thus entering into our feelings and circumstances,—we beheld the living God. Not *some* unseen power—some angel or divine creature who might have been sent down on a message of mercy to our little corner of the earth, or to us poor fishermen of Galilee—it is not such a being whom we saw hidden under this human form; we declare that we saw the glory of the Father, of Him who made heaven and earth and the sea, of Him who has been, and is, and is to be; of Him to whom all nations and kindreds belong, and who shall be at last acknowledged as the one living and true God of all. We say that the Father revealed himself fully and perfectly in this man, that he was with him before the worlds were, that he held unbroken converse with him while he was upon earth, that he is upon the right hand of his glory now. He told us that when we saw him we saw the Father: the lowliest of men told us so, and we believed him. We are certain that all the Love and Grace and Holiness of God came forth in Him; we are certain that he exercised the power of God; and we are appointed to declare this truth to all men, that they may believe it and rejoice in it. We say that God has made himself known to men, and that in the flesh of Jesus Christ there is a bond between all creatures and their Creator.

That a meek, humble man, who believed that nothing was so horrible as to trifle with God's name, should have spoken such words as these, so boldly, and yet so calmly, with such a certainty that they were true and that he could live and act upon them, this is wonderful. But yet, this might have been, and the world might have gone on as if no such sounds had ever been proclaimed in it. What is the case actually? These incredible words have been believed. In the east, in the west, in the north and the south, men there were, who said, "They are and must be true." Though all their interests went the other way, they said so; though they had to give up the most cherished notions and feelings, they said so; though they had to believe despised men of a despised nation, they said so; though the world was against them and would not leave them quiet in their faith, they said so. The world could not leave them quiet in their faith; for it was not a faith about themselves, but about the world. They did not say, 'The Son of God has been made flesh for *us*.' They said, 'By this act He has redeemed our race, He has declared that mankind is created in Him, that men have a new eternal life in Him. He has proclaimed himself the King and Lord of the universe. And we do not live and die to claim some glory for ourselves because we are good men or saints. If we are good men or saints, it is because we renounce all pretensions to goodness and saintship in ourselves, because we say that all we have is in Him who has been made flesh, and in that flesh has made us one with Him, that we might receive the Spirit of the Father and the Son. If we are saints and good men it is because we will have no honour but what we claim for the poorest beggar who will enter into God's covenant, and put on Christ by holy baptism.' You see, then, it was not a question whether this man or that should hold a certain opinion. The question was, "Who is the Ruler of the world?" The apostles said, "This Jesus of Nazareth is its Ruler." Their words prevailed. The masters of the earth confessed that they were right. Here in England, at the other end of the world, the news was heard and received. Then the day which said the Word has been made flesh and has dwelt among us, became the queen-day of the year. All the joy of the year was felt to be stored up in it. Every man, and woman, and child, had a right to be merry upon it.

And has this right ceased? There are some who will tell you that it has; and it seems the general opinion, that people are not as merry now on this day as they used to be. One says that this is a grievous thing, that we should try if we can to bring back the old times. Another says, 'This cannot be, people are wiser now. They know that one day is no better than another; the thing is to be real Christians in our hearts.' Another tells us 'Christmas day is forgotten, because that of which Christmas day speaks does not signify so much as it once did. It was good for the people who lived a thousand years ago to believe such tales; but we have better and more solid things to care for.' Brethren, I will tell you what I believe is the truth about these notions, which different people will puzzle you with. To those who say, 'Let us bring back the old times—let us be merry as we used to be,' I would say, 'Well! but we cannot be merry merely because we try to be so. We cannot be merry unless there is something to make us merry. If our hearts be glad we shall find ways to express our gladness, but we do not make our hearts glad by pretending that they are so, or by putting on the outward signs of jollity.' Now, this is what men have been endeavouring to do, and they find that it is a vain thing. They have heard from their forefathers that Christmas day was a good day; a day when children and parents, brothers and sisters, should meet together and rejoice; they have, accordingly, met and kept holiday. As long as they remembered that they were kinsfolk, and liked coming together for the sake of greeting old friends, and looking at the happy faces of children, they had the savour of Christmas day in them, even though they might not always recollect in whose name they were assembled, and what his coming into the world had to do with their good fellowship. But by degrees, the song, and the cup, and the dance, which were signs of the pleasure that friends and brothers had in seeing one another, were more thought of than their friendship and their brotherhood; then the joy wasted away, and went so much the faster because they were trying to invent ways of keeping it up. Good hearty English gladness must have some root. If we care about nothing but ourselves, we shall not be merry at Christmas time, or at any other time.

And therefore, brethren, I do not know what those mean who say, that we are to be good Christians in our hearts, but are not to think about Christmas day. That seems to me like saying that we are to be very good Christians for ourselves, but that we are not to care whether our neighbours have any share in the blessing or not. Now how a man can be a good Christian and only be concerned about himself, I do not know. These days are witnesses to all men, everywhere, young and old, rich and poor, of a blessing which God has bestowed upon them : if there be no such blessing we ought to say so plainly ; but if there be, it is a base and miserable thing not to like the plain, simple testimonies of it which come down from generation to generation, and which all alike may own and rejoice in whether they have book-learning or no. And mark this, also, brethren ; they who would cheat us of these days, and send us to a book, though it be the best book in the world, for all our teaching, soon forget that our faith is not in a book, but in Him of whom the book speaks. They forget that the Word is a living person, and that he was made flesh and dwelt among us. These days bear witness of that truth—bless God for them.

Yes, bless God for them! for he is a liar who says that the words which St. John speaks to us to-day, are not as fresh, as living, as necessary now as they were when he first wrote them down. It may be, brethren, that easy, comfortable people make less of Christmas day than they once did. Perhaps they will presently make less of it than they do now. If the Bible be true this was to be expected. If Christmas is a real and true thing it was to be expected. For hear what Isaiah says, and St. Peter repeats the words, " The grass withereth, the flower thereof falleth away, but the Word of our God endureth for ever." As if he had said, 'All that has grown out of this root shall drop off in order that it may be seen how deeply the root itself is fixed in the soil.' We do not keep Christmas in the bright, sunny time of the year, but now in the heart of winter, when everything is bare and dry. And our Lord himself is said to be " a root out of a dry ground," that, indeed, from which all the blossoms of hope and joy are to come, but which must first be owned in its own nakedness before they shall appear. If then, brethren, men have begun to fancy that their gladness has another root than this, it is meet that for a time they should be left to try whether they can keep it alive by any efforts and skill of theirs. If Christmas joy has been separated from Christ, it is no wonder and no dishonour to Christ that it should grow feeble and hollow. But Christmas is not dead, because the mirth of those who have forgotten its meaning is dead. It is not dead for you, it is not dead for people who lie upon beds tormented with fevers, and dropsies, and cancers. It is not dead for the children in factories, and for the men who are working in mines, and for prisoners who never see the light of the sun. To all these the news, "The Word who was in the beginning with God and was God, in whom is life, and whose life is the light of men, by whom all things were made, and without whom was not anything made that was made, became flesh and dwelt among us, entered into our poverty, and suffering, and death,"— is just as mighty and cheering news now as it was when St. Peter first declared it to his countrymen on the day of Pentecost. You want this truth, brethren, you cannot live or die without it. You have a right to it, no men can have a greater. By your baptism God hath given you a portion in him who was made flesh; by your suffering he is inviting you to claim that portion, to understand that it is indeed for you Christ lived and died. You may live as if no such news as this had ever been proclaimed in the world, but it is not the less true that it has been proclaimed, and proclaimed for you. And blessed be God, this proclamation is not made merely through weak, mortal lips; that altar bears a more deep and amazing witness of it than it is possible for these words of mine to bear. There you may learn how real the union is which the living Word of God established with the flesh of man; how truly that flesh is given to be the life of the world. Christmas day declares that He dwelt among us. To those who there eat his flesh and drink his blood, he promises that he will dwell *in* them, and that they shall dwell in Him. This is the festival which makes us know, indeed, that we are members of one body; it binds together the life of Christ on earth with his life in heaven; it assures us that Christmas day belongs not to time but to eternity.

SERMON II.

THE UNBELIEF OF THE GALATIANS.

(Preached at Guy's Hospital.—The 19th Sunday after Trinity, 1839.)

For ye are all the children of God, by faith in Christ Jesus.
GALATIANS iii. 26.

THE Galatians, to whom St. Paul wrote this Epistle, had heard the Gospel from his own lips; and when they first heard it, nothing could exceed their astonishment and delight. St. Paul says they would have plucked out their own eyes to have given them to him. If you consider, I think you will not wonder that it should have been so. These men had been worshipping gods of whom they knew nothing, but about whom they had many guesses. They thought some of them were friendly to them, and some were enemies; they thought they had need to persuade those who were their enemies to forgive them, and to keep those who were their friends in good will to them; they could not tell in what way they should make themselves most acceptable to either, but they had traditions of their ancestors respecting the offerings and sacrifices which were most suitable, and they could add to these new plans of their own. But all this could not prevent the world and their own lives from seeming to them most dark and unintelligible, and miserable. If they thought of the past, there was something in them which said, 'Then, on such a day, you sinned and displeased the gods;' they thought of the present, and every storm which they heard in the heavens, and every sorrow and sickness which befell men upon earth, seemed to testify that there were powers above which were offended with them; they thought of the future, and death stood staring them in the face, and saying, 'You shall one day be mine, and whither I shall lead you none of you can tell.' Supposing some one had come among them and said, 'All this that you believe is a dream, there are no such powers as those you speak of; foolish men have told you of such things, but they do not mean anything; send them out of your minds, take your ease, eat, drink, and be merry;'—supposing some one had said this to them, would it have comforted them, would they have been ready to pluck out their eyes to give them to such a person? Possibly some of them might, possibly for a short time such tidings might have sounded very welcome, and been most heartily received; but in a little time, I think, all would begin to say to themselves —some would have said it at the very first, 'Well, supposing it be so, can you take this secret accuser from within us, can you make out that the things which he says are delusions? What if there are no gods over our heads, there is this tormentor in our hearts, and if you say he is not there, we feel, we know, that you are liars. And if there be no gods that raise the storms and send sickness and suffering among men, yet the storms do rise, and sickness and sorrow do

come, and your words do not change them in the least.
And supposing, as you say, all our dreams about death
are nothing, yet can you deny that death is, or can
you teach us how to hold him off from us, and defy
him? But if you can do none of these things, your
news that there are no gods is worth nothing, yea, it
is most dismal news; for though we know nothing of
them, yet even to think that they are, is some relief
and comfort from the oppression of this world about
us, and our hearts would become hollow and desolate,
and would soon become like the hearts of beasts, if you
took this away from them.' But supposing a man
should have come to them and said, 'These notions of
yours that the winds and the waves are not moved by
themselves, that diseases and sorrows do not come of
themselves, are perfectly true; this witness in your
consciences that there is some one against whom you
have rebelled, is true; your feeling that sorrow, and
misery, and death, are connected with the evil of which
your consciences speak, is true; yea, even the tradition
of your fathers, that there must be some way of reconcil-
ing God to man, and that way an offering or sacrifice,
this also is true. And now I declare to you, that He
who has spoken to you in your consciences, He against
whom you feel that you have rebelled, He who rules
in heaven and earth, has made himself known to us; I
testify to you, that he has sent his own Son to claim
us for his children, that that Son has taken our flesh,
and gone through our sorrows, and died our death,
and has risen again, and is sitting on the right hand of
God. I tell you that this Son hath offered that
sacrifice with which God is well pleased, even the
sacrifice of himself. And now in this Son he hath

declared himself satisfied with men; through him he hath declared that he holds intercourse with men, and that men may hold intercourse with him. That sin, of which your consciences testify, has separated you from God because he is holy, and loving, and pure. But in Christ is no sin, and we united to Christ are righteous with his righteousness. In him he forgives you the past; he gives you a new life now; he promises that that life shall last in you for ever. He has made himself one with you by taking your flesh. In that flesh he has overcome sin and death, and now God in him makes an everlasting covenant with you. He says, "I will be to you a Father in Christ, and you shall be to me children in Christ, and I give you the seal of baptism as an assurance that this is so. And I promise with this baptism to give you my Spirit, that you may be able to feel to me as children, and call upon me as a father."' Do not you see that this would be a different kind of tidings from the others? Do you not see that this met exactly the needs and distresses of their spirits, that this was just the word which they had been waiting and wanting all their lives to hear? But this was the word which St. Paul spoke to them; are you surprised that those who received it should have thought him the best friend they had ever had, yea, should have been willing to pluck out their eyes and give them to him?

A few years, perhaps less, passed away, and these same Galatians began to look upon St. Paul, whom they had so dearly loved, as an enemy. What had happened to cause this change? Had his character changed? Had he shown that what he told others he did not really believe himself? Or had he changed his language, and brought them some other message from that which he first delivered as God's ambassador? No! none of these things had happened. St. Paul's life showed that the Spirit which he said God had poured out upon men governed and inspired his own heart; every day he grew more humble and more loving; every day his assurance became stronger that the word which he spoke was not his own word, but in truth the Word of God. But there had come other teachers among these Galatians, who said to them, 'This Paul has been deceiving you. These words which he has spoken, telling you that you may receive your baptism, as a proof that you are in a new covenant with God, are not true words. If you would have any benefit from God's promises, or from Christ's coming into the world, you must enter into that covenant which God made with the Jews. You must be circumcised, and must keep God's law, otherwise all the blessings which Paul has promised you will never be yours.' Now the persons who brought this report to their ears had many very plausible arguments to urge in favour of their opinion. They would say, 'God made this covenant with his people the Jews. He chose them out of all the nations of the earth more than nineteen hundred years ago. He gave this people a law, and he commanded them to obey it; and he said, if they obeyed it they should be blessed, if they disobeyed it they should be miserable. Do you think it at all likely that he would at once set aside this covenant and this law of his, and that he would send a message to you, men who have been living as heathens, worshipping false gods, that he receives you into his family, and accounts you his children? Do you not see there must be a long preparation for such blessings as these, and that if you would really receive them, and be worthy of them, you must put yourselves into God's school and practise his law, and learn to overcome your wicked dispositions, and be cured of your ignorance. Then, indeed, Christ's coming will benefit you, but not otherwise.' So these persons would speak to the Galatians. And this effect followed. They felt that they had not really lived as if they had those privileges which St. Paul told them of; they had not been living as if God was their Father, and they were his children. Therefore it seemed to them probable enough that all they had heard was a delusion. They could not doubt that there was such a blessing as that which St. Paul had announced, but it seemed as if he had not told them how they were to attain it; as if, in order to get favour with them, he had pretended that they were already possessed of it, and might save themselves the trouble of seeking and labouring after it. Surely these, they said, are good men who put us in the way of procuring this blessing from God. And Paul is an evil man and a deceiver. In proportion to the vehemence of their affection to him before, was the greatness of their dislike to him now.

Brethren, you may think that perhaps these Galatians, though they were fickle in their feelings towards St. Paul, yet showed an humble and praise-worthy temper respecting themselves. Was it not humble of them to think that they were not worthy of those great names and high honours which the Apostle said God had bestowed upon them? Was it not humble of them to think, 'We must do something much more than we have ever done yet to please God and entitle ourselves to these blessings before we assume them as our own'? No, strange as it may seem, this temper which seemed so very humble, was, in fact, the fruit of the deepest pride. They did not like to feel—It is of God's pure mercy and grace that we are made his children. They wished to obtain this privilege by some efforts of their own, instead of receiving it with shame, and wonder, and thankfulness, as a blessing from him. They secretly liked the thought—If we become circumcised, and submit to the law of Moses, and train ourselves diligently, then we shall have a right to account ourselves God's children,—the glory of being so will be ours; whereas, if we believe that we are so simply upon the warrant and assurance of this baptism, the glory is not our own, we have done nothing. This feeling was working secretly within them. They had not found it out in themselves. They gave themselves credit for great modesty and diffidence. But yet it was the secret root of all their thoughts, and their aversion to him who had given them such proofs of love was the natural fruit of it.

St. Paul, who knew them far better than they knew themselves, saw how the case was with them. But he saw more than this. He saw, that if he let the doctrine of these teachers prevail, there would be no Christianity left in the world; the life, death, and resurrection of his Master would have been all in vain. He therefore at once undertook to confute them, and to assert again that truth which they had denied. He showed the Galatians that these teachers were not honouring God's old covenant, but that he was honouring it. God had made a covenant with

Abraham that in him and in his seed all the nations of the earth should be blessed. All the holy men among the Jews had lived and died in the hope that this covenant would be fulfilled. If Jesus, the seed of Abraham, did not fulfil it, none ever had fulfilled, none ever would fulfil it. If he did fulfil it, then Paul had a right to tell all the nations of the earth that they were blessed in Him. The law of Moses, which was made four hundred years after this covenant with Abraham, could not set it aside. It was made to warn people of the sins by which they had transgressed God's covenant. It was given that those who heard it might feel that they were sinners, and might seek to be delivered from sin, that they might feel they had a flesh which was striving against their spirits, and that with their spirits they must cry out for a Lord and friend to help them. It was given that they might seek God's Spirit, and might serve God in the strength of his Spirit, not in their own strength. And now he says God having prepared us in all these ways for his Son, having made us feel that we need a deliverer—need some one to unite us to God—hath sent forth his Son, made of a woman, made under the law to redeem us, that we might receive the adoption of sons. He adds, "Now you are children of God by faith that is in Christ Jesus." 'And when I tell you so, I tell you that God hath been faithful to the covenant and promises which he made to Abraham, and hath fulfilled the purpose of the law which he gave by Moses. And these teachers who tell you that you are not the children of God, who would send you back to the law which was your schoolmaster to bring you to Christ, these men, whatever they may pretend, do not really believe in God's covenant or care for his law. They do not think that He meant anything by them, or had any intention of accomplishing them.'

But, besides his arguments from Holy Scripture, St. Paul would appeal also to their own hearts. When they believed his gospel and were baptized, the Spirit of God had been shed abroad in their hearts. There were outward signs granted them at that time of this Spirit's presence among them. He took possession of their understandings and of their lips, and they were able to speak with other tongues. But a far higher witness than this was given them by the trust and confidence they had in him, and by the willingness they had to serve him. This was the fruit of believing the truth which he preached to them, the truth that they were God's children in Christ. Now did not they know that it was by forgetting this—by not standing fast in the liberty wherewith Christ had made them free, by not calling upon God as their Father in Christ, that they had fallen into strife, and debate, and envying? While they remembered that they were the children of God's covenant they were able to keep his law; they were able to love God with their heart, and soul, and strength, and their neighbour as themselves; when they forgot this, when they began to doubt of it, when they began to think they must do something in order to get the right of being his children, then they lost the feeling that they were spiritual beings, then they lost all fellowship one with another. Then pride, and hatred, and malice, and revenge, which are the fruits of the flesh, took the place of meekness, gentleness, and love, which are the fruits of the Spirit. But if this were so, they were not to lie against the truth;

they were not to say that God had not made them his children, because, by not acting as his children, they had fallen into sin.

Brethren, why do I speak to you of what happened in a country thousands of miles from our own nearly eighteen hundred years ago? How can such a record concern you? Because, this truth which St. Paul preached to the Galatians is precisely the truth which I have to preach to you. Because, if we with our hearts received this truth, it would cause as much thankfulness to God and to those through whom it has been delivered and preserved to us, as it did at first in the Galatians. Because, the very same causes which hindered them from believing this truth, or holding it fast when they had once believed it, are at work in our hearts too. This is the message which we bring to rich and poor, to high and low: "Ye are all the children of God by faith in Christ Jesus." By your baptism you have been admitted into the family of God; the right of calling God your Father has been conferred upon you; the right of believing that he has redeemed you and reconciled you to himself; the right of approaching him at all times and in all places through his well-beloved Son. I know that these are the words which men want to hear; that till they hear them and believe them their hearts will be full either of stupid ignorance and sensuality, or of the most miserable restlessness and confusion, or of both together. I know that I have a right to speak these words, and that I do not speak of myself but upon the authority of God's word, upon the witness of his sacraments, and that his Spirit testifies with your spirits that they are true.

And why then do they seem to men as idle tales? Because they know that they have not been living as if they were God's children in Christ; that they have not been loving him and loving their brethren. Therefore when we tell them of this glorious covenant into which they are brought at their baptism, and of the assurance it gave them that God was their Father, and that they are redeemed by Christ, and that the Spirit is with them to teach them and guide them —to soften and humble their hearts, to fit them for receiving God's word, and for doing all the works he has given them to do, it seems to them as if we were mocking them, as if such things could not be meant for them. And then when any sickness or sudden trial wakens them, for a moment, out of their sleep, they are ready to listen to persons who will tell them that they are not the children of God yet, but, that they may become so by and by, if they will believe or do certain things which they teach them.

Brethren, such words seem most reasonable to men who feel that they have wandered from God's covenant, and have been rebellious and disobedient to him. But they are not true words, they are not God's words, and they will not profit you any more than they did the Galatians. They seem humble words, but it is the pride of our heart which makes them acceptable to us. We feel that if we are indeed God's children, our sin in revolting against a gracious and loving father must be, indeed, terrible, and though it is this faith which alone can enable us to turn to God and believe that he will receive us, yet we do not like to confess how great our departure from him has been. This is pride, and it is pride, also, which leads us to think that by some act of ours, by believing something, or by uttering some prayers, or by doing some works, we can make ourselves children of God; when, in truth, we are commanded to do all these things because we are his children. I beseech you, then, to receive this as the testimony of God himself, made known to you by the death and resurrection of our Lord, ratified to each of you by his baptism, that you are the children of God by faith in Christ Jesus. That is to say, if you believe Christ to be the Son of God, you will, and must believe yourselves to be the adopted children of God in him; one belief includes the other. Either you believe that He who was crucified under Pontius Pilate, and dead and buried, was not the Son of God, or you believe that by those acts he came to claim men as God's children. Be assured that, if you hold this truth fast in your hearts you will grow in the knowledge of all other truth; if you lose this you will lose all other truth; it will become, first, a mere word and name to you, then you will lose the very word and name. Claim this right as God's children, to draw nigh to him as a Father in Christ, and men may tell you what they please about the difficulties and contradictions in the faith of Christians, you will find the great difficulty, the eternal contradiction, is to be without Christ; without a mediator. You will find that all other doubts and contradictions disappear as your own mind gets clearer and brighter, and you will look forward to a perfect day in the clear brightness and sunlight of which they will vanish altogether. Claim your rights as God's children, not deterred from doing so by the feeling of your own past sinfulness, but humbly acknowledging that before him as the ungrateful return of a child to its loving Father, and your whole lives will gradually become clear and happy. Every work you have to do for yourself or for your fellow men you will feel is his work. It may be a high occupation or a low. It may be the service of the most high and honourable profession, or the service of the labourer, still it will be the service of a Father, that to which he has appointed you, for the good of his children. You will go about with the confidence that you have his Spirit working with you, both to will and to do, making the labour of your minds or the labour of your hands alike a labour of love. Claim this privilege, of being God's children, and you will find, indeed, that you have mighty temptations to struggle with—a world, and a flesh, and a devil, fighting with you day by day and hour by hour. But you will find, also, that the great effort of all these is, to rob you of the faith and feeling that you are the redeemed children of God; you will find that God has provided you with means for strengthening and deepening that faith in you, for enabling you to live in conformity with it, for enabling you to overcome every enemy. Claim this privilege of being God's children, and every relation in which God has placed you here upon earth will be changed into a new relation. You will look upon your parents as the witnesses of God's presence with you, as the bonds to connect you with the past, and make the thought of it not painful but joyful. You will look upon the relationship of brothers and sisters as witnesses of that bond which has been established between you and all mankind in Him. You will look upon the relationship of husband and wife as a witness of that love which is between

Him and his Church — of that union which he established in his death and resurrection, and which will go on becoming more intimate through eternity. You will look upon children as connecting you with the times to come, when you shall have passed out of this world, but when God's love shall not have passed from it, but shall be still watching over it and binding those who are in it with those who have left it. Finally, this faith of being God's children will hallow every work, and thought, and affection, and cross, and will prepare you to understand more and more what it is to be formed in his image, and how, by beholding that image in his Son, you may be changed into it from glory to glory.

SERMON III.

WHO DID SIN: THIS MAN OR HIS PARENTS?

(Preached at St. Pancras Church.—August, 1841, for the North London Dispensary.)

And as Jesus passed by he saw a man which was blind from his birth. And his disciples asked him, saying, Master, who did sin, this man or his parents, that he was born blind? Jesus answered, Neither did this man sin nor his parents, but that the works of God should be made manifest in him.—St. John ix. 1, 2, 3.

The question which our Lord's disciples proposed to him on this occasion was a very natural one. They had been taught that every transgression received a just and exact recompense; that the law if it were violated by disobedience must be fulfilled in punishment. It had been one great object of the Jewish history to fix this lesson on their minds. And though they knew that sin might be forgiven, and put away, when the offender humbled himself before the Lord, yet they knew also that absolution from guilt was not necessarily connected with deliverance from its outward consequences. David was pardoned for his adultery and murder; a clear conscience and a right heart were given him; but the child of his sin died, and the sword never departed from his house. Moreover the national crimes of the Jews had always brought upon them national judgments. The words of the commandment against idolatry, that the sins of the fathers would be visited upon the children unto the third and fourth generation, had been literally accomplished; and the sensuality, corrupt practices, and evil education of one age, could be distinctly traced in the misery of the next. Was it then strange that men, with these facts before them, should carry the analogy into all the cases which fell under their observation; that they should suppose every instance of physical suffering to be the result of some moral evil, and that their only doubt should be, whether that evil was to be sought for in the sufferer or in his parents? Oftentimes the relation between sin and disease was evident. Was it not honouring God to presume that it existed always, and to feel a certain degree of alienation from any one who bore about him the signs of the divine displeasure?

The feeling was undoubtedly most natural. Yet if the disciples had looked carefully into those records which seemed to warrant it, they would, perhaps, have found a correction of it. The law, it is true, denounced regular and certain punishments against those who transgressed; but those punishments proved that the Jew had been taken into a divine order—that by this order he was united to his neighbours and to his Lord, and that every act which injured them was an outrage against Him. Judgments were, in like manner, brought down upon the nation generally, when its members forgot the relation in which they stood to each other; by the rebellion of children against parents, the indifference of parents to their children, the infidelity of wives and husbands, the feuds of brothers. So that every sentence in his law, and every fact in his history, reminded the Jew that he should not look upon himself as a separate creature, having separate interests from his countrymen; that the sins of each man affected the commonwealth; that the suffering of every member was the suffering of the whole body. Now the disciples knew that this blind man was their countryman; they should have known, therefore, that if his blindness came from the sin of himself or his parents, that sin was affecting them, was doing injury to their country, was to be mourned for by all who loved it. Whatever might be the right or the wrong of their speculations about the divine counsels, this principle which immediately concerned their own conduct was certainly true, and any maxim which hindered them from acting upon it was certainly false. They might make some other good use of their notion respecting the connexion of physical suffering with sin; this use they certainly could not make of it; they had no right to let it interfere with the thought that every suffering and every sinful Jew was their brother.

This feeling of the disciples, then, was not true, because it was natural; like many natural suggestions, it had an evil root, and though they might propose it to their Lord for the wise purpose of being satisfied for ever by a word from his lips, yet it showed that they had studied in another school than his. He had often, you will remember, encountered this temper before. He had encountered it in express words. "Think you," he said, of those Galileans, whose blood Pilate had mingled with their sacrifices, "that they are sinners above all the Galileans? or that those eighteen upon whom the tower in Siloam fell are sinners above all that dwell in Jerusalem? I tell you nay, but except ye repent ye shall all likewise perish." This was the true remedy for the disease of judging men by the accidents that befel them. 'These accidents are meant as warnings to yourselves. You cannot tell what they signify in reference to the past life of those whom it pleases God they should visit. You can get a meaning and a warning from them in reference to your own future life. These judgments are God's voice against sin, not against that sin of which you imagine other men are guilty, but against that of which you know you are guilty.' Nothing could be added to these words as an appeal to the conscience against the falsehood and hypocrisy of that mode of judging which seemed so pious and reasonable. But the evil fruits of it required a different treatment. A man might reason himself into the conviction that he was really as guilty as any diseased man whom he saw suffering God's chastisements, and that, therefore, he ought not to withhold his compassion. But what hearty sympathy could grow out of such a calculation as this? How easily the conscience might be bribed to favour the suppression of it by the hint that, after all, there must be some good cause why this particular individual was taken out of the common condition of humanity. Now little as the disciples had yet penetrated into the mystery of their Lord's being, they were convinced that He hated sin infinitely more than they did—that He had seen infinitely further into the divine counsels than they had—that all his words and acts revealed the mind of the Most High. Surely, then, they must have expected that every sickness would rise up before Him stamped with the black mark of the sin which had produced it—that the loathing which the suspicions of other men taught them to entertain, would be inconceivably aggravated by his knowledge—and that as He could not apply to Himself the warning and the call to repentance which the divine judgments contained for them, He would not hesitate to show how entirely he sympathised with the sentence of God's justice. How strange it must have seemed to them that the deaf man, the palsied man, the lunatic, were those towards whom he testified the most continual tenderness and affection—that the leper, whom God's law had forbidden to approach any one, could dare to approach him—that there was no line drawn even in the cases of those whose diseases had been produced by self-indulgence, or were connected with moral corruption—that the unclean spirit was cast out, the madman, whom no man could bind, restored to his right mind, the sick man, who laboured under the conscience of a heavier burden, relieved from that also by the still mightier exercise of power, " Son, thy sins be forgiven thee."

The first sight of these acts, (if any reflection upon their nature was not lost in the mere admiration of the power which was shown forth in them,) must have been very startling. But gradually an impression will have been left upon the minds of those who beheld them with honest faithful hearts, which they must have felt to be right, however little able they might be to reconcile with it notions which they had adopted previously. They had thought of God as the punisher of sin. These miracles taught them to look upon him as emphatically the deliverer from it. They had believed that plagues and sufferings were the effects of sin. Christ taught them that they were, indeed, the effects of it, but that on that very account He who desires to rescue his children from the cause, is also willing to set them free from the effects; that all things came originally from his hands free from disorder and contradiction, and shall be restored to that state again; that only the evil Will which refuses his mercy shall be left to its darkness and misery; and that, in the meantime, the restoration of health and peace is a more wonderful witness of his presence than the loss of them. Such was the lesson which must have slowly, but surely, worked itself into their minds as they perceived that our Lord, instead of standing aloof from human calamities, entered into the very depths of them—instead of treating them as the sentences of God's wrath, which he was to ratify, spoke of them as the bondage of Satan, which he was to unloose.

But the language of the text leads us, I think, to the discovery of a higher truth than even these acts would, of themselves, have made known. This man, says our Lord, is born blind, not for the sins of himself or of his parents, but that the works of God should be made manifest in him. As if he had said, 'You wish to penetrate into the meaning and the purposes of God. You wish to know why he appointed this special calamity to this individual man. I will gratify your curiosity. I will tell you the ultimate end of this infliction. It is that the love and power of God may shine forth in this man to you who see him, and to generations that are to come. You thought that this blind man was one from whom you might turn away, because contact with him might be mischievous to you. I tell you that he is sent here to be your benefactor. He has been without light so long himself, that he might impart a new light to you. Learn to look upon him with reverence, as one who is intrusted with a special message from God to you.'

There are several ways in which the works of God might have been made manifest in this man. His blindness was a manifestation to other men of the source and the preciousness of their sight. It was a witness to them if they would have received it, that common, daily blessings are not things of course; that they are not less, but more wonderful than those which come to us suddenly; that He who gave sight can withhold it; and therefore that every time in which men are able to take in the wonders of earth and sky, would be, if they were in a right state of mind, a fresh occasion for thanksgiving. The dull, useless eyeballs are a silent and perpetual admonition of these truths. It is a sad blindness in men that the lesson does not reach them, but whether it do or not, God means it for them. He is in this way manifesting his works through every blind man.

Again, the subsequent history of this sufferer teaches us another way in which God's works were manifested in him, not merely for other men's good, but for his own. There are many striking traits in the character of those whom our Lord healed while he was upon earth, which are recorded by the Evangelists with their usual simplicity, and which we do not easily forget. The Syrophenician woman—the woman who had suffered from the issue of blood—the leper who returned to give glory to God,—are all living pictures in the minds of those who have read the Gospels with any interest and affection. But there is no character of which we have so clear and beautiful an outline, as that of this blind man. His answers before the Jewish Sanhedrim; his words, "One thing I know, whereas I was blind, now I see;" above all, his answer to the question, whether he believed on the Son of God, "Who is he that I might believe on him?" are as touching indications of brave, simple faith, as any that we meet with in the whole Bible. Now the discipline which had brought out all these qualities was surely, if anything deserve that name, a work of God. Physical suffering had produced its intended effect. A softening, sanctifying power had gone forth with it. The loss of the outward eye had led the man to desire more that his inward eye might be opened, and with it he had been able to read more of the meaning of God's word than those who had been poring over it for years.

But though both these exercises of divine power may be hinted at in our Lord's words, unquestionably they refer most directly and obviously to the miracle which he was about to perform. The great work of God which was to be manifested in the blind man was that which restored him to sight. His life up to that moment had not been a wasted one, but yet it may be truly said, that he existed for that moment, that till it arrived the purpose for which he was sent into the world had not been made evident. Then it was indeed clearly displayed. He was one of those whom God had chosen as an instrument for declaring his Son to men, for proving that light was come into the world, and that the Man of Sorrows, while he entered into all the calamities of the poorest of his creatures, had all power in heaven and earth.

Perhaps it may seem to you that *this* view of our Lord's words can have no possible application to our own circumstances. They seem to have been directed first against a Jewish prejudice, and secondly to have been used in illustration of a miracle. The prejudice, it may be said, has in all probability passed away. At any rate, it would not influence any enlightened persons now, and the use of miracles ceases as soon as they have convinced us of our Lord's divine authority. I do not think either of these positions is true. I fear that a feeling very like that which led the disciples to ask, "Did this man sin or his parents that he was born blind?" prevails as much in England as it did in Judea; as much among the most cultivated classes as among the most ignorant. And I am convinced that we have much to learn from the miracles of our Lord, after we have adopted, or think we have adopted, the most assured faith respecting his person and his offices. I will say a few words on each of these points, and then speak of the charity on behalf of which I am to solicit your help this morning.

I. It is very true that we are not in the habit of referring every sickness, as the Jews did, to a divine judgment. Whether the change is owing to greater clearness in our minds respecting the ways of God, or only to a more utter forgetfulness of Him and unwillingness to believe that He has anything to do with the ordinary affairs of men, is a question of some importance, and one which each should diligently ask of himself.

But without entertaining any notion of God's displeasure, we may commit the same injustice and uncharitableness which the Jews committed when they attributed outward evils to it. We may not indeed dwell much upon the thought that sickness and suffering spring from guilt or imprudence, for these belong to all classes. We feel that in judging harshly of them, we should be condemning our kinsmen and ourselves. But are we not very apt to associate poverty with imprudence and guilt? We have seen numerous instances in which it could be traced to those causes. Is there no inclination in our minds to fasten upon these instances, and to make them reasons for abstaining from any troublesome efforts of compassion, any zealous exertions to diminish the amount of misery? Nay, do we not feel the more disposed to recollect these facts and to make these excuses, when we see poverty and suffering multiplying around us? When we are living in a village where there are a few cases of want that seem easily to come within our reach, we are less anxious to trace out all the circumstances of carelessness or improvidence or positive evil which may have helped to aggravate the distress. But when we are surrounded with a whole mass of suffering human beings in a great city, it seems as if our consciences could find no comfort till we had persuaded them that really all this calamity was chiefly owing to the thoughtlessness and the intemperance of the sufferers; that it was the sin either of them or of their parents that they were born poor. Alas! we can discover evidence enough in support of our position. If we are cunning in seeking out these reasons against benevolence, we shall be sure to find them. There is all this recklessness and self-indulgence that we complain of. It is true that where the poverty has become most fearful and terrible, these moral evils may be found side by side with it—each continually reproducing and augmenting the other. But before we draw the inference which seems to some to follow inevitably from these premises, before we stint our charity on account of our neighbour's sin, it would be needful to inquire whether the self-indulgence which we accuse him of, though different in form, is greater in reality than that which we practise ourselves; whether it is more inexcusable because it is practised by those who are more ignorant; whether it is only then to be pardoned when we have no sharp stings of suffering to urge us into it. We should have to inquire further, whether the greatest or the first sin was in the poor man or in his parents; whether we who have not helped to cure his improvidence, helped to supply some healthful satisfaction to the cravings of nature, helped to awaken other and nobler cravings, and to satisfy them with the bread of life, have not the worst sin to answer for and to repent of. We ought to inquire, lastly, whether this misery, to whatever cause it may be owing, above all if it be owing, as we say it is, to moral corruption, is not the misery and plague of our nation, the misery and plague therefore of ourselves, and whether if we shrink from the responsibilities which the sight of it involves under pretences, however plausible, it will not visit every class, in some terrific national judgment. We may then, I think, learn a lesson, not inapplicable to our own condition, from the ignorance and prejudice of our Lord's disciples.

II. But I believe a still more important lesson is contained in his own words. "Neither did this man sin nor his parents, but that the works of God might be made manifest in him." I cannot think that we turn the records of our Lord's acts upon earth to their right account, when we look upon them merely as strange and portentous evidences of his Messiahship. No doubt they were this. They proved that the poor and humble man, who was sailing in the ship on the Lake of Gennesareth, was Lord of the winds and waves. They proved that He who himself felt hunger and thirst, was he who gave bread to his people; and gave them the living power to receive it, and to be nourished by it. But this was not merely a demonstration for that day; to silence the unbelieving Pharisee and Sadducee. It was an evidence to all times who it is that is with the sailors on the deep, who it is from whom we receive every day our daily bread. And therefore, too, those powers of healing which he exercised, were not merely witnesses to those who saw them, that a great Prophet had risen up among them, and that God had visited his people. They are witnesses to all who read of them at this day, from whom it is that the gifts of healing come; who it is that enables the cripple to walk, and takes away the impediments from speech, and bids the fever and the madness depart. As the poor man reads of them in his Bible, or hears of them in the church, he feels and knows that a power, silent, mysterious, gracious, is about his bed; and, that through whatever human hands the blessing may be administered to him, it comes down at last from the Great Physician and Lord. And just so far as this belief prevails, is it intelligible to us why the Physician does not mainly resort to mechanical contrivances for the purpose of dealing with disease—why he studies mysterious processes and powers, and knows that by acting upon them he is producing the outward effects which he desires upon his patient. We believe that a God of order is the prime mover in all the changes of the human frame, and therefore we can believe that the processes by which he acts are mysterious, and invisible, and orderly.

It is then a work of God that sickness should be healed in our day, as much as it was when our Lord openly and visibly wrought his cures upon the bodies of men. And if the sight and feeling of these cures help men to acknowledge God, we have a better reason why physical suffering exists, than we can ever discover by regarding it as a punishment for individual sin. We may look upon every suffering person as existing in order that the works of God may, by some means or other, be made manifest in him.

But we are never to forget that our Lord's miracles, though in the highest sense the *works of God*, were also the *works of man*. That as one object for which they were performed was to teach men to refer all things to an invisible source, another, which could not be separated from it, was to prove that the invisible being was manifesting himself in human acts; that the Lord of all had taken their own flesh, and become their brother. In like manner it is our business and duty to believe that the acts of mercy which He performs now on earth take place through human agents and instruments, and that one great purpose of them is to connect men by closer ties of affection, of reverence, and of sympathy with those of their own kind. Let us believe, my brethren, that in this sense men are born poor and blind, that the works of God may be made manifest in them. Let us believe that the poor shall never cease out of the land, because we need them to awaken in us those sympathies and charities which it is the highest grace of God to communicate to his creatures. Let us think, when we see any form of sorrow or sickness, The man who is enduring these things is suffering for my sake—suffering, to awaken in me feelings that might else be dormant—suffering that I may be drawn into closer ties of brotherhood with my fellow men—suffering that I may seek for more of the mind and spirit of Him who lived and died for him and for me—suffering that I may know more of the meaning of the Covenant of Baptism into which he and I have been admitted—suffering that I may learn to feel how far more blessed it is to give than to receive—suffering that I may enter more into the mysteries of that communion, which rich and poor, high and low, are invited to partake of together, in the body and blood of their suffering Lord.

My brethren, if these be the uses of affliction and poverty, not only to those who feel it, but still more to those who behold it and have the power of relieving it, I feel that I am doing you the best of all possible services when I tell you of any means by which your charity towards your poor and sick brethren may be profitably exercised.

In the district which surrounds your church, there are thousands of sick and suffering people. You have an opportunity of showing to-day that you do not look upon their sickness and their poverty as sins. You have an opportunity of showing that you have received the benefit which they are meant to confer on you. You have an opportunity of making yourselves God's instruments in these works of mercy which he has intended should be made manifest through those whom he, for our sakes, has afflicted. This dispensary has been working for years silently and unobtrusively; its blessings are felt by hundreds; its funds are very inadequate to the demands which are made upon them.

You cannot say that it is a distant object lying beyond the range of your daily experiences and ordinary sympathies. You cannot say that it is a party object appealing to any narrow prejudices. It rests its claims on the ground that those whom it helps are your countrymen, your neighbours, your brethren. It is not safe to reject such claims. The influences of the world are very hardening; whenever you forego an occasion of doing good, they become more irresistible. The cry of the poor must either be heard by us, or it will ascend up against us into the ears of the Lord of Sabaoth. May he not answer it in judgments! rather may He dispose your hearts to love your brethren for his sake, and bestow upon each of you the blessing of the cheerful giver.

SERMON IV.

THE FLESH AND THE SPIRIT.

(Preached at Guy's Hospital.—The 8th Sunday after Trinity, 1839.)

> Brethren, we are debtors, not to the flesh, to live after the flesh. For if ye live after the flesh, ye shall die: but if ye through the Spirit do mortify the deeds of the body, ye shall live. For as many as are led by the Spirit of God, they are the sons of God. For ye have not received the Spirit of bondage again to fear; but ye have received the Spirit of adoption, whereby we cry, Abba, Father. The Spirit itself beareth witness with our spirit, that we are the children of God: and if children, then heirs; heirs of God, and joint-heirs with Christ.—ROMANS viii. 12.

ST. PAUL is telling us here that there are two masters, either of whom we may serve, but one or other of whom we must serve. Christ is one, sin is the other. Christ is the Lord of our spirits. If we claim him for our Lord and serve him, then we must live as if we were spiritual beings, trusting, hoping, loving, holding our bodies in subjection: if we serve sin, then the body becomes the master and the spirit dies; we eat, and drink, and sleep; faith, hope, and love, perish. "But," says St. Paul, "it need not be so with any of us. Christ the Lord of our spirits saw that the spirits of men were dead within them, that they were living as mere fleshly creatures, and he came down and lived on this earth and died on it that he might deliver these spirits out of death, and bind them to Him." "Now," adds St. Paul, if we do believe this, and do verily claim Christ for our dead and risen Lord, "then we are debtors, not to the flesh to live after the flesh:" that is to say, we are debtors, but this flesh, this evil nature of ours is not our creditor, we owe it no service, we are not bound to please it and follow its will; it is not our lord, it is our slave. But we are debtors still, we are debtors to Him who has redeemed us and made us one with him; we owe to him the free service of the spirit, the service of trust, and hope, and love. And this is a debt which we shall go on owing and paying through eternity, and which we shall always love to owe and be able to pay, because there will be always fresh love to call forth ours, and to bind us closer to him. This is what St. Paul means by the first words of my text. Now let us consider them a little more particularly, and also those which follow them.

You see St. Paul declares that there is a spirit within every one of you. You would all have known this if he had told you, at least, you would have known it in a certain way; you would not have had a happy comfortable knowledge of it, but you would have had a restless painful feeling of it. All men have had this; you and I have had it. Every poor savage on the earth who had never heard of a soul, or of Christ, has strange thoughts within him; he cannot tell whence they have come or whither they are going. He sets out with his bow and arrows to get himself food, and he thinks this is his business. But while he is out on his hunt, wonderful feelings come upon him;

some of them are feelings of anger and revenge against men who he thinks have injured him; some of them are stranger still, as if he heard one speaking to him and telling him, 'That is wrong; you ought not to have those feelings of revenge, those men are your kinsfolk and brethren;' sometimes they are feelings of kindness and affection towards those who are of his own flesh and blood, or have done him a kindness. And then, along with all these, are thoughts of some great spirit who must have sent him these thoughts, and these reproofs, and these feelings of affection, but whether he sent this revenge into him also, or not, the poor man cannot tell; oftentimes he thinks Yes, but when he is happiest he says No, it cannot be. All this goes on in the poor savage, and therefore whatever he may fancy about himself or other people may fancy about him, he is not sent into the world mainly to hunt for food or to cook it, or to eat it. There is a spirit in him, and he wants some one to meet that spirit, and speak to it, and tell him what it is, and what is to become of it. And what was in this man, I say, has been in you, and in me. Yes, and those things which we have in common with the savage, do more concern us than many of the things in which we boast of differing from him. He may never have seen a city, and we may have lived all our lives in one; he may know a very few things, and we may have heard about a great many. But, depend upon it, these questionings in his heart are more to him than all these things would be if they were given him at once, and if we understand the matter rightly, they are more to us. These thoughts that stir within us, these feelings and cravings and wants which all these things that we see and hear do not satisfy, these are worth all the world to us if we only know what to do with them, if we only know to whom we can carry them. I do not say they make us happy, they do no such thing, they have made you very restless and unhappy, and you know it. But yet they are the way to happiness, and the man who is without them, never can be happy. A hog may be a happy creature, but a man who makes himself a hog never can be, for he was not meant to be this, but something else.

You see then what I mean when I tell you that there is a spirit in each of us, and that we should all have felt this to be so in some way or other, even if the Scripture had not told us about it. The Scripture is not sent to tell us this, but it is sent to tell us who is looking after these spirits, and what he has done for them—what he is doing, what he means to do for them. It is sent to tell us how these spirits may be free instead of being in bondage, how they may live instead of dying, how they may be at peace instead of being at war.

This is what St. Paul is speaking of. "We are debtors," he says, "not to the flesh to live after the flesh." We are not bound to live as if eating, and drinking, and sleeping, and getting money, were the business of our lives; for if we do this we shall die: that spirit within us which is longing, and striving, and hoping,—which wants an immortal Being to sympathize with it, this will die within us; every day will make its struggles for freedom weaker; every day will put heavier chains upon it, every day will make it more degraded and wretched, till at last it will die; that which was the life of it will go away, its hope will go, its love will go, and yet it will last on in this state of death, and when the body leaves it, that will not end its misery; its death will continue, a death that is felt and known by it, though it can feel and know nothing else. It will feel that it has not peace, or joy, or God, and that it was meant to have them, and that it has lost them. Brethren, this death is going on around us at every moment, God grant that it may not be going on within any of us. You see the breath leaving men's bodies continually; you see them carried out before your eyes; it is a mournful sight, but still, if that be all, the end of so much suffering is surely blessed rather than grievous. But, oh! do you not see men dying about you in another way? Do you not see sinful habits and inclinations extinguishing the life of their spirits, destroying the affections and good desires and longings after God that were once in them? Do you not see this death and unbelief in all good things creeping over men's spirits? Do you not see a subtle poison getting deeper and deeper into their hearts, and at first making a fever there, then leaving all bitterly cold? I said, do you not see it? I should have said, have you not felt it? Do we not know that such changes as these, worse, ten thousand times worse, than a change from the most perfect health to the most miserable sickness of the body, have gone on within us? Have we not known what it is to have life dying and death living in our hearts?

And if so, my brethren, where was the help? what was the end of it? This is what the Scripture is written to tell us, this is what St. Paul is preaching to us here. He says this death need not come over you; it need never have overtaken you; and yet in the very jaws of it there is still a deliverer. He into whose name you are baptized, of whose death you are made partakers, he who died that your sin might die, who rose that your spirits might rise and live, He is still with you, the Lord of your spirits, still unchanged and unchangeable. Believing in him, claiming that right in him which he gave you in baptism, and which he has never withdrawn from you since, claiming your union with him who has died unto sin once, but who now dieth no more, for death hath no more dominion over him, your spirits may shake themselves free from this oppressor who is holding them down. Death shall have no dominion over them, as it hath no dominion over him; sin shall not be their master, as it is not his. With your spirits you can trust in him, with your spirits you can hope in him, with your spirits you can rise up with him and ascend with him, and reign with him. And then if they have tasted this liberty they would wish to enjoy it continually; and that they may do so they will desire to mortify the deeds of the body, which has kept them from enjoying it and would keep them from enjoying it still. They will desire to give up their spirits to be ruled by his Spirit, to be filled by him with all holy desires and good thoughts, and prompted to all just works.

Feeling themselves to be spiritual beings they will feel that they want this mightier Spirit to guide them continually, to teach them how to know themselves, and know their brethren, and know God.

They will feel that they need him to dwell with them continually wherever they are, whatever they are doing. They will feel, therefore, that they need that he should be renewed in them day by day, and they feel that they may ask for this renewal, because, being led by the Spirit of God, they are the sons of God, and because Christ has said, "If ye being evil know how to give good gifts to your children, shall not your heavenly Father give the Holy Spirit to them that ask him?"

Now, the nature of this Spirit, and his effect upon us, St. Paul describes in these words: "Ye have not received the spirit of bondage again unto fear, but the spirit of adoption whereby we cry Abba, Father." When you first felt that you had spirits, and you did not know what they were, or how you came by them, a strange fear took hold of you. You felt as if you were very wonderful beings, and yet it seemed very terrible to be so wonderful; you wished you could be like the other creatures without any such spirits. Then, after this, you find that these spirits are in bondage. They want to be free, but they are not; they want to be thinking, and hoping, and loving, but they cannot. They have fallen under some power which hinders them from doing what they would. You begin to ask, What brought us into this bondage? and the answer which comes is, Sin brought us into this bondage. We have lived separate from God, and therefore have we fallen into it. But this answer very much increases our fear, and that fear itself becomes a new and a most terrible bondage. You see then what St. Paul means when he speaks of a spirit of bondage again unto fear. And what is to banish this spirit from us? Nothing can but believing that the God from whom we have revolted, against whom we have sinned, has himself sent to claim these spirits for his children, to take them out of their bondage, to make them free and happy again. This is the good news which your baptism preaches to you, and which we on the warrant of your baptism declare to you, that God has adopted you to be his children, that he has sent his Son to bring you into his family, and that, therefore, through Christ you may call him Abba, Father. And it is while you are calling him so, and feeling to him as a Father, that his Spirit beareth witness with your spirit that you are the sons of God.

If you live away from your Father's house you shall never know that he is your Father. If you come to him and draw nigh to him as a Father you shall feel that he is one. So that this spirit is given to us that we may be able to pray to him saying, Our Father, and to trust in him as a Father, and while we do this we know that we have his Spirit. You must not wait to pray to him till you think that you have this Spirit to pray with. You must believe that you have it and pray because you believe so, and then you shall know that you have it. Believe that you are not debtors to the flesh, to live after that flesh, but that you are united to Christ, and bondsmen and debtors to him; and act as if it was so, thanking him for having redeemed you and blessed you, and then you shall rise above the flesh and be able to mortify the deeds of it, and be able to trust in him. Do not say, I will crush my evil inclinations and desires when I have something better in me than them. But be assured that there is something better in you, and lay hold earnestly of that with your heart's desire, and then in God's strength cut off every right hand and pluck out every right eye which hinders you from possessing it. Do not say, If we are God's children we will call upon him, but say, We are, and therefore will we call upon him.

And do not stop even here. St. Paul says, If we are children then are we heirs, heirs of God and joint-heirs with Christ. What does this mean, brethren? If you think that I cannot tell you, and you may well think this, come to that altar, and let God tell you what it means. This mystery of being heirs of God, of entering into his love and joy, this mystery of being joint-heirs with Christ, of being partakers with him in his life and his death, is the mystery of that holy sacrament to which I have just invited you. It is a mystery which angels may desire to look into, and into which they can see but a very little way, and yet it is a mystery in which every poor suffering child of Adam is besought and conjured by God himself to be a sharer.

All that I have been saying to you this morning, all that I have ever said to you about life and death, the flesh and the spirit, Christ and sin; about that Spirit which is given to us, that we may be the sons of God; about the blessedness of calling him Father, all this is contained in that holy feast. I speak it to you in words here, God speaks it to you indeed there. It is not a vain thing: it is your life. It is offered not to others but to you, to you who are here this day. A suffering Lord and Master presents to you, suffering men, the pledges of his having been one with you, one in your sorrows, one in your death. He gives you these tokens that you belong to him, that he has purchased you, and redeemed you of old, and that he is now bearing you in his bosom, and if you will submit to him will carry you home to his fold. Then you will know what indeed it is to be heirs of God and joint-heirs with Christ; what it is to see him who was the Lamb slain upon earth, surrounded by his saints in heaven, and sitting down to the marriage feast with those whom he has brought out of much tribulation, having washed their robes and made them white in his blood.

But you may know something of it now, you may be joint-heirs with him now. He is seeking to make you so by making you partakers of his sufferings. Oh! understand his gracious and loving purpose. Receive this second token of your sonship; this baptism of fire by which he confirms and makes effectual his baptism of water, and to which also he adds the seal of his Holy Spirit. Receive it as his own call to you to take up the privileges of children, to come to him in faith as those who know that they are not debtors to the flesh to live after the flesh, but to the Spirit to live after the Spirit, as those who believe his own sure word, that if they suffer with him, committing the keeping of their souls to him as to a faithful Creator, they shall live and reign with him for ever.

SERMON V.

THE FOOLS AND THE WISE.

(Preached at Guy's Hospital.—The 20th Sunday after Trinity, 1839.)

See then that ye walk circumspectly, not as fools, but as wise, redeeming the time, because the days are evil.—EPHESIANS v. 15, 16.

IN the words immediately before those which I have just read to you, St. Paul had told the Ephesians that all things were made manifest by the light; wherefore he says, Awake thou that sleepest, and Christ shall give thee light. And then he adds, "See that ye walk circumspectly, not as fools, but as wise." Here then is contained the secret of wisdom. There is a light about every man, and a darkness about every man. As there is a light in the sun, without which our eyes would be useless, and would not show us anything; so there is another light, without which our understandings would be useless, and would show us nothing. This is that light which makes known to a man what is passing in himself. This is the light which shows little children to know when they have done wrong, and causes them to tremble and be ashamed. This is the light which has frightened men with thoughts of the past and of the future. This is the light which will not let them go on comfortably and peaceably in following their own selfish plans and inclinations. This is the light from which men run away into pleasure and vanity and sin, because they dare not look at it. For as there is a light, so there is a darkness about all of us. A man can hide himself from this light if he will; he may busy himself about a multitude of things, and forget it a while altogether —forget it till his strength fail him, and he can do these things no more, and he become sick or disappointed: then the light begins to scare him again, and he must find some other way to get rid of it. A man may even tell himself this light is not there. 'That which seems to lay bare these evil thoughts within me is nothing but some words I heard long ago from my nurse, or from my mother.' And he can persuade himself of this, and half believe it; nay, he may die in this thought, holding the light firm down in his darkness, till the darkness covers him in altogether. Nay, he may do more even than this: he may tell himself that this light comes from his own understanding, that it is he himself who has been so clever as to find out all his own sin; yea, he may compliment himself upon being a sincere and honest man for acknowledging it, and being content with it. Nevertheless, brethren, the light is there entering into the hearts and understandings of each of us; and St. Paul says that a man is a fool who turns away from this light, or denies that it is there, or boasts of it as his own, and that he is wise who opens his heart to this light, and permits it to lay bare the evil that is in him, and confesses that it is a good and glorious light, and believes that this light is Christ himself, who is the light of the whole world, and in whose brightness all things are bright. Awake, he says, thou that sleepest, thou that art lying hid and buried in thy darkness, only receiving this light into thee to scare thee in thy dreams. Awake, own this light of Christ which is shining upon thee; go up to it, invite it to come to thee, and it will come to thee, and scatter thy darkness, and fill thee with its own clearness. If thou once understandest that there is actually a living person speaking to thee through thy conscience, that he is thy Lord and thy friend, then will this miserable feverish, restless dream of thy life be at an end, thou wilt be an honest, living, waking man. The light which seemed to thee so terrible, will be the only thing which gives thee comfort. Thou wilt feel that it cheers and warms thee, as well as shows thee where thou art going. Instead of flying from thy home to get out of its reach, thou wilt come to it from all the confusions and perplexities which surround thee, to dwell in it for ever.

Now then you may see a little what wisdom is, and how poor men and rich men, high men and low men, may all be wise, or may all be fools. This light of Christ is that which hath distinguished everything, that which hath given to everything its order and its beauty and its life. If thou wouldst see anything in its order and beauty and life, it must be by conversing with this light; it must be by drawing near with thy heart to him in whom all wisdom dwells. Christ is nearer to thee than he is to all those things that thou seest about thee; nearer to thee than he is to the sun and the moon, and the stars, for he made them to glorify him, but thee he made to know him, and be like him. If then thou wouldst understand them, seek first to be acquainted with him; but if you do not want to understand them, you should at least enjoy them, for they are given to the peasant as much as to the scholar, and that you may enjoy them, you must first enjoy him who created them. But before you can do either of these things, you must know yourself, and be at peace with yourself, and here is He who is the great teacher about thyself, and the great peacemaker. Believe that He who is speaking to thee in thy heart and conscience, is thy friend, and Lord, and brother, one whom thou mayest trust, one whom thou mayest rest upon in all troubles, one whom thou mayest fly to in all temptations, one who can purge thee from all sins; and thou hast the secret both of knowledge and of peace. You no longer need be a coward, refusing to acknowledge the sin that is in you, trying to justify it, and making excuses for it: you will long to confess it, that you may be delivered from it, and you will know that as your sin was living apart from your righteous Lord and friend, our goodness is to trust in him, and live at one with him. This is the wise life; the other is the foolish mad life.

Now then you will see what St. Paul means by exhorting the Ephesians to walk circumspectly, not as fools, but as wise. This good news had been declared to them, Ye are children of the light and of the day: Christ, the light of the world, has showed himself in the world, that you might know him and claim him for your Lord and your light. You have been baptized, or, as they used to say at that time, "illuminated," brought out into the light. Now then remember this, remember that upon you this light is continually shining. As surely as the sun is shining over your heads, and making plain to you the ground at your feet, so surely is this other brighter light with you at all times, so surely is it marking out a clear bright track for you to go in, and making all your thoughts and all your doings clear and distinct. But remember that the darkness is also about you, just as much about you as about any heathens who never heard of this light. Our new position does not make the least difference in this respect; it only makes us understand better how around us and within us there is something which shrinks from this light, which hates it, and which would drag us down into itself, and keep us shut up for ever. This is your state,—the state of men who have Christ near them, and may believe him, and trust him, and become one with him, and whose hearts may grow clearer and brighter every day, and who have the world with you, and sin and self with you, and may grow at one with them, and become darker and narrower every day. In God's name, if you are reasonable beings, be circumspect, have your eyes about you, be thinking with yourselves, 'What is it which is likely to separate me from this light? What is it which is likely to harden and stupefy, and deaden this heart within me? What is it which is likely to blind me, so that I cannot discern this light? What is it which is likely to derange my spirit, so that I shall hate it?' My brethren, St. Paul knew there were acts which he might do, that there were thoughts which he might cherish, that there were feelings and habits which might grow into him, that would have this effect. He knew it about these Ephesians—I know it about myself and about you. I know that there are lusts in your hearts and in mine, to which we may yield, and that if we do yield to them, there will come a blindness and deadness and stupidity over us which will make us incapable of beholding this light, and therefore will make all things else confused and dim to us; yea, most confused and dim when we fancy we have marked them out most accurately. I say then, be circumspect. These lusts are ready to spring out upon us, and overcome us. They are able to put on fair faces and seemly guises; they are able to present themselves as natural, reasonable, nay, laudable. Know and thoroughly consider with yourselves what you are doing when you listen to them. Know that you are making a lie, that you are quenching the light within you, that you are determining not to be wise but fools. There is again in each of us connected with these lusts a disposition to delight in the things which our eyes see and our ears hear and our hands handle, and to say, These are our gods. Be circumspect. This disposition is in one of us and in all of us; at every moment it is working within us. Give it its head, let it have its way, and this light is no longer owned and honoured. You fancy you trace it in the pictures and images of the world, and truly all the brightness they have comes from it; but in pursuing them, you lose the light itself; you cease to own Christ as the Lord of your hearts; you see him broken and divided into a thousand forms; you do not feel that he is the light of men; you forget that you are a man; you become the slave of the world, and He would make you its master. Again, there is in you, and in me, and in every man, a Spirit of pride, which is ever waiting and watching about us, ready at every moment to persuade us to exalt ourselves, to boast that we are something when we are nothing, deceiving ourselves. Be circumspect. This spirit lurks in corners where you think not that it dwells; when you fancy that you are furthest from it, then is it nearest to you. When you think that you have vanquished it, then has it got you most surely within its gripe; and when you have let it prevail, it doth not only make you turn from the light, but hate the light. There is nothing it would not do to put out this light for ever, because it witnesses of our insignificance and meanness, because it tells us that we are beasts, when this pride would make us out to be gods.

But if we have such enemies about us at all times and in all places, what securities have we against them? St. Paul speaks of this in the next clause of the verse, where he says, "Redeeming the time because the days are evil." By time here he means the season, the occasion, the opportunity. He means to tell us that we are surrounded with seasons, and occasions, and opportunities, for bringing us into acquaintance and fellowship with this light, for delivering us out of this darkness. But these seasons, and occasions, are in the midst of days which, in themselves, are evil, and which will be evil to us, if we do not buy up or redeem these occasions out of them, and by so doing turn them to good. The witnesses for God are in the very midst of all the things which oppose and contradict Him. "Out of the depths," says David, "have I cried unto the Lord." In the depths of his confusion, and despondency, and despair, he discovered one of God's occasions, or opportunities; he redeemed it, and his soul rose out of the darkness into the light. See that you do the like. Look upon any trouble or confusion which besets your mind as a season in which God would be speaking to you, seize this season, buy it out from among the evil by which it is surrounded: so will the very things which would make you foolish and forgetful of God, help you to become wise. In the midst of the noise and tumult of this city you see God's churches rising up, speaking of his name, testifying to you of the light which is shining around you, inviting you to come and claim your place as children of the light. Here is an occasion, a season vouchsafed to you that you may redeem out of the evil days. Do not let it go. Prize these proofs that God is, indeed, among us, that he is still the Lord and King of our nation. You know not how long this witness may stay among you. You know not how soon God may leave us to worship the mammon which we have loved better than him. Oh! while it is the light let us walk in the light, for indeed the days are evil, and will be more evil yet. Around us there are men combining with each other not for love but for destruction. Yet God spreads his table for us in the midst of our enemies; he invites us to meet as brethren, at his feast of love, he promises to give us his spirit of unity within us, he gives us the sacrament of the body and blood of his Son. Redeem the occasion; lay hold of this blessed season; prize God's sacraments, for the days are evil. Men are binding themselves in the devil's sacraments, and, if we are not circumspect, we may be binding ourselves in them too. I have told you a few occasions that we are, especially, to redeem —a few of the tokens of God's light, and God's presence, which, if we will use them aright, may keep us from becoming fools in forgetting and denying him. And these occasions, if you rightly profit by them, will turn all others to gold. Evil days of sickness, evil days of solitude, evil days of ungodly company, evil days of national calamity, will all be turned into blessings, will all be means in God's own hands for leading us nearer to himself, for teaching us to trust him more entirely, to know him and love him better. For the path of the just is as the shining light that shineth more and more unto the perfect day. And those who have walked circumspectly, cleaving to him who is the only true wisdom, the only clear light, and redeeming all occasions which he gives them, will see him, when he shall appear as the true Sun of the world, and when all evil and darkness shall have passed away for ever.

SERMON VI.

THE KINGDOM WHICH CANNOT BE MOVED.

(Preached at Southampton.—August, 1835.)

Wherefore we receiving a kingdom which cannot be moved, let us have grace whereby we may serve God acceptably with reverence and godly fear; for our God is a consuming fire.—HEBREWS xii. 28, 29.

IT can scarcely escape the observation of any one who reads the Evangelists, that our Lord is continually speaking of a kingdom. Each of his parables is intended to illustrate some mystery of his kingdom. When his disciples went forth on their first mission, they were to preach his kingdom. When he was examined before Pontius Pilate, every question and every answer had some relation to his kingdom. When he was hanging on the cross his enemies were compelled to see him designated as King. Besides all this, his forerunner came in the wilderness declaring the approach of his kingdom. And, after his ascension, his apostles went everywhere, speaking of that kingdom as already come, and speedily to be ratified by a judgment on the nations, especially on his own. The constant recurrence of such expressions should, surely, lead us to some earnest questionings respecting their import. We may easily explain them away, or substitute for them some loose phrases of our own, but it is not easy to satisfy ourselves that language which Christ and his apostles used habitually, and which they seemed to think big with meaning, language, too, which connects itself with all which we read in the Old Testament, and with the analogy of God's dealings—it is not easy to satisfy ourselves that this language has not some great and serious signification for us who live in this day.

In our text we find the writer of the Epistle to the Hebrews using it, not accidentally, but in close connexion with all that he had been saying throughout his letter, and, especially, in those magnificent chapters of it, this and the foregoing one. In that splendid muster-roll of holy Israelites, contained in the eleventh chapter, each person is identified as a faithful descendant of Abraham, by his sharing in that hope of a city having foundations, whose builder and maker is God, by which the founder of the nation was sustained. And in the twelfth chapter, when he exhibits those whom he had been previously bringing before us in long and grand procession, as a united body of spectators watching with intense interest the race and the conflict in which their brethren below were engaged, in this chapter, after many cheering exhortations to the Christians of Palestine not to be disheartened by trials, which were the signs of their adoption, and means of their purification, and many solemn warnings not to let a fleshly Esau spirit grow up among them and produce an indifference to their glorious birthright; he winds up the whole with the wonderful passage, "Ye are come unto Mount Zion, to the innumerable company," and then in the words of my text assumes that fact as the basis of an exhortation. "Wherefore we, receiving a kingdom which cannot be moved, let us have grace to serve God acceptably, with reverence and godly fear, for our God is a consuming fire."

I propose, to consider, *first*, what the apostle means by saying that we receive a kingdom which cannot be moved.

Secondly,—how this is a reason for seeking grace, that we may serve God acceptably, with reverence and godly fear.

Thirdly,—in what way this representation of God as a consuming fire, becomes a confirmation of our faith, and an additional reason for seeking this grace.

I am to inquire, *first*, what the apostle means by saying that we "receive a kingdom that cannot be moved."

I. You will see at once that this question is not, whether the kingdom of Christ is hereafter to be manifested or acknowledged in some remarkable manner. That expectation it may be lawful and cheering to entertain, but our text does not suggest it. It speaks of Christians, even in that day, as receiving a kingdom—it teaches those to whom the Epistle is addressed, that their faith in this kingdom, their confident persuasion of its reality, the assertion of their privileges as members of it—were the most certain tests of true discipleship. On the other hand, doubts respecting the existence of this kingdom, ignorance of the grounds upon which it rested, indifference to the position which they occupied in it, they are told again and again, were symptoms of present heartlessness, and coming apostasy. What, then, is meant by this kingdom? and how does the inspired writer prove its establishment?

In the beginning of the Epistle it is affirmed, that He who was born at Bethlehem, and died on Calvary, was no mere superior, angelic person, such as some of the Hebrew teachers, tinctured with Rabbinical fables, had dreamed that He might be; but that He had been repeatedly addressed before his coming in the flesh, by titles appertaining only to Godhead. With equal earnestness it had been asserted that this same person was an actual man, that his birth was a real birth, his death a real death, that by everything He did, He asserted a participation in the lot of those whom He was not ashamed to call his brethren. The writer of the Epistle had gone on to show, how this man, thus uniting together the invisible Godhead with humanity, was fitted to fulfil the office of a perpetual High Priest, substantiating all that had been shadowed forth in the priesthood of Aaron—how He that had been the perfect priest had also been the perfect sacrifice—how he had entered into the true holiest of the holies, the presence of the absolute and invisible God—how by this means he had established a perpetual intercourse between heaven and earth—had made it possible for man to approach with a pure conscience and a clean heart into the presence of God, and possible for God to hold communion by his Spirit with the spirit of man. It had been shown how hereby the first covenant, which had dealt with man as a fleshly creature, had been set at nought, and how a new covenant had been established with him as a spiritual creature—" Behold I will write my laws in their hearts, and in their minds will I write them, and I will be to them a God and they shall be to me a people "—how the law of a carnal commandment had been transfigured into another law, carrying with it the power of an endless life. It is upon this grand and solid foundation that all the subsequent assertions and exhortations of the letter are built. Our Lord had declared, in the days of his flesh, after St. Peter had made the memorable declaration, "Thou art the Christ, the Son of the living God," " On this rock, that is to say, the rock of my divine humanity, I *will* build my Church, and the gates of hell, or confusion, shall not prevail against it." On this rock our Epistle affirms that the risen, ascended, and glorified Christ *has* built his Church. It is set down as a fact which stands good and unmoveable, whether man will believe it or no; and then this fact is made an argument for all faith. This is the doctrine of the whole Epistle, 'It is so, therefore believe and enjoy the truth—believe the truth, and the truth shall make you free — believe that Christ has justified your race before God, and that he is now the Head and King of that race, the everlasting Mediator, by whom your spirit may ascend up to God, and his spirit may come down to you. Believe that you are not under a curse, but under a blessing; believe this, and be happy. But whether you believe it or no, it is the fact—it has been asserted and demonstrated to be the fact by the most wonderful events the world ever saw: by the death, resurrection, and ascension of the Son of God. He is the Lord and King of your spirit, and of every man's spirit, whether you will acknowledge him or no. You have no right to look upon yourselves as natural creatures. It is believing a lie not to believe that his glory and inheritance are yours.'

Now, brethren, it is this kingdom which the Apostles, in all their epistles, and in all their preaching, are declaring to be set up in the world. It is this kingdom which your parents and your sponsors claim for you at baptism. It is this kingdom which we assert and claim for you now, and which we beseech you to assert and claim for yourselves. We say, that you and all men are bound to claim for yourselves the dignity of being members of Christ, and children of God, and inheritors of the kingdom of heaven. We entreat every one of you not to deny, or doubt, or qualify the words of the Apostle, "That you are come unto Mount Zion, unto the city of the living God, unto the heavenly Jerusalem, unto the innumerable company of angels, unto the general assembly and church of the firstborn which are written in heaven, and to God the Judge of all, and to the spirits of just men made perfect, and to Jesus the Mediator of the New Covenant, to the blood of sprinkling which speaketh better things than that of Abel." We entreat every one of you to believe that you are free of this blessed society—that all the rights and glories of this citizenship appertain to you. We ask you to try yourselves, not whether you have a *right* to be in this faith, for you have a right to be in it, for you have a right to assert this honour for yourselves, but whether you *are* in this faith—whether you are claiming this honour, and living in the daily enjoyment of it—whether you are calling upon God as a reconciled Father —whether you are keeping up union and fellowship with your Head — whether you are seeking for his Spirit to sanctify you, and guide you into fellowship with the Father and Son, and with all the members of his Church, militant and triumphant.

If these things seem to you a dream, if you ask us, 'Where are the signs of this kingdom? what are the proofs of its establishment on the earth?' we answer you boldly, every church that you see around you — every baptism to which you bring your children — every sacrament by which you bind yourself, and by which you see others bind themselves, to the Head and Lord of the whole body, is a witness of its establishment. We answer further, every privilege of your national life—all the order of society—all the fellowship among men—all kindness—all gentleness—all reverence—all courtesy—everything within us which is not brutal—everything around us which is not miserable, are the fruits of its establishment. And whether or no you will receive this evidence now, we are certain you will acknowledge it hereafter. For if ever a time should come, and how many signs proclaim that time to be at hand, when the belief of this kingdom shall vanish from among men, or, at least, from those laws and institutions which have hitherto recognised it, whenever Christ shall be disowned and openly denied by kings, and magistrates, and legislators, who have hitherto reigned and decreed justice under the awful sanction of his name and authority, then we are certain you will find there has been a kingdom amongst you—then you will know, by the dissolution of all social relations, all family ties, that this invisible Sovereign was indeed exercising power; a gracious, restraining, healing power, even amongst those who despised him, and that hence all our peace, and safety, and blessedness proceeded. Then will it be manifested, as it was manifested in the Christ-denying city of Jerusalem, that without him those affections which we are apt falsely to call natural utterly disappear,—that the mother has no compassion for the child she has brought forth. Not that when all this shall have come to pass, the kingdom itself shall be shaken; that cannot be moved, unless the divine humanity of Christ should cease—unless he should cease to be God, or cease to be man—unless the acts which he has already performed, the work which he has already accomplished, could be undone. No, the power, and grandeur, and permanence of this kingdom will be never so completely manifested as when they are brought into collision with the whole power of evil in the world, the flesh, and the devil. But though men cannot destroy this kingdom, they can destroy themselves by separating from it; they can learn the excellence of that which once was theirs, by their bitter feelings of misery, when they have shut themselves out of it for ever. Oh! let it not be by such proofs that you are convinced that there is indeed such a kingdom of righteousness, peace, and joy. Be convinced of it by the inward experience of its blessedness. Be convinced of it by becoming really bound in heart and spirit to him who is your King. Be convinced of it by becoming his faithful soldiers and servants unto your life's end. Be convinced of it by eating his flesh and drinking his blood.

Be convinced of it by seeking and finding daily supplies of grace to uphold you in your daily duties, and to give you power and freedom of access to his Father's throne.

II. And this leads me to the second point on which I was to speak. I am to show that in our receiving this kingdom is a reason for seeking grace that we may serve God acceptably, with reverence and godly fear.

There is an apprehension in a great many minds, that those who announce boldly and bravely that Christ has a kingdom upon earth — that it is an *universal* kingdom — a kingdom of which we may register our children citizens before they exhibit one sign of intelligence or grace, and that in doing so, we render homage to the finished work of Christ; there is an apprehension in some minds that those who use such language as this are depriving men of all motives to watchfulness and holy obedience. If men, they say, can be thus installed freemen of the new Jerusalem without any act of their own, why may not their lives be passed in slothful confidence? If men may thus enter upon their honours as upon a birthright, what witness do you bear, that we, and all men, are by nature children of wrath?

Now, if it be true, as I have endeavoured to show, that the Apostles and first teachers of Christianity, used this language without diffidence or hesitation; if it be true, as I might show easily, were this a fitting time, that such also is in substance the language used by the Reformers in the sixteenth century, modified indeed to suit the circumstances of the times in which they lived, and the errors with which they were contending; if it be true, that this is the regular and consistent language of all our devotional services compiled by holy men in the best ages of the Church, that they all proceed upon this principle, and are unintelligible if we do not admit it; I think these objectors may dismiss some of their fears that we are asserting anything inconsistent with practical holiness on the one hand, or with the deepest conviction of human depravity on the other. For where will you look for practical holiness if not in the lives and deaths of those Apostles, Confessors, Reformers; where, if not in their writings, will you look for the deep and humiliating confession, that in us, that is, in our flesh, dwelleth no good thing? But if we consider for a moment what the nature of this kingdom is, the unreasonableness of such an alarm will be evident to us all. What is this kingdom but a kingdom of righteousness, and peace, and joy in the Holy Ghost—a kingdom, of which the privileges are admission into the presence of a holy God, union and subjection to a holy King, communion with a holy and sanctifying Spirit? What are its privileges, but the privilege of not being under the dominion of the world, the flesh, and the devil; the privilege of entering into that service which is perfect freedom; the privilege of not having hearts full of pride, vain gloryings, envyings, debatings, jealousies; the privilege of receiving those fruits of the Spirit, meekness, patience, gentleness, faith, hope, charity, against which there is no law? Surely it is a strange thing to say that those who tell men they have these mighty blessings conferred upon them, are thereby depriving them of that holiness which, if the report be true, is their life and their glory. And if you remember upon what foundation we affirm that this kingdom stands, and what are the facts which prove its existence, you will see that it is not less strange to suppose our assertion of it inconsistent with the recognition of man's fall and debasement. For what is it that we say has preceded its establishment and without which its establishment was impossible? Nothing less than the incarnation, the passion, the resurrection, the ascension of the Son of God. All these stupendous transactions must have taken place before it was possible for men to assert an inheritance in this kingdom. And what events can attest the depravity of man or his ruin, with such awful evidence as these? Or if, passing from facts which have reference to the whole human race, we appeal to the experience of each man, I would ask whether any one does know what the plague of an evil heart—what the bondage of nature upon his will is—what the tyranny of the world is— what the temptations of Satan are, until he believes that he is a redeemed and reconciled creature? Whether any one knows what the exceeding sinfulness of sin is, till he understands it to be the rebellion of a child against a loving and merciful Father? If so, how can we more effectually aggravate man's sense of his own depravity, than by bringing him this message, that he *is* a reconciled and redeemed creature—that he *is* adopted into the family of a loving and merciful Father? And in reference to the immediate words in my text, I would have you earnestly reflect that if we do need grace whereby we may serve God acceptably with reverence and godly fear, there must be some way of obtaining that grace. But I know of no way of obtaining it, except by seeking it of God as a Father, through the Son of his love: of no warrant for obtaining it, except the assurance, that if a son ask bread of a father, he will not give him a stone. Is it not then a mockery to tell you that you must serve God, and that you must seek grace, if we do not accompany it with this cheerful message, that you are children, and that therefore it will not be refused you?

We dare then to use the language which the Apostles used—we dare to make not the vague hope of obtaining a kingdom, but the fact that it has been obtained for you, the ground of our exhortations to you to become holy servants of God. We tell you that holiness is necessary to you. "Without it no man shall see the Lord." And at the same time we justify God's ways by telling you that this necessary thing is not denied to any of you—that it is freely given you of God. We address you, not as outcasts, but as children; not as aliens, but as adopted citizens. We tell you that these are your titles. By these you will be judged at the last day. And because we know these are your titles, and that such, and so mighty are the responsibilities appertaining to them, we adjure you by His holy name to seek grace, that you may serve Him with reverence and godly fear.

III. I am to inquire in what way the representation of God, as a consuming fire, becomes a confirmation of our faith in this kingdom, and an additional reason for seeking this grace. There is something very remarkable in the Apostle's language. You must often have been struck with it. "You are not come," he says, "unto the mountain that might be touched, and that burned with fire;" and he adds immediately after, "for our God is a consuming fire." The inspired writers are never afraid of seeming to contradict themselves. They give the captious, disputatious heart of the natural man, all advantages—they let him amuse himself with their apparent inconsistencies, as much as he will; for they know well that if they left out either of two apparently opposite assertions, the other would be false, and that only by meditating upon both, can the spiritual man rise to a vital apprehension of the truth. So it is in this instance: the Apostle uses the very same word in both cases; on purpose that you may be startled with the inconsistency; on purpose that you may be led to search out its meaning. And if you do search it out, you will find that the fact of God being a consuming fire, is absolutely necessary to the support of that other truth that we are not come to blackness and darkness, and a flame; but that we are come unto Mount Zion, unto the New Jerusalem.

The feeling which the Apostle wishes to convey to your minds, I apprehend, is this. The holy, and righteous, and sin-hating God, revealed himself on Mount Sinai to the Jews, as one who is carrying on a mighty conflict with sin, that very sin by which they felt themselves continually enslaved. He showed them that they were sinners; and, therefore, every word that he launched against sin, every flash of lightning and peal of thunder that ratified this word, seemed to be directed against them. This was the effect of his revelation upon their sin-stricken minds.

It was not that even then, he wished them to feel thus. He had brought them with a mighty hand, and a stretched-out arm from the house of bondage, He had carried them upon eagle's wings, had fed them with manna, had proved himself their Almighty deliverer, preserver, and friend. But sin had darkened their minds, and in spite of these gracious demonstrations, they could not help feeling that He, who they saw was the determined enemy of sin, was in some sense their enemy. Now, says the Apostle, the case is changed; *He* is not changed; the holy, righteous, and sin-hating God is the same, yesterday, to-day, and for ever; but that righteousness which he then manifested, simply in its opposition to sin, he has now manifested for your justification and deliverance out of it. In Christ, he has shown that this righteousness, this sin-hating, sin-destroying righteousness, is not something from which you are to fly, but something in which you are to confide. In Christ, he has revealed himself to you as your Father; in Christ he has justified you as his children; and now he does not permit you to consider that his rage and wrath against sin, are rage and wrath against you. He entreats you to believe that he does not impute your sins to you; that he loves you with the very same intensity, and for the very same reason that he hates them. That state which he always intended for man, his original state, his real state, the state of members of one family, united in one head, contemplated, loved, only in Him, this estate he now permits and calls upon you to assert for yourselves, and to renounce for ever that vile independence which your first father set up when he disobeyed the command of his Creator, and which it is the nature of each one of you to claim for himself. Henceforth, therefore, consider yourselves in this new character, as redeemed out of the flesh, as his adopted, spiritual children, consider all the evil within you, as something distinct from yourselves, as his enemy and your enemy. If you do this you will rejoice to think that God is not changed, that he is still the same consuming fire as when he revealed himself to Moses in the bush, and to the Israelites on Mount Sinai. You will rejoice to think that he is carrying on a deadly and exterminating warfare against your foes, and that he will not cease from that warfare until he has utterly destroyed them. You will rejoice to think that he has sworn with an oath to drive evil out of the world; you will delight to think that you are interested in this oath, and that he will vex and plague the evil that is in you, till he has thoroughly subdued it and cast it out of you. Now, if this be the Apostle's mind, you see at once how needful it was to assert this truth, not only in order to vindicate the character of God, not only in order to show that he does not alter, but in order that you may be driven to take refuge in this kingdom which he has established for you, in order that you may feel that there is an everlasting protection and security for that kingdom against the foes that are beleaguering it round, in order that you may feel that this safety consists in the ability to seek, and the certainty of finding "grace to serve God acceptably, with reverence and godly fear."

Brethren! before I conclude, I must remind you that you especially are under solemn responsibilities to believe and hold fast the truth which I have at this time been setting before you. For to you it is no novelty, whatever it may be to others. Sunday after Sunday it is brought before you in the services of the Church. It is brought before you in your first confession which you make to God as revolted children to a merciful Father. It is brought before you in the Absolution, where that Father declares by the mouth of his ministers that he himself receives you back and casts your sins away from you. It is brought before you in your joyful ascription to the Father, Son, and Holy Ghost, as it was, and is, and shall be. It is brought before you in every Psalm, where we are all assumed to be members of one family under one Father, members of one body, rejoicing in one Head; and by virtue of their common union with him, sharing in each other's sorrows and delights. It is brought before you in that grand song in which you join with "the apostles, prophets, and martyrs," in giving glory to the "Father of an Infinite Majesty, his honourable, true, and only Son, and the Holy Ghost the Comforter." It is brought before you in the Litany, where you pray to One who has already redeemed you with His most precious blood, and where you appeal to him by the most solemn adjurations as members of one kingdom, fighting against his foes and yours. It is brought before you in the Creed, where you declare that you believe in the Holy Catholic Church, the communion of saints, the forgiveness of sins. It is brought before you in the service of the Holy Eucharist, where you join with angels and archangels round the throne in giving thanks for a salvation already accomplished, in feeding upon a sacrifice already offered up, in owning together a King who will reign for ever and ever. These are the witnesses to you, the continually repeated witnesses, that you have received a kingdom which cannot be moved. By these the Spirit and the Bride are continually exhorting you to seek for grace, that you may "serve God with reverence and godly fear." By these, that God who will not clear the guilty, and who is a consuming fire, is promising to all of you that you shall be to him a people and he will be to you a God. "See that ye despise not him that speaketh, for if they escaped not that refused him that spake on earth, how much more shall not we escape if we refuse him that speaketh from heaven?"

SERMON VII.

THE RACE AND THE PRIZE.

(Preached at Guy's Hospital.—Septuagesima Sunday, 1839.)

> Know ye not that they which run in a race run all, but one receiveth the prize? So run, that ye may obtain. And every man that striveth for the mastery is temperate in all things. Now they do it to obtain a corruptible crown; but we an incorruptible.
> I therefore so run, not as uncertainly; so fight I, not as one that beateth the air.
> But I keep under my body, and bring it into subjection; lest that by any means, when I have preached to others, I myself should be a castaway.—1 CORINTHIANS ix. 24—27.

VERY near the city of Corinth, where the people lived to whom this letter of St. Paul's was written, certain games were celebrated every three or every five years. These games were of various kinds; some were of leaping, some of wrestling, some of throwing quoits, some of darting, and some of running. They were very famous games, and they were held on a neck of land which joined the two parts of the country of Greece together, so that people came in great numbers from both sides of it to see them. We may fancy they were going on at the very time this letter was written, so that those who read it would have seen some of these exercises, or at all events would have heard much talk of them.

Indeed, all their lives long they had heard talk of them. When children they were told what a great thing it was to win a prize in these games, though the prize itself was but a branch of a pine-tree, and what famous songs had been written about the persons who had got these prizes, and what pains men took to prepare themselves for them. They knew especially that those men who sought for the prize in the foot race, took wonderful care of themselves beforehand, eating very sparingly, and even putting their body to great suffering that they might be the lighter and freer to run.

I tell you these things that you may see how well the Corinthians would understand what St. Paul meant when he said, "Know ye not that they who run in a race run all, but one obtaineth the prize;" and "every man that striveth for the mastery is temperate in all things." They did know both these facts. They were reminded of them every day, for they heard every day of some man who had been the winner, and of others who had been disappointed; and they knew it was not by accident, at least in general, that one got the crown, and the others lost it; that it was because one had been watchful and careful, and had kept the prize constantly in his mind, and lived as if that were the thing he was living for; and had not grudged trouble and suffering for the sake of it; the man who had kept under his body and brought it into subjection.

Now, says St. Paul, "They do it to obtain a corruptible crown, but we an incorruptible." He means to say, 'We are running a race as well as they. It is a different kind of race in many respects, the rewards of it are different; but it is like in this; some will win the prize, and some will miss it, and those who miss it will miss it because they run uncertainly, or if they are fighting, fight as those who beat the air. Those who obtain it will obtain it because they keep their end steadily in view, and go steadily and right on towards it, and are ready to give up and throw over anything that makes them less fit to run, and therefore less likely to reach the goal.'

Let us try to consider all these points which St. Paul brings under our notice.

I. The prize, in the contest that St. Paul speaks of, is a different kind of prize from that which these Corinthians were seeking after in their games. I wish you to attend to me while I am speaking on this point, for men are apt to make great mistakes upon it, much greater than they fancy. When I say that the prize in the race St. Paul speaks of was not like the prize which men contended for in such races as these, I do not mean that they only contended for the branch of a pine-tree, and that we contend for much greater and higher prizes and rewards than that; I do not mean this. The little branch was not the thing they really contended for; they contended for the honour and esteem of their fellow-citizens; they contended to be thought the greatest men in all the country round; to be praised and wondered at by all who saw them and all who heard of them. It was not a light thing, as men call lightness, which these racers sought after. The man who seeks to be wondered at because he is so rich, or because he is so learned, aye, or even because he is so kind and charitable — this man seeks just the same sort of reward that the runners and the wrestlers, and the leapers and the throwers among the Corinthians coveted. It does not signify what the sign of people's approbation which they receive may be; it is this which they desire, it is for this they labour. Do not then account these runners very silly people for wasting such time and trouble in hopes of such a paltry reward. They were just as wise as any other men who are striving after the honour and esteem of their fellow-creatures. The means they took to get it were far more honourable than those which many take, and they were so far better than other men who have the same ambition, that they were willing to receive a branch with a few withered leaves on it, as the only pledge and token of their labour and their glory.

St. Paul, then, means to take these runners at the Corinthian games as specimens of men who are striving after all the rewards which men of this world seek for, when he says, "They do it that they may obtain a corruptible crown, we an incorruptible;" he means to say, the poor faded leaves, for such, we are told, they were which formed the garlands of these conquerors, are signs and specimens of the pride, and wealth, and glory, for which men here are toiling, for which they are content to spend themselves by day and night, which through years of toil and suffering they are pressing after, and which at last only one here and there out of a number of those who have desired them, ever obtains.

But what, then, was that prize which St. Paul said that *he* was struggling for, and which he bade these

Corinthians struggle for, and of which he said, that instead of being faded and withered, it would be ever green, and fresh, and new, and flourishing throughout eternity? I know what you will say. You will say that this prize was the joys of heaven, while the other prize was the joys of earth. Yes, brethren, but what do you mean by the joy of heaven? Do you mean something that is like the beautiful pictures we sometimes see in our dreams? Something that sounds much more pleasant in words than the good things that men of the world rejoice in, but is less real and substantial than they are? If you mean this, you do not mean what St. Paul means. Or do you think that the joy of heaven is to be idle and free from pain, after the work and suffering of this world is over? If you mean this, you do not mean what St. Paul means. Or do you think that the joys of heaven consist in having all the good things that our eyes see, and that our ears hear, and that our hands handle, only in a much better and more perfect state than we have them here, and being able to feast upon them and enjoy them without becoming tired and exhausted? If you mean this, you do not mean what St. Paul means. No, and you do not speak of the things that you want, or that any man wants. You do not speak of things that are worth living and dying for. You speak only of shadows and phantoms that are just as perishing as those leaves which the conquerors won at the foot-race.

St. Paul was a man who had as hard a fight to fight in this world as you have. Dreams would not have satisfied him any more than they would you; he wanted realities, he complained of the things men in general are seeking after, not because they are too substantial, but because they are not substantial enough, because there is no food in them to content the appetites of hungry men. And this was not because his heart was not formed like the hearts of other men, because he did not thirst for honour and approbation and love as they do. He did crave after all these things, and he believed that his Heavenly Father had put that craving into his heart. But he felt, 'These smiles which are so pleasant for an hour while they are greeting me on my return from the race, or which reward me for being rich or wise or charitable, these will last but a little while and I shall be left cold again. I want to live in the light of a countenance which never ceases to smile upon me; I want to behold one and behold him constantly who will not love me to-day and forget me to-morrow, but who will be the same at all seasons; who will be "the same yesterday, and to-day, and for ever." I want honour, but if I am merely honoured for something that *I* do, for some labour that *I* undertake, I feel how poor and weak I am, how utterly undeserving of that perpetual honour which I desire, and without which I cannot be content. Oh surely I must long to behold the honour and glory of another, to delight myself in *that*, to lose myself in *that*, to forget that I am anything, in my delight to see him exalted, to find all the blessedness I seek for not in myself, but in him.' Brethren, this was the prize St. Paul desired; he tells us so himself; he says, "I press to the mark of the prize of my high calling of God in Christ Jesus, that I may be found in him, not having my own righteousness, but the righteousness which is of God by faith."

He desired to know God. To know him in whom is all life, and light, and honour, and glory; to dwell in the light of his countenance, whose name is love, who was love, is love, and shall be love for ever and ever. And desiring this, he did not desire a vain thing; he desired the most real of all things, he desired that which *is*, because *God is*; he desired that which the spirit of you, and of me, and of every man in this earth is desiring, and which we must have or perish discontented and miserable. And, he was desiring that which God hath promised to give, which He hath given us in His Son Jesus Christ, in whom dwelleth all His fulness, in whom all His love and His glory are manifested, and who is "made unto us wisdom, and righteousness, and sanctification, and redemption." This was that incorruptible prize which he told the Corinthians so to "run that they might obtain."

II. I have shown you then how this race differed from the race to which St. Paul compared it. Now I will show you wherein they were alike.

1. They are alike in this, that the prize is set before all. All, he says, run; every one may be a candidate for the race who pleases; one as much as another may have the prize. It was as in these games near Corinth, every one who run knew that he might have the pine-branch. It is so in the contests of this world—any man may, if he will, set to work, and try to win the approbation, and honour, and wonder of his fellow creatures. But it is most true of all, with reference to that race for the incorruptible crown which St. Paul here speaks of. A lame man might have been allowed to run at Corinth; but he would

have been a fool for his pains. The prize was there, but he must have known he could not win it. A poor man may try to make himself rich; here in England at least there will be no laws to prevent him from succeeding. But he starts at a great disadvantage. Other people who have money, may make it more, but he who has not anything to begin with, will only now and then rise greatly in the world. But this prize of the "knowledge of God in Christ Jesus our Lord," this prize of durable riches and righteousness, is indeed proposed to all, and no one that hears of it need say, I have some disadvantage which makes it impossible for me to obtain it. For if he say, I am no scholar, I am a poor ignorant man; unto poor ignorant men the Gospel is preached, and Christ declares himself to be their wisdom; and he says, "If you lack, ask of God, who giveth to all men liberally, and he will supply you." If a man say, I am a sinner, we meet him again with these words, This righteousness of God, which is the "prize of thy high calling," is declared in Christ for the forgiveness of sins. By believing in this righteousness, by cleaving to it, thou becomest delivered from the plague of thy sins. By looking up to this brazen serpent, thou art healed of the bite of that serpent which has been stinging thy conscience so long. Thou risest up a new man, having the new and pure and righteous life of Christ imparted to thee. If a man says, But can I lay hold on this prize? how can I embrace it? This knowledge of God seems higher than heaven, how can I reach it? deeper than hell, how can I enter into it? Lo! God bringeth the prize near to thee: he says, In my well beloved Son is contained all the excellency of my goodness and glory; in his body and blood, freely offered on the cross, are contained all the love and holiness that thou requirest, and behold that body and blood, I, by my ministers, do set before you; I invite you to come and partake of it; I ask you to come with repentant and thankful hearts, and I myself promise to feed you with that bread and water of life, of which whoever partaketh, shall never hunger or thirst. And if any one says, But this too is out of my reach, it is with my heart, not with my lips, I must eat, and that heart must be repentant and thankful, but it is cold and dead, this also we meet; for He promises by his Spirit to give you repentance, to give you thankfulness, to enable your heart "to feed on him by faith with thanksgiving."

2. I say then this prize which our spirits require, and which alone is substantial and enduring and incorruptible, is set before us all, is freely given to us all. But here is another point in which this race resembles the other race we were speaking of just now. All run, but some only receive the prize. It was not so in the games, as I have said already, because the prize was denied to any; there was great care to prevent partiality; there were special judges appointed to see that each man had fair play, and to award the prizes to those who had really won them. You may say, It is otherwise surely in the contests of the world; many get on in it by sheer cheating; and so no doubt it is. Still, on the whole, those who have laboured most diligently, are most likely to win the things they labour for. And yet in both these cases, it is one that winneth the prize, and many are disappointed. How is it in that race which St. Paul

bids the Corinthians run? There, as I showed you, "the prize of the knowledge of God in Christ Jesus" is freely held out to all; it is conferred on all of pure grace, and there is a most just Judge of the course, who will see that none fails through any misfortune; nay, who desires nothing so much as that all should win. For remember, that this is a prize, which all may win—the success of one does not exclude another; all may possess this glory together, as all may enjoy the light of the same sun together. And yet it will be true here also, that many run, and some only win the prize. Why so? Because some only care for the prize, because some only believe and steadfastly remember that the knowledge of God, the possession of his eternal righteousness and love, the "seeing him as he is," are the rewards which they want, and without which they cannot live. They disbelieve or they forget this, and, therefore, they set their hearts on the pursuit of other prizes which are not incorruptible, garlands in which there are only leaves that are withering or already withered; and because their hearts become wholly enamoured of these, wholly absorbed in them, it becomes impossible for them to think of that higher good, which is yet ever offering itself to them, ever coming near to them, wooing them to accept it, giving them a taste of its own sweetness, making them feel for a moment the paltriness and pettiness of all other things that they long for. But,

3. There is yet another point in which this prize and this race resemble the other. It is in the conduct of those who do win the race and obtain the prize.

They keep under their bodies, and bring them

into subjection. I told you how literally this was the case with the runners in these games—how carefully they restrained themselves from ordinary gratifications that they might be fit and free from the contest. I hinted to you, also, that men, in striving to be rich, or powerful, or wise, do, in like manner, submit to great hardships, and give up many things which their inclinations are lusting after. Now St. Paul says, if a man has this prize of the knowledge of God steadily in view, he also will do this. His body does not crave after this prize; it longs after things to taste, and smell, and handle. If you give it its way, if you let it have the mastery, these will be your objects, for these you will be striving. It is mere common sense, therefore, to see that you keep this body under, that you teach it to be a servant, and not a lord, which is not to tell you, but to be told by you what is good. St. Paul does not make it any merit to restrain this body from its indulgences and lusts, it is merely a point of plain wisdom which no one who is really in earnest, really means to seek God and his glory, can neglect. We do neglect it, alas! but we do it at our peril—we neglect it, because we neglect, at the same time, the thought of the glorious prize which God is offering us: that prize of being found in Christ; that prize of "awaking up in his likeness, and of being satisfied" with it.

My dear brethren, God himself is bringing your bodies into subjection. He himself is taking from you the power of indulging and gratifying them; yea, even of enjoying that, which, when you were healthy, he put within your reach. Oh take advantage of the moment, prize the lesson he is teaching you. Believe that he, himself, is your teacher and trainer—that while he is breaking down these bodies of yours, he is holding out to your spirits that blessedness, respecting which St. Paul declared, that he "counted all things but as loss, yea, as dung, that he might win it." Believe that your heavenly Father is not dealing hardly with you, that by this discipline He is claiming you for his children, is fulfilling the promise of your baptism, is teaching you what it is to be "inheritors of the kingdom of heaven." As the commissioned minister, as the ambassador of Christ, I beseech you to submit yourselves to God's holy Spirit, to receive his discipline, to let him bring your bodies into subjection that he may raise up your spirits to embrace Christ, and to feed upon him, that he may finally raise up those bodies and spirits together to make them like unto his own glorious body, and his own glorious Spirit.

And now having fulfilled this duty which I owe to you, let me tell you very earnestly that you owe a duty to me. Those are dreadful words with which St. Paul concludes this passage of his letter to the Corinthians. He does not say, Bring your bodies into subjection lest you be cast away; but he says, "I do this lest, having preached to others, I myself should be a castaway."

If St. Paul, called of Christ himself, God's own Apostle, used this language of himself, do not you think that we all of us ought to use it too? If we do not use it and feel it, must it not be because we have not enough of the spirit of St. Paul? Should not you earnestly desire for us that more of that spirit may be given us, that we may have more holy fear, more watchfulness, more sense of the grandeur of the prize which is set before us, and of the horror of losing it after we have been permitted to present it to you. O, pray, for the honour of Christ our Mediator and Advocate, that not one of those whom he permits to declare his own Gospel to men, to come to them when they are sick, to offer to them his own blessed body and blood, may be found wanting in that day "when the chief Shepherd shall appear," and when all who have waited for him shall receive his crown of righteousness.

SERMON VIII.

THE PERFECT SACRIFICE.

(*Preached at Guy's Hospital.—The Fifth Sunday in Lent*, 1840.)

> For if the blood of bulls and goats, and the ashes of an heifer sprinkling the unclean, sanctifieth to the purifying of the flesh, how much more shall the blood of Christ, who through the eternal Spirit offered himself without spot to God, purge your conscience from dead works to serve the living God?—HEBREWS ix. 13, 14.

AT the beginning of Lent I told you that it was especially set apart as a time for confessing sins and for humbling ourselves before God. But I told you also that it was connected with our Lord's life as well as our own, that it brought him before us more than ourselves. It would be unlike all the other seasons of the Church if it did not. In Advent, though we were to think of a deliverance that had been wrought for us, and of a judgment that is to come upon us, we were to think first of Him who came to deliver, and will come to judge. At Christmas, though we prayed that we, being regenerate, and made God's children by adoption and grace, might be daily renewed by his Holy Spirit, yet we were able to pray this prayer because He had sent forth His Son, made of a woman, made under the law, that we might become children of God in Him. In the Circumcision and the Epiphany it was still the same. Because He had submitted to the law for us, we might ask for the better circumcision which is made without hands; because he had been manifested to take away sins, we might look for the final manifestation of the Sons of God. Lent, then, is only like all the other periods which the Church has been leading us through in this, that it unites our Lord's acts to our acts.

And, brethren, the Church would not be a Church if she did not follow this rule, and teach you to enter into the meaning of it. If we were allowed to fancy that any act of ours was good for anything when it was separated from His acts, or that we were good for anything when separated from Him, the Gospel, our baptism, the word of God, and the Church of God, would all lose their meaning, and become nothing to us. Understand, then, where your strength lies. Christ was baptized, and in his baptism was pronounced to be the Son of God. Believing that, you can believe that your baptism proclaims you to be the sons of God in Him. Christ subdued His flesh to the spirit; believing *that,* you can subdue your flesh to the spirit. Christ was tempted; believing that, you can pass through temptation.

The Epistle of to-day teaches you the same lesson. Lent, I said, was a time of confession. A time, that is, in which those who are feeling the inward burden of sin are invited to come and cast that burden away, that they may rise up as freedmen, able to do the work which God has set them to do. If we understood well what it meant, it would be to us, of all seasons, nearly the most blessed and the most comfortable. At all events, it would remind us of the most comfortable of all duties, the greatest of all privileges; how each man may come with his own secret load which none else can tell the weight of, which he can impart to no other creature, though the most dear to him, and may lay it bare before Him who knows exactly what it is, and what is the length and depth of the misery of him who suffers it; who knows all this far better than we know it ourselves, and who desires that we should be freed from our burden more than we desire to be freed from it. If we looked at it in this way, should not we feel the voice which invited us to come and confess, the softest and the most soothing one that we ever heard in our lives? Would not every sick man and poor man say, 'That is the very word which I have wanted to hear—the word, that there is one to whom I can tell this grief which is gnawing here at my heart—that there is one who will understand me when I tell it—one who, besides understanding what I mean, will actually take away that which is oppressing me'? But how is it, then, brethren, that when you hear of Lent, there comes into your mind some feeling of sadness, and darkness, and reproach? How is it that men either think nothing at all about it, or think this: 'Here is a time which brings things to my mind that I would rather not remember—which tells me of an enemy whom I had well nigh contrived to lose sight of—which frets and torments me with things done and thoughts thought years ago, and seems to say that they are present now, and that they will be with me in years to come'? Have not we often said to ourselves, 'Christmas and Easter are pleasant enough, but this time I do not like; I wish it were away'? And even those who have not remembered the time enough to have such thoughts passing through them have the like feeling at other times. If they do not hear the voice of the Church calling upon them in Lent to confess, yet there are other voices speaking the same language. There is a voice within them speaking it, and there are echoes of that voice in every sick bed and in every open grave. You know you do not like to think of these; and that which makes them painful makes this time painful.

And what is this, brethren? It is that which my text speaks of when it says, "men have a conscience of sin." It would be very pleasant news that we might come and tell our griefs into the ear of a friend, and whether we could see him or not, whether we could look up into his kind face and hear his friendly sympathizing voice or no, yet the belief that he was near us, was listening to us, and feeling with us, this would be an unspeakable relief. But what if this grief we were going to tell him of was a wrong done to himself? Nay, more than this, what if we felt within us a secret dislike and aversion to him who invites us to come into his presence? What if we said to ourselves, 'These very thoughts, and feelings, and acts, which press upon me and torment me, are thoughts, and feelings, and acts of strife against him, of acts of resistance to his will; he who calls me to come and tell him my sorrows says he is my master, and that I have broken his laws; that he is my benefactor, and I have not thanked him; that he is my father, and that I have wandered from his house.' Brethren, it is a very different thing to tell a grief to a friend, and to tell such a kind of grief as this. If you but think a person kind or tender-hearted, you may say, 'I am weak, or poor, or helpless, or ignorant,' and may believe that he will attend to you. If you think all that, and more than that, of God, you may make known these complaints to him, and feel sure that he will give heed to you. But this "conscience of sin" is another matter altogether. It is a secret sense of separation from God himself, a sense of war between your heart and his, a sense of hatred on one side or on both. And here lies the confusion of it. A man who has this conscience of sin, does not know on which side the hatred lies; he cannot know. His mind within him is angry and restless, and everything that he sees and thinks of seems to him like himself. He feels that he is wrong, yet he cannot tell where the wrong is. He thinks it is everywhere; sometimes he has a glimpse of a Being full of love and gentleness, and then he has a pleasant sensation that, perhaps, all may be well, that there is nothing very false or evil within him after all; sometimes he has a sense of a Being who is just and true, then he thinks that that Being must regard him with the most intense displeasure. But in either case it is impossible for him to declare what a worm is secretly preying at his heart, because when he persuades himself that God is merciful, he thinks for a time that he has no wrong to tell of; and when he thinks that he is just, he dares not tell it Him.

Brethren, this is the conscience of sin. Surely every one of us has known something of what it is; for it is not a thing merely written of in a book, though it is written of in every book which has ever appeared in the world, and most of all in God's book. It is a state within us which may be talked of, and written about, and called by great names, or by little names; but it is there after all, and it must be got rid of actually, and not in pretence, if we are to be honest and happy men.

I say, if we are to be honest men—for you see what a confused dishonest thing this feeling of sin within us is. And yet is it better that a man should not think himself a sinner when he is one?—Would that make him honester? You cannot believe that. How strange this is! God requires truth in the inward parts; He cannot then require us to have these untrue feelings about ourselves, and about Him; He requires us to have truth in the inward parts; how then can He permit us to think ourselves better than we are?

Now, listen to my text: It speaks, first, of the way in which God dealt with the Jews. It says, He appointed that they should offer sacrifices to Him of bulls and goats, and that on certain occasions they should sprinkle the ashes of a heifer before his altar. Why was this done? It was done to remind men of sin, it was done that they might have the feeling awakened within them, 'We have wandered from God, we have broken his law.' It was done for this end partly, but not wholly. It was also done that they might feel 'God, who takes care of you, and has brought you into one family and one nation together, does not wish you to be separated from Him. He does not overlook your transgressions, but He forgives them; and He has appointed this way in which you may come to Him and confess your sins, and in which He may signify to you His forgiveness.'

This the text calls "sanctifying to the purifying of the flesh." The Jews, whose priests had offered up the bulls and goats at God's altar, and had confessed their transgression before God, might go away with the feeling, 'God has forgiven the transgression.' That was a good feeling to have; unless a man had it, all would have gone wrong with him. But yet these sacrifices and offerings only made the Jew think more about sin. They made him ask himself, 'Why is it that I committed these transgressions? Surely there is some root of evil in me, otherwise these fruits would not have appeared. I should not have done this wrong act against my fellow-creature, if I had not had something wrong in the very heart of me towards him. I should not have broken God's law, if there had not been something within me that was at war with him.' So that, while the Jew got the feeling of being pardoned for that particular act, he got the feeling of being a sinner against God more and more into him too. He got the feeling, 'There is something wrong at the root, and I must be set right there.' Was he never right, then, in his heart within him? Yes, when he believed God's word, when in the strength of God's promises he drew near to him; when he felt, 'Somehow or other there is a bond between me and God in spite of this sin which seems to separate me from Him;' when he prayed to God to deliver him from his enemies, and felt indeed, that his sins were his enemies; when he remembered that he was the child of God's covenant, then he had a right and clear heart within him, and then he began to understand that God does not only pardon our acts of sin, but that he means to take away sin itself from us; to cut up the root as well as to cut off the branches.

Now this is what the other part of the text speaks of, where it says, "Shall not the blood of Christ, who, through the eternal Spirit, offered himself up to God, purge your consciences from dead works to serve the living God?" These sacrifices which the Jews offered year by year continually made them feel as you have seen, that there was a separation between them and God, and yet that they were meant to be at one with him. The sacrifices could not do away with the separation, because there was something wrong in those who offered them; and that, whatever it was, must be given up. But what if this wrong in every man was his *own self*, how could this be given up? How could this be got rid of? The text answers, "Christ, through the eternal Spirit, offered *himself* to God." He made that wonderful sacrifice; he gave up, not something else, but himself. And this was not done by some mighty effort of his own. "By the eternal Spirit he offered himself up to God:" he merely yielded himself to God's will; God himself prepared the sacrifice.

And how does that benefit us? How can we give up ourselves the more for knowing this? We give up ourselves when we acknowledge that we have no power to give up ourselves; that it is Christ alone who could make the sacrifice for us all. Each one of us does not try to do something in himself, he does not try to draw near to God in himself, he is content to own that he has no life except in Christ, that he can draw nigh to God only in him; and he owns that even this he cannot do by any effort of his own will, he can only do it by the eternal Spirit which is in Christ, and by which he moves the members of his body.

Now, brethren, this faith does not merely take away particular sins, it takes away the root of sin; it takes away that conscience of sin of which the Apostle speaks. For the root of sin is our self-will; the conscience of it is finding out this self-will in ourselves. When we approach God as our reconciled Father in Christ, who accepts us for his sake, and bestows his Spirit upon us for his sake, we give up our self-will, we acknowledge that our life is not in ourselves but in him, and that from him must come forth the power which enables us to enjoy the new life that we have in him. It is thus that the life-blood which is in Christ purges our consciences from dead works to serve the living God. For separate from God all our works must be dead, but this blood of Christ testifies that we are united to him. Where the will of God does not inspire our wills all our works must be dead. But this blood of Christ is a stream of life coming forth from God himself to quicken the spirits, and souls, and bodies of his creatures.

All these words would be very confused and incomprehensible to you if God had not provided you with helps for understanding them. But he has provided very wonderful helps. For he has given you your baptism, which is in the name of the Father, and the Son, and the Holy Ghost. This tells you that the Father of all has made you his children, but that you are his children in his Son, and that it is the Spirit of the Son who unites your will to his. Here is one lesson, and if you had learnt it rightly the next would not have been needful for you, at least in the same way. But you have not learnt it; you have tried to have a will of your own; you have not understood that you lived only by Jesus Christ, and that you could only do right works by the power of his Spirit. Therefore your works have been evil, or, as St. Paul says, dead. Lent comes to remind you of this, to bid you confess these dead evil works to God, to cast away your evil conscience, to seek a new heart, a new power to serve the living God. When you have obeyed this invitation and learnt this lesson you will be able to profit by the third and highest of all. The Communion of the Lord's Supper is the true teacher of all these mysteries. How we may present the spotless sacrifice of Christ before God, how we may partake of that sacrifice, how the blood of Christ may purge us from dead works, and fill us with a new, and pure, and heavenly life.

And I wish you, brethren, to take this thought away with you, as the fruit of what I have been saying. In one sense the recollection of our Lord's sacrifice is a preparation for Lent, since we cannot truly and heartily confess our sins till we know that God is our reconciled Father, that all the enmity which has separated us from him is on our side, that he is willing to destroy that enmity. In another sense Lent is a preparation for the recollection of our Lord's sacrifice; since, till we have confessed our sins and turned to God, we cannot know what his love is, or enter with any real thankfulness in the mystery of Good Friday.

SERMON IX.

THE SICK MAN'S PRAYER.

(Preached at Guy's Hospital.—The Second Sunday in Lent, 1810.)

O Lord, I am oppressed, undertake for me.—Isaiah xxviii. 14.

THESE are some of the words which King Hezekiah wrote when he had been sick and was recovered of his sickness. In a psalm of praise to God he describes what his feelings were in that sickness, and so clearly and freshly did they come back to him that you would fancy he was actually suffering the pain at the moment he is speaking of it. There are many passages in that psalm which some of you would be well able to enter into. You would say at once, We know what that means. But this short sentence seems to contain the marrow of it all. He tried to set forth his complaint before God, and there was relief in that. But he found that his words did not answer to his thoughts. He seemed to himself to be chattering like a crane or a swallow rather than to be uttering intelligible language. Then he looked up, and said, "O Lord, I am oppressed, undertake for me." What all this weight and burden at my heart mean I cannot tell; I cannot describe it much as I long to do so, I can only say I am oppressed; there is a weight here of some kind, and I believe Thou art near me, undertake for me.

This is surely a good prayer for a sick man, and it is a good prayer for a healthy man too; for if we understand what sickness is we shall find it is sent that we may learn what is good for us when we are well. A man is broken down then that he may learn his true condition at all times. He feels the burden of death then that he may know he is carrying it about with him continually. He is brought to understand in whom it is that he must take refuge then, in order that he may believe there is a refuge for him in all time of his tribulation and all time of his wealth. The Church to-day gives you a prayer, which is a little longer and fuller than this sentence of Hezekiah's; but which has the same sense in it, and will, perhaps, help you to see more clearly what it means. The prayer is, 'Almighty God, who seest that we have no power of ourselves to help ourselves, keep us both outwardly in our bodies and inwardly in our souls, that we may be defended from all adversities which may happen to the body, and from all evil thoughts which may assault and hurt the soul, through Jesus Christ our Lord.' When we have considered this prayer we shall see, I think, why it is particularly suitable to this season of Lent, and yet how suitable it is to all seasons; how good it would be for us if we got the savour of it into us, and made it a part of our own selves.

In these collects there are always three parts: first, we turn to God and remember what He is; then we remember what we are and what we want, then we connect both these recollections together in a petition.

It must be so in every true prayer. That is no prayer which dwells only upon ourselves and does not carry us up to God. That is no prayer which does not express some necessity of ours. That is no prayer which does not ask that our want may be satisfied out of His fulness. I do not want you always to think distinctly upon each of these points. I know that you cannot do it, oftentimes you must cry to him who is at hand to help you, without staying to think at all. Still if you do that out of a full heart you will find that there are these three parts in your prayer: a feeling of there being a sufficiency in God for your need, a feeling that there is something which you do need, and that you may ask for it. But these prayers of the Church are given you that you may think them over in your minds; that you may know what an act this of prayer is, how awful it is, and yet how needful it is, how much it carries us above all our own reasonings, and yet how reasonable it is still.

1. Now the thought respecting God, which is set before us in this Collect, is one that we are reminded of in many of the other Collects, especially in that on Sexagesima Sunday, of which I spoke to you lately. It is contained in the words, "Almighty God who seest." The recollection that God knoweth the very want which we are going to tell Him of, is at the bottom of all prayer. You may think it strange that it should be so, and it is strange, because prayer itself is the strangest and wonderfullest act that a man can perform. It is wonderful that I should need the assurance of God understanding the whole depths of my heart before I can find courage to make them known to him. But yet that was exactly Hezekiah's

feeling; "O Lord, I am oppressed, undertake for me." 'I cannot tell my own wants yet there is something that I do want, and thine eye can take the full measure of it. Thou canst perceive exactly what it is.' Brethren, it is in God's light that we see light. It is when we believe he is looking into our hearts, that we begin to know something of what is passing there. Else all is darkness, all is confusion. We have a sense of some pain, a dull heavy pain, but what it is, or where it is, we know not. We have a number of random thoughts and feelings, of recollections and desires, moving backwards and forwards within us; but there is no order or distinctness in them; we do not know what we are desiring, hardly what we are remembering. Then comes that thought into our minds which came to the Egyptian maid Hagar, as she sat alone by the fountain in the wilderness, "Thou, God, seest me," and light and clearness follow. We begin to know ourselves, because God knows us; and then this feeling that He knew us before we knew ourselves, and that our knowledge comes from his knowledge, helps us to pray.

2. In that Collect for Sexagesima Sunday which I alluded to, the words were, "O Lord, who seest that we put not our trust in anything that we do." I explained to you at the time that there is an evil inclination within us which leads us to be trusting in the things that we do, and in our own selves. Now this inclination puzzles a man exceedingly. For he feels weak, and he wants one to strengthen him; and yet there is this in him which says, 'Thou must do something thyself; thou must

put forth some strength of thy own;' but what strength it does not tell him. The effort he ought to make, is the effort of trusting in another; and yet he feels as if he could not make this. But when he says, "Thou God seest," the cloud begins to disperse. For though he could not distinguish the better trusting mind in himself from the other bad self-righteous mind, he feels that God can distinguish it. He can look up and say, 'Thou who seest that there is one praying to Thee, though against the inclinations of an evil heart, who puts not his trust in anything that he does, mercifully grant, that by thy power he may be defended from all adversities.' Here is an instance of a man getting into clearness respecting himself, by looking up to him who is all clearness, in whom there dwells no darkness at all. The Collect to-day is somewhat different. It supposes a man who has suffered trials without and temptations within, who has found that he has a poor suffering body of death with him continually; and what is worse than a body of death, a weak heart, an inconstant will, unequal to all the ten thousand dark and evil thoughts which are assailing it. It supposes him, after long striving with himself to know how he may overcome this evil and weakness, struck with the thought, 'But God knows that I have no power of myself to help myself.' The weakness of this body is no secret to Him; the ignorance, and folly, and treachery of this heart are all naked and open before Him. He knows it, and remembers it all. What, you will say, can comfort come out of such a reflection as that? Is it not a great increase of our sorrow to know that He, in whose sight the angels are not pure, is acquainted with all our iniquity? Can this be any help to us in drawing near to him? Can this give us any encouragement that he will hear us? Yes, brethren, it can: for when you say, 'God sees that we have not any power of ourselves to help ourselves,' you mean, He does not intend us to help ourselves; He did not send us into the world that we might learn to help ourselves, but to depend upon Him. If men had done that from the first, these bodies would not be the burdens to us that they are. Death has entered into them, because they have become separate from God—because they have not simply trusted in Him. And what is it that we feel our hearts are weak and treacherous in? Is it not in their unwillingness to trust in Him, and depend upon him? In their foolish, mad attempt to live on without Him? Well, then, is not this experience of our weakness and evil mercifully given us, that we may throw away the vain confidence which has caused it—that we may see our own weakness, even as God sees it—and that we may learn wholly to give up the keeping of ourselves to him?

3. You see, then, how the second part of this Collect is connected with the first. First, we remember in what way God beholds us; then we feel rightly and truly sensible of our own wants. And what are those wants. First, To be kept outwardly in our bodies. One would think I need not say many words to you about this part of the prayer. Every day tells you how some little accident, the falling of a tile, the breaking of a rope, the slipping of a ladder, may destroy one of those limbs which are so curiously and wonderfully made, and set all the rest of the body ajar, and lay a stout man, who a few minutes before

was equal to any work, helpless, and in wretchedness upon his bed. Every day tells you of still stranger accidents than these, of sickness entering into men they know not how, creeping through their blood, and destroying all the life that was in them, so as to make them cry and roar for disquietness of heart. One would think, I say, that you cannot need to be told that these bodies want some keeper who knows more about them than the owner of them, or than any physician in the world. And yet, perhaps, it is even more necessary to remind you of this than other men. You cannot, indeed, fancy that all is safe; but you may easily fancy that all is accident; that there is nothing to determine what happens to this man or to that—that there is no real protection over any of us. You may get into this habit of mind. The devil will be trying to make this hospital, and all that you see here, a means of leading you into it. Your consciences are telling you that there is such a protector—that these things which happen do not come by chance—that the misery and falsehood of your lives have come from fancying that they do. And your hearts are secretly supporting the testimony of your conscience, though they may have been bribed to speak the other way. They are saying, 'We want this protector, we cannot live without him, it is anguish to think he is not there.' Do not cheat them of what they want. Assure them that they have this protector; let them realize the fact by crying to Him. Let this be the cry, 'Our bodies are in Thy keeping, defend them from all adversities that may happen to them.'

But then while we have been learning how much

we want this prayer, we have been entering into the other too. Keep us inwardly in our souls, that we may be defended from all evil thoughts that may assault and hurt them. What these evil thoughts are, we have partly seen. They are summed up in the thought, 'We have no friend to whom we may look up, none who will take care of us if we ask him, none to whom our cries will reach.' These thoughts are assaulting all of us continually. Sometimes they express themselves openly; sometimes they put on seemly shapes and disguises; but every one who knows anything of himself, knows that he has them, and that they do not change their nature when they change their garb, and that they keep him from all right and true and comfortable acts, and that they are the root of all else that is vile within him. Therefore, we desire, above all things, to be defended from these, and we believe assuredly that there is one who can grant us this wish, who can deliver us from our atheism; yea, the very act of calling upon Him is itself saying, 'We cannot be without God, we will not be without Him.' It is saying 'These bodies want His care, but these souls want Him much more.' The life of the body perishes unless He preserves it, but the life of the soul perishes unless it is trusting Him to preserve it, unless it is understanding His care and love, and resting in Him. And thus we are able to know for what end it is that he afflicts the body with those accidents and diseases. It is that He may call out the sense of dependance and trust in the soul, without which it cannot move or breathe. When this work is accomplished, the trials of the body have done their work, the great lesson has been taught that in

Him we live and move and have our being; we have been taught to say, "O Lord, we are oppressed, undertake for us;" we have been brought into that state of humiliation into which Lent is intended to lead us. He has laid low, and in due time He will exalt. The soul will be delivered from the evil thoughts which assault it, and will know Him as its reward and its joy; the body will be made like unto the body of our Lord by that mighty power whereby He is able to subdue all things unto Himself.

SERMON X.

THE CHRISTIAN COVENANT THE GROUND OF NATIONAL EDUCATION.

(Preached at Trinity Church, Newington, for the National Schools.— The Second Sunday after Easter, 1839.)

Only take heed to thyself, and keep thy soul diligently, lest thou forget the things which thine eyes have seen, and lest they depart from thy heart all the days of thy life : but teach them thy sons, and thy sons' sons.

Specially the day that thou stoodest before the Lord thy God in Horeb, when the Lord said unto me, Gather me the people together, and I will make them hear my words, that they may learn to fear me all the days that they shall live upon the earth, and that they may teach their children.—DEUTERONOMY iv. 9, 10.

THE Book of Deuteronomy, which we are reading on these Sundays after Easter, is a key to all the books which precede, and to all which follow it.

A light is thrown back from it upon the dealings of God with the patriarchs, upon the deliverance from Egypt, upon the national law and priesthood and sacrifices, upon the sins and the discipline of the people in the wilderness. A light is thrown forward from it upon the causes of the nation's prosperity and misery under its first judges, in the brilliant times of David and Solomon, in the period after it became divided, in the days of its captivity, in the time when its faithful members began to look for the more spiritual glories of the second temple, in its present downfall and dispersion.

If we inquire whence it derives this importance as a part of the canon of Scripture, we shall find, I believe, the answer to be this. That it is especially intended to set forth the condition of a people who are in covenant with God; to tell what is their strength and their weakness, their danger and their refuge, what are their responsibilities and their hopes; how this one fact in their history is connected with all the other facts of it, how it affects all their actions, interprets all their sufferings, and gives a purpose and a meaning to their whole lives. The Church has been very careful in her selections from this book. On these Sundays after Easter, she has taken pains that the chapters which she reads shall unfold to you the intention of the rest. In the chapters especially for the services of this morning and this evening, we have very distinct indications of its object. Amidst abundant proofs of tenderness and affectionateness in the mind of the old legislator for the people whom he had guided forty years through the wilderness, you see one thought possessing and almost overpowering his mind, that of the grandeur and awfulness of the position into which it had pleased God to bring his nation. As his narrative compelled him to notice his own absence two successive times for forty days in the Mount, and the intimate communion which he had enjoyed with the Lord God of Israel, you might have supposed that he would have dwelt on these his personal privileges, and have scarcely remembered that the people who had remained below when he went into the thick darkness, had been acknowledged by God at all. On the contrary, he passes rapidly over those events, he touches upon them only as they affect the condition of the Israelites; and the feeling which is nearest his heart, is one of wonder that not he, but the whole nation, should have been brought so nigh to the Lord of heaven and earth. "For ask now of the days which are past, which were before thee, since the day that God created man upon the earth, and ask from the one side of heaven unto the other whether there hath been any such great thing as this thing is, or hath been heard like it. Did ever people hear the voice of God speaking out of the midst of the fire, as thou hast heard, and live? Or hath God essayed to go and take Him a nation from the midst of another nation, by temptations, by signs, by wonders, and by war, and by a mighty hand, and by a stretched-out arm, and by great terrors, according to all that the Lord your God did for you in Egypt, before your eyes? Out of heaven He made thee to hear His voice, that He might instruct thee, and upon earth He showed thee His great fire, and thou heardest His voice out of the midst of the fire."

You may see, if you look with a very little attention at this chapter, that it was not the terror of these outward spectacles which impressed the mind of Moses himself, or which he wished to impart to his countrymen. These had no doubt imposed on the senses of the other Israelites; that which made Moses to quake and fear when he heard the trumpets sound loud and long, and saw the fire upon the mountain, was not the sign, but that which it signified, not the devouring element, but the presence of God into which it showed that they were brought. He is most careful, therefore, to impress upon the Israelites, that the wonder continued, though the sign was departed, that they were as much standing in the awful presence of God then, as when the covenant was first made, and that all generations afterward were as much to feel that they partook of this awful blessing as if they had themselves been brought out of Egypt, and kept the Passover in the wilderness. In fact, this is the very point to which his whole discourse tends; this, he teaches them, is the very meaning of their being brought into covenant with God; they were to feel themselves continually nigh to Him, continually under his protection and discipline, and they were to declare to their children's children that they, like their fathers, were a people of inheritance unto the Lord.. Now that you may understand why he lays so much stress in my text upon their remembering this covenant, and upon their teaching it to their sons, let us take notice of some of the blessings which he says appertain to those who have received this benefit.

I. He connects with this, all clear knowledge and apprehension respecting God himself.

"Unto thee it was shewn that thou mightest know that the Lord he is God, there is none else beside him."

He describes this, as the primary benefit of God having chosen them, and united them to himself, that, thereby, it became possible for them to have a distinct knowledge of him who created them. I say, a distinct knowledge, for it is implied in these very words, and we are taught in all the rest of Scripture, that the heathen had a knowledge of God, that their consciences witnessed to them of him, and that they worshipped him. The privilege of the Israelite is said to be that he worships the Lord, and *none else*—that is to say, that he does not confound the unseen Being of whom his conscience and his heart speak, the Being of whom he feels himself to be the offspring, with the works of his hands; that he looks upon all things in nature as inferior to himself, and to God as above himself; that he feels himself the lord of creation, and the servant of *the Lord*. This was the great privilege of the Jew, and it was a privilege which rested wholly on his being in covenant with God. We may fancy that it is an easy thing to think of God as the one God—an easy thing to rise above the low animal conceptions of God which we read of as prevailing among people in old times and now. But history shews us that it has been a most difficult thing for other men; and if we look into our own minds, we shall find that it is a most difficult thing for ourselves. Nay, more, if we look into history and into our own minds, we shall find that merely to have a notion of God, as One Being, merely to abstain from bowing down before idols, is a very worthless thing. The heathen nations of old were better, happier, more godly, when they were confusing God with the sun and moon; and all the hills and fountains around them, than when they began to think of him merely as a cold dead name of which they knew nothing and who cared nothing for them. In the first case they did ignorantly honour him, in the last they ceased to honour him altogether. In the first case they dimly revered the true God, though they could not distinguish Him from the things which they saw and handled, in the last they worshipped with their hearts and minds the things which they saw and handled, and those only, and they utterly forgot God. How then can a people really learn to distinguish God from his creatures, and to love and fear him the more instead of the less for doing so? I answer, it can only be so when he pleases to bring them near to himself, to make known to them how intimate the relation between them and him is, to make them understand that he is indeed their God, and that they shall be his people, when he becomes himself their guide, and teacher, and friend, when he makes the events which befall them the means of revealing to them his own character. It is God's covenant then, which was the means of making known to the Jews what manner of Being he was, and of withdrawing them from the worship of things beneath them to a mighty Person above them.

Again, Moses teaches them in this Book, especially in this and the following chapters, and in that beautiful song which occurs at the close of it, that it is in virtue of this covenant they could be a nation at all. They owed to it the feeling of union among themselves, or of being connected with their forefathers or their posterity. He shows them that the acknowledgment of one God over them was the only security of their being one people. The moment they forgot that they were related to this God, that he was their Lord and King, and that he had taken them to be a people unto him, that moment they would become divided and helpless, losing all respect for each other, and a prey to their enemies. The faith of this covenant, the faith that God watched over them, and loved them, and had "brought them out of Egypt with a high hand and a stretched-out arm," the faith that he was with them now, as he had been in past times; this would give them the brave hearty feelings of men, this would make them understand that they were brethren; two would then chase a thousand, and ten put ten thousand to flight; for they would feel that the Lord was their Rock, and the Most High God their Saviour. But when through forgetfulness of this covenant, through the want of faith in God as their God, and in his care for them, they began to corrupt themselves, and to make graven images, "doing evil in the sight of the Lord their God, and provoking him to anger. Then he called heaven and earth to witness against them, that they should soon utterly perish from off the land, whereunto they went over Jordan to possess it, that they should not prolong their days upon it, but should be utterly destroyed; and the Lord should scatter them among the nations, and they should be left few in number, whither the Lord should lead them; and there should they serve gods, the work of men's hands, wood and stone, which neither see, nor hear, nor eat, nor smell." All courage and union as a nation, then rested on their faith in this covenant.

Once more, he says, in the 6th verse, that by keeping this covenant, they would be reckoned a wise and understanding people in the sight of the nations. That is to say, the other nations would

THE GROUND OF NATIONAL EDUCATION.

perceive in them a clearsightedness and vigour of mind, which, beginning from the highest subjects, would extend to the most common and earthly affairs. They would be free from the vague terrors which men must needs feel who mix together visible things with invisible, and who fancy that every powerful thing around them may be a god. Feeling their own relationship to their Lord, knowing that he was their Friend, the thought of his presence which made other men tremble, would make them calm and bold. They would look steadily back upon the past, and forward on the future, because they would feel that One, "who is, and was, and is to come," had been, and would be, their protector; they would sow the ground, and wait for the appointed weeks of harvest, believing that a regard to his ordinances would bring a fulfilment of his promise; they would go cheerily into untried regions, if his providence called them thither, assured that if they took the "wings of the morning, and went to the uttermost parts of the sea, still his hand would guide them, and his right hand would uphold them;" they would feel an interest in all the works of God, "from the hyssop on the wall, to the cedars of Lebanon," because they would regard them as his works, who was their guardian and deliverer; "Day unto day would utter speech to them, night unto night would show knowledge." Above all, they would be wise in their own hearts; the mysteries which others shrunk from examining, they would rejoice to meditate upon, because they knew that those secrets of the human heart and conscience which "no fowl knoweth, and the vulture's eye hath not seen," are all "naked and opened to him with whom they have to do;" because they knew that to commune with their own hearts, was the way to become acquainted with him, and to be at peace.

Whatever, then, entitles men to the praise of wisdom and understanding, clearness in their practical judgments, earnestness in seeking after those things which God hides, that man may search them out, or freedom from the superstitions or fears of ignorant men, these would belong to them just in proportion as they remembered the covenant of their God, and walked in His ways.

But I said that there were responsibilities, tremendous responsibilities attached to this privilege. The first was this very one, of remembering that they possessed it. A deep responsibility indeed, which if rightly discharged, enabled them to fulfil almost every other; for to remember the covenant of God, was to remember God Himself; to remember that they were weak without Him, and that they had all strength in Him; to remember what He had as yet made known of His character; to remember the appointed means for approaching him, of sacrificing to him, of praising him; to remember how he felt to their brethren, as well as themselves; to love him, and to love them for his sake.

Rightly understood, this duty included the second, which, nevertheless, was of such importance, that it had need to be mentioned separately, and to be pressed upon them again and again. They were to *teach their children.* In this way they were to ensure the continuance of their nation, and to make it felt that the blessings of one generation were the property of the next. And, therefore, the legislator does not leave us to doubt for a moment what kind of teaching this was to be, and for what end it was to be communicated. If the knowledge of the covenant was to be the means by which they attained the distinct knowledge of God, if the knowledge of the covenant was to be the means whereby they would be a brave and united people, if the knowledge of the covenant was to be the means whereby they would become a wise and understanding people, the first lesson to their children must be, 'You are in this covenant; God hath taken you into it. Whatever its blessings are, he wishes you to be possessed of. See that you do not through neglect, or of choice, abandon them.' This, I say, must have been, we know that it was, the foundation of all Jewish education. In this way only, did they hope to educate at all. For in this way only could they hope to draw minds, naturally prone to sensuality, to feel the glory of their own position, to feel that they were more than the beasts that perish; in this way only could they make the records of divine revelations and of human faith in their sacred oracles of any avail to their children. If once they felt that they were interested in the covenant made with Abraham, Isaac, and Jacob, then did the lives of those holy men, and all that God had spoken to them, become to them like their necessary food; if once they felt that they were under the government of him who redeemed their fathers from the house of bondage, then would the story of that deliverance be more to them than the records of their own family: if once they felt that the law, and the priesthood, and the sacrifices, and the tabernacle, were gifts and ordinances of God, in which they were permitted to have a share, every precept respecting them would be studied with the most affectionate diligence. If they were really citizens of the state, every portion of its polity had a living worth for them; but without this the words of the sacred book, however solemn and momentous, would either seem to them idle tales, or be listened to with pain, as carrying a significance which they felt to be most deep, and which they were utterly unable to realize.

It was only then, so far as they began with teaching their children the fact of their being in covenant with God, that they were able afterwards to use the Scriptures as an instrument in their education. It did, no doubt, happen, through the good providence of God, above a thousand years after the delivery of the precepts contained in this book of Deuteronomy, that the Scriptures were translated out of the language of the chosen people, into that language which was most in use among the heathen nations. It is very probable, though we have no means of ascertaining the fact, that these Scriptures, in this new dress, excited a spirit of thought and inquiry among those who were not included in the Jewish covenant. But we have no warrant for believing that these Scriptures by themselves educated the soul of a single person into the knowledge of God, who had not been previously received into the privileges of the Abrahamic family. And we need not be at the pains of fancying that this must have been the purpose of God in allowing that great work, because, within a very short time it pleased him to make that translation available for the use of persons who were brought into a grander and more perfect covenant than that into which he had entered with the Jewish nation.

II. This is the second point on which I propose to speak to you. I have shown you what the privileges of the Jewish nation were, and how entirely they were grounded on their covenant. I have shown you what their responsibilities were, also grounded on that covenant, especially in the matter of education; and I have shown you what the nature of the education was which it became them as heirs of this covenant to communicate. And now the question remains for us to consider whether our position is in this respect different from theirs; if not, whether our responsibilities be in the same direction as theirs; whether our education is to rest upon the same principle as theirs, or upon some other. My brethren, consider for one moment what we should be saying if we said that we are *not* as much in covenant with God as the Jews were. Seeing that it was the great blessing which he bestowed upon them, to bring them near to him, to make them his people, and to declare himself their Lord, we should be saying that the incarnation, and death, and resurrection, and ascension of our Lord have left us in a worse condition than they were in who lived before His appearing. We should be saying that God, by revealing himself as so directly related to man, in the person of his Son, had put us at a greater distance from him, had declared that we are no longer as much at one with him as they were. We should be saying that all the promises which were made to the fathers, and in the expectation of which they lived and died, had proved abortive. For were not all these promises tending to this point, that in the latter days a more perfect and intimate communion should be established between earth and heaven than ever had existed before; that men should be more completely made the subjects of God's discipline and education than they had ever been; that an everlasting covenant should be established with them, and that this should be the tenor of it—" I will write my laws upon their hearts, and on their minds will I write them, and their sins and iniquities will I remember no more."

Was not the difference as to the nature of the covenant to be this, that whereas heretofore God had declared himself the King of one nation, now He would own himself as the Father of all in his well-beloved Son; that whereas he had admitted the Jews to call themselves his servants, he would now invite men to look up to him as sons? Was not the difference this, that instead of merely reigning over them he would dwell in them; that instead of having one temple upon Mount Zion, he would make the whole Church and the bodies of every one of its members his temple; that instead of a priesthood which was built upon a carnal commandment, there should be a priesthood built upon the law of an endless life, and established by an oath in the person of an ascended Mediator; that instead of sacrifice offered up in the expectation and foretaste of a perfect sacrifice, there should be a sacrament admitting into the fruition of that sacrifice now completed and accepted?

Does it occur to you that because Christ died for all mankind, therefore no particular body can look upon themselves as now in covenant with him? You might as well say that because all men are in truth the servants of God, the Jews might not look upon themselves as taken into his covenant and recognised as his people. Where, I ask you, would be the blessing to mankind of Christ's death if there were none to bear witness of it, none to claim the universal fellowship which it is meant to establish? We see that the world is not united in the acknowledgment of God or of the Mediator, not united to each other in one Lord or one faith. How, think you, can it be shown to them that there is such a Lord, such a Mediator, such a bond between all men, unless there be some who feel themselves successors to more than Jewish privileges, taken into covenant with God, his appointed witnesses? And who must these be? I answer, all nations who, through God's mercy, have heard the Gospel of Christ, and have confessed it to be true; all who by baptism have claimed the privilege of belonging to his Church. Unless these have a right to consider themselves in covenant with God, unless they are *bound* to consider themselves so, and commit a sin when they abdicate their rights, the condition of the world, I must say it again, is worse than it was when there was one elected nation of witnesses. The Gospel has not been the declaration of a fact—there is no Church existing among men. But if it be so, then, I say, our responsibilities must be the same in kind as those of the Jews; greater in degree, because our covenant is greater and nobler. We have that new and special obligation laid upon us, of going into "all nations and preaching the Gospel to every creature, baptizing them in the name of the Father, and tho

Son, and the Holy Ghost." We have the old obligation of remembering his covenant, which in our case means remembering that we are "the children of God, the members of Christ, the inheritors of the kingdom of heaven." We have the old obligation of teaching our children the same lesson that we have received ourselves. And thus, my brethren, we are come to the point which it behoves me to press upon you this morning.

III. In all that I have been saying hitherto, I have been explaining to you your own position. I have been setting before you your own duties. I have been pleading for that kind of education which is established in your parish. You may have heard two objections to this education. Some may have said to you, It would be far better to give your poor children an education merely in human knowledge, because upon the manner of communicating this all are agreed. Some may have said, It would be far better to give them merely a knowledge of the Scriptures, without the use of any catechisms, because in this way all Christians would be agreed. I think, in what I have said, I have replied to both these complaints. To the first I have answered, We want to make our people a wise and understanding people, we want to give them an interest in all the works of creation, a knowledge of their own hearts and minds, a sound and practical wisdom in the conduct of life. And therefore it is that we begin with teaching them this catechism, which tells them that they are in covenant with God—that they are members of Christ, the children of God, and heirs of the kingdom of heaven. For we are sure that if they know and believe this, they will have a living interest in all things; they will reverence their fellow-creatures and themselves; they will walk firmly through the world as men who know for what purpose it was made, and what work they have to do in it, they will be a wise and understanding people. And without this we fear they will never be so; without this we fear they will be an ignorant and a superstitious people; yea, not the less so if they be an infidel people. For men must worship something; if they do not worship an unseen Being who loves and cares for them, they will worship the works of their own hands; they will secretly bow down to the things that they see, and hear, and taste, and smell; these will be their lords and masters, these will be their cruel tyrants.

To those again who say that you are to teach the Bible and the Bible only, I have answered. The greatest object in our education is to interest our children in the Bible, in every prophecy and gospel and epistle which it contains. And we are sure we cannot do this unless we give them a property in the Bible, unless we tell them that they are one with those of whom it is written, one with the band of apostles and prophets and martyrs of whom it speaks, one with Him who is the head of the whole Church throughout the world; in other words, unless we tell them that they are the children of God's new and better covenant, the children of the second birth. I have answered them again, We cannot disobey the Bible in order to honour the Bible, we cannot reject the system of education which the Bible points out and then say to our children, 'Take the Bible for your guide.' The Bible commands us to lay the foundation of our education in teaching them the covenant of the Lord. Therefore we take this course. We do not interfere with the plans of other people, we do not say whether they may or may not be justified in substituting another method of teaching for this; but this has been given us, and we do not mean to abandon it: we do not mean in our own spheres, within the region over which our influence extends, to lay aside that instruction which all history teaches us is the one best fitted to make a wise and understanding people.

This is the language which I believe every parish has a right to adopt. I trust you will show this morning that it is your language. You will come forward to support the schools of which you are the proper guardians, and by doing so you will give a pledge of your determination that they shall be really and in fact what they are in principle—schools for training children to be true and brave men, by training them to be servants of the living God.

SERMON XI.

CHRIST IN THE WILDERNESS.

(Preached at Guy's Hospital.—The First Sunday in Lent, 1839.)

Then was Jesus led up of the Spirit into the Wilderness, to be tempted of the devil.—MATTHEW iv. 1.

I WILL read you the words immediately before those that you may understand what the time is that is here referred to. "Then cometh Jesus from Galilee to Jordan unto John to be baptized of him. But John forbade him, saying, I have need to be baptized of Thee, and comest Thou to me? And Jesus answering, said unto him, Suffer it to be so now, for thus it becometh us to fulfil all righteousness; then he suffered him. And Jesus being baptized, went up straightway out of the water, and, lo! the heavens were opened unto him, and he saw the Spirit of God descending like a dove, and lighting upon him. And, lo! a voice from heaven, saying, This is my beloved Son, in whom I am well pleased."

You see that the temptation of our Lord immediately followed his baptism. Before his baptism very little is recorded of him. We are told only of his miraculous birth; how the shepherds and the wise men adored him; how he was presented in the temple and received by old Simeon and Anna; how he was carried into Egypt; how he settled at Nazareth; and how, at twelve years old, he tarried behind his parents when they had gone up to Jerusalem, and was found by them in the temple among the doctors, hearing them and asking them questions. This is all we know of his early years, and all we need to know. We want to be assured that this wonderful child was really a human child, that he grew to be a boy, that in all respects he was made like one of us. More minute information than is just enough to prove this would probably do us harm; we should be forgetting who this Jesus was; we should be forgetting that he came to be the Head of a universal Church, the Lord of men; we should be forgetting, above all, that he came into the world to manifest God unto us. This the evangelists will not suffer us to do. They tell us in a very few words all that is needful to teach children, and boys, and young men, that their Lord has partaken their nature and felt their sorrows, and then lead us quickly on to that event which declared to all the world that in this being of their own race they were to behold Him who created them.

This event was his baptism. John had come baptizing in the wilderness and saying, "Repent ye, for the kingdom of heaven is at hand." The object of his baptism seemed to be to rouse the Israelites to a recollection of the covenant which God had made with them, to make them feel how they had forgotten him, to show them that He still remembered them, to assure them that He received them back and owned them as his people, and put away their sins when they turned to Him. I say, this *seemed* to be the object of

John's baptism, and was the object of it. But yet John himself said, "That Christ may be manifested to Israel, *therefore* am I come baptizing with water." So that his baptism was not merely a call upon the people to turn to their King, but it was the way of showing the King to his people. They were to be baptized, that they might receive remission of their sins. He was to be baptized, in order that they might see in whom it was that God gave them remission of their sins. They were to be baptized, in order that they might be fit to receive God's revelation of himself to them; he was to be baptized in order that he might be fitted to reveal God to them. They were to be baptized confessing their sins; he was to be baptized as a testimony that he had fulfilled all righteousness. They were to be baptized in order that they might show that they did not rest upon their privilege as children of Abraham, but that they looked for the higher glory of being children of God; he was baptized that he might be declared to be the well-beloved Son of God, in whom he was well pleased. They were baptized with water unto repentance, that they might afterwards be baptized with the Holy Spirit; he was baptized that that Holy Spirit might descend upon him, and that through him it might, by the same means, be given to all the members of his Church.

The mystery of our Lord's baptism is wonderfully connected with the mystery of his temptation. And it is equally true, that the mystery of his temptation is connected with the mystery of all our temptations. I desire, with God's help, to set these truths before you in three or four discourses.

All good men who had ever been in the world

had believed that they were in some way or other united to one whom they could not see; that they were good, and right, and true, so far as they trusted in Him, and guided their steps by the light He gave them. But every man knew that there was something in him which hindered him from exercising this trust, something which said, 'Thou canst live without it.' Every man in the world had obeyed this voice, had set up himself and lived for himself. Some had done this habitually; they had chosen their own ways, they had said, "Our words are our own, who is Lord over us?" Some had struggled hard with their inclination to be solitary selfish creatures. They had felt it was an enemy, an enemy who was threatening to destroy them, and they had cried aloud to be delivered from it. That cry was deliverance; it was returning to their right place; it was beginning to renounce themselves and to rest upon another. But how was this? Each man was fighting with himself, fighting with his own evil inclinations; it seemed as if he had nothing to do with his neighbours, it seemed as if the desire he had to resist was one that no one else could possibly share in. And yet it was this same desire which every one of his neighbours was feeling too; it was this to which he was either giving himself, or else which he was trying, with such might as he had, to baffle. How strange! Every one was alone in this war, and yet it was the common war, the war of all mankind.

God taught his servants to see their way out of this perplexity. He brought them into families—he made them into a nation. The father felt that he was to trust in God for his children as well as himself; the king felt that he was to trust for his subjects as well as himself. The father felt that his children's enemies were his enemies; the king felt that his subjects' enemies were his enemies. Each man was not struggling alone; others were interested in the battle. The father was struggling against the disposition in himself to be apart from his children, and against the same disposition in them to be apart from him; the king was struggling against the disposition in himself to be a tyrant, and against the same disposition in his people to be' rebels. Thus men got the feeling, by degrees, wrought into their minds, that they had common enemies, because they were men, and that they had a common friend who must sustain them all against this enemy. This feeling grew up in them slowly, and it was hard to keep it when they had gained it. For each man knew in himself that the sin he committed was his own. He could not be deceived about this. His conscience said clearly and strongly to him, 'Thou hast done it; thou art answerable for it.' All he could do was to lay hold of the promises which God had given, to come and seek his forgiveness in the appointed way—to repent and turn to God; then he felt that he was right again; his sin was his enemy, and was not a part of him any longer; and he could pray God to destroy it in himself and every other man.

And now there was a Person in the world of whom the voice said, 'He is perfectly one with ME, he is my well beloved Son, in him I am satisfied.' This was as much as saying, In him there is none of that distrust; none of that desire to set up himself which there is in every other; the evil thought in them is not in him; he is altogether like me. But in such a one what could there be like *us?* What battle could he have to fight? How could he possibly sympathize with the creatures who are continually separating themselves from God, continually trying to make themselves independent of Him? Think, brethren, and your hearts will answer at least one of these questions. How could he sympathize with men? Rather say, who else could sympathize with them? What hinders sympathy but this selfishness? What hinders men from being at one with each other, but the desire in each to have a way of his own? He that was without this, was without the thing which had kept the members of families apart, and the members of nations apart, which had hindered men from knowing that they were brothers. He that was without this, must be that common friend, that Lord of all men, whom in every different place and time they had been crying after.

But there was another question. What fight could he have to fight, seeing that the very thing which all other men had been contending with in themselves, was not in him? Remember what I said to you just now, and you will be in no difficulty here. The men who trusted in God had a hard battle to fight, because they felt evil to be their enemy; those who did not trust him, fought no battle at all, because they let the sin dwell in them as if it was meant to be there, as if it was a part of themselves: when the good men yielded to it, and it got into them, they ceased to fight too, and did not take up their arms again till they recollected that God had called them to be his servants, and that, therefore, sin was not to be their master. Well then, if there was one in the world who entirely hated evil, who had never entertained it in his heart at all, would not you think that he would have the greatest fight of all?

And do you not see what kind of fight this must be? Do you not see that he would be able to feel fully what each one had felt imperfectly, that he was fighting the *common* enemy—fighting an enemy who was entirely separate from him, who was the most entirely unlike him, and who, therefore, was assaulting him more directly than he had ever assaulted any other being? Other men had particular foes that troubled them. Perhaps these were actual human creatures, backbiters, or tyrants. If so, it was hard to feel that it was not the man who was God's handiwork they were to hate; but the man's enemy, that which was destroying him. Or it might be some particular besetting sin of their own which troubled them; one from which their neighbours seemed to be free; then it was hard not to feel that God had given them some different constitution from other people, and that it was this which they had to alter. But He who was perfectly free from the least grudge against any human creature, who had perfect fellowship with a God of love, he must have felt at once what it was in every human creature which was against God, against love, and against the man himself, and must have regarded that as the thing which was abhorring Him, and which He was to abhor. And He that was perfectly separate from sin, would see down to the root of each particular sin, and would know that it was this which was seeking to destroy him, and which he was come to destroy. His conflict, therefore, would be with the very Spirit of Selfishness, and Division, and Disobedience. This is the awful battle which you hear of in the Gospel of to-day.

I shall not speak in this Sermon about the way in which it was possible for this spirit to hold converse with Him in whom dwelt all love, unity, and obedience, and to tempt him. This you will learn from the verses which follow the one I am now speaking upon; but I have one or two remarks to make, for the purpose of preparing you profitably and reverently to enter upon the study of them.

The first has reference to our Lord's fasting. It is said that he fasted forty days, and the Collect you have been repeating to-day asks that we may be able to use such abstinence as may subdue our bodies to the Spirit. To enter into these words, we must again go back to our Lord's baptism. He had been acknowledged as the Son of God, in whom his Father was well pleased. He was not this because he had a human body; he was this before he had any human body, and the voice declared that he was still the same now that he had taken that body. By humbling his body, then, he asserted this privilege which had been declared to be his. He claimed his power of holding communion with Him, who is a Spirit. In doing so he did not put dishonour upon his human body, he put the highest honour upon it; he showed that it had been taken into union with one who could call God his Father; that it was his servant to do his will; that it should share his suffering and his glory. But as he fasted to make manifest his Sonship to the Father of all good, so did he fast also before he entered into direct strife with the source of all evil. For this battle, as I have told you already, was a battle of his Spirit with the spirit of selfishness. It was to this the devil spoke; it was this which answered him. You will understand better what I mean when I speak of the particular temptations. But it is needful to hint thus much now, lest you should suppose that because the tempter said, "Command these stones to be made bread," he was addressing merely the appetite of our Lord's body. He did tempt that, as I hope to show you hereafter; and our Lord's fasting made him capable of feeling the temptation. But the voice went much deeper; it spoke to him as the Son of God. Again, our Lord's fasting was at the beginning of his ministry; it was to arm him for the great work which he had come to do. You think that he went into the wilderness to be alone. Certainly he did. But then it was to redeem solitude from any taint of selfishness. It was to show us that solitude is given us as a means of binding ourselves more closely to our brethren than we can do while we are living amongst them in their hurry and bustle.

Our Lord's fast, then, was not to gain anything for himself, but to maintain a glory which belonged to him; to fit him for engaging with our enemy; to fit him for going about doing good. Even so must it be with his disciples. When they fast it must be not to obtain a privilege, but to realise one which God has freely bestowed upon them; not to save themselves from temptation, but to prepare themselves for it; not to separate themselves from others, but to fit themselves better for helping others. And you who are poor and sick men, upon whom God oftentimes lays fasts much severer than we can invent for ourselves, or than the Church ever devised for any, do you desire that these may be turned to your good, so that they may lead you to claim your privilege as God's children, may fit you for resisting evil, and for doing or suffering God's will; then when all bodily food is loathsome to you, the bread of life will nourish your spirits more and more.

This was one point upon which I wished to speak; the other refers more directly to our Lord's temptation. Do not go away with the thought that what I have said about our having a common enemy, and about that enemy being the one by whom our Lord was tempted in the wilderness of Judea does not concern you, even if that were all, and there were no particular lessons to follow from it afterwards. If I have said anything to you which has puzzled you, while I have been trying to make you better acquainted with this subject, I am sorry; but the thing itself belongs to your daily life, and if you are honest men, that will interpret it to you. If there be no such spirit of evil as he whom we hear of in these days of Lent, then each man must be left to fight as he can with his own sin, no man can give any help to his fellow man. Then we are alike in our faces and our forms, in our hunger and thirst, in our feelings of heat and cold, but we are alike in nothing else; all that is most sacred and terrible in us our neighbour has nothing to do with; we cannot condemn the same things, or even know that we mean the same thing when we use the same words. Then the man who lies in the next bed to you has one set of evil things to tempt him, you have another, and though you may perhaps pray a confused, desperate prayer for yourself now and then, your cries will not help him in the least. But if it be as the Church and the Bible says that it is, then your battle and his are the same. The same spirit of selfishness and falsehood is striving to separate you from the same God of love and truth: the same prayers which you send up for yourself are prayers for him. Then we are not a set of solitary divided creatures. You and I can pray for a poor creature who is now turning from her evil ways at the other end of London though we never saw her face or heard her name. We can pray for people in America and people in New Zealand; the poor man can pray for the rich man; here in this little chapel we may ask blessings on the Queen and Parliament and peace for all the nations of the earth. We lift up our voices for them as well as ourselves when, having gone through the evils of pride, vain glory, hypocrisy, uncharitableness, of fornication, of rebellion, of schism, of contempt of God's word and commandments, which destroy the heart of individuals, of nations, and of churches, we cry, "By thy baptism, fasting, and temptation, good Lord deliver us."

SERMON XII.

COMMAND THESE STONES TO BE MADE BREAD.

(Preached at Guy's Hospital.—The Second Sunday in Lent, 1839.)

And when the tempter came to him, he said, If thou be the Son of God, command that these stones be made bread.—MATTHEW iv. 3.

I MUST ask you to remember what I said last week respecting the connexion of our Lord's temptation with his baptism and his fasting. In his baptism he was declared to be the Son of God, with whom his Father was well pleased. By going into the wilderness and fasting for those forty days and nights, he claimed the honour which had thus been put upon him; he proved that he had another life besides his human life; he entered into wonderful converse with the Father, who had given him his Spirit. Then began that conflict with the Spirit of evil which is recorded in this chapter, and which we remember in these forty days of Lent. He had withdrawn from the society of men, so that these were not his tempters; he had humbled his flesh, so that this could not be his tempter. It was then the Spirit of evil speaking to his Spirit—the Spirit of disobedience contending with that Son of God, in whom the Father was satisfied. If you keep these things in mind, I shall be able, through God's assistance, to set before you the meaning of this first temptation, "If thou be the Son of God, command that these stones be made bread."

But, before I begin, let me make one remark to you. You are not to suppose that there was any bodily figure before our Lord when these temptations were presented to his Spirit. Nothing is said of this in Scripture; and without the authority of Scripture, we have no right to imagine it. I wish you all to know and believe that it is not the things which we see with our eyes that are the most real. I see the eyes and lips of you who are sitting here to-day : I see your figures and the clothes which cover them ; but if you were all dead carcases, you might have still the same eyes, and lips, and figures, and clothes. There is a living person within each of you who uses these eyes and these lips, to whom this figure and these clothes belong. I see him not ; but I know he is dwelling in each one of you. When he departs, it will be said of these bodies that they are dead; but nothing will destroy your life; that will go on for ever and ever. It is not, then, that which we see in our fellow creatures which is most precious to them, or to us. It is not that which we love—it is not that which is kind to us, or pities us, or does us good. No! it is that which we cannot see—that which our hearts tell us of, but not our eyes. And as it is with our fellow creatures, so it is with our Lord. He had (as I have often told you) a real body which really lived, and suffered, and died ; but it was that which was within this body, that over which death had no power, but which was able to bring his body back out of the grave, it is this which was truly our Lord; it is this which loved us, and died for us, and gave up himself for us; it is this which was tempted for us. There was no need that He should see the tempter with his eyes. He was not misled, as we are, by the shows and shapes of things. He knew that the most true and awful things are those of which our eyes tell us nothing. Why do I say this? That you may understand, brethren, that this tempter is with you, even as he was with your Lord, though there is no bodily shape near you, and this also, that your Lord himself is also with you; speaking to your spirits, and sustaining them in that temptation, though your eyes would be quite unable to bear the vision of his glorified body.

In the Evangelist St. Matthew it is said that when our Lord had fasted forty days and forty nights, "He was afterwards an hungered;" but in the Gospel according to St. Luke, it is said that he was forty days "tempted of the devil." These words do not contradict one another; both are true. You are not to suppose that our Lord was not often hungered during the course of his long fast; but only that his hunger became particularly painful at the end of it. Therefore this temptation, which was addressed to his hunger, may have been presented to him again and again. The thought may have been hovering before him continually. It may have been continually driven back. Only there will have come a time when it will have thrust itself more directly before him, when his Spirit will have become engaged with it as in a battle for life or death. A man may be walking all day under the heat of a burning sun; but near the end of his walk, as he is standing bare-headed, there may come a sun-stroke and smite him to the earth. So it was with our Lord. All those forty days he was fasting—all those days he was tempted. But just at the close of them, the whole power of the temptation gathered itself up into the words, "If thou be the Son of God, command that these stones be made bread." And it became, indeed, a battle between the Lord of Life and the Lord of Death.

"If thou be the Son of God." In a wilderness not less desolate than this in which our Lord now was, the children of Israel had wandered for forty years. They had been most rebellious against the commands of God—they had complained of him for bringing them out of Egypt, where they sat beside the flesh-pots. They had murmured against him, and against his servant Moses. Yet had this people been fed day by day with bread from heaven, and when they thirsted, the rock had been struck, and the waters had gushed out. In a wilderness, not more solitary than this, the Prophet Elijah had been sustained with food and water by an angel; yet, he too had been a murmurer, and had wished that he might die. Here was one who had committed no disobedience, who had been led by the Spirit into that wilderness; could it be that there was no manna to satisfy his wants, no one to bring him food? And what had the voice at his baptism said of him? Had it declared him to be dear to God as the children of Israel were dear to him? Had it said that he was a great prophet, as Elijah was a prophet? No! but it had said, "This is my beloved Son." That is to say, 'This is he whom Abraham expected,' the seed, in whom it was promised 'that all the nations of the earth should be blessed.' This is he who made himself known to Abraham, as he sat by his tent-door in the heat of the day. This is that angel of the covenant who went with the children of Israel on their journey through the wilderness, and whose presence they were told to fear, because God's name was in him. This is that Word of God who spake in visions to Elijah, and all the prophets. This is he, for whose sake alone, God was well pleased with Abraham, in whom, and for whose sake he loved the children of Israel, and bore with their murmurs in the wilderness, and for whose sake the prophets (though they were but earthen vessels) were permitted to carry his name. All this, and more than this, must have been meant by the words, "This is my beloved Son, in whom I am well pleased."

But surely if this were true of him, he must be able in some way to provide for his own wants. If manna and cakes were sent to the servants, surely the Son had a right to expect what he needed. They were to take what was sent them, and they might confidently hope that it would be renewed day by day. But he could surely command a supply of what was needful; as Elijah had been enabled to give others food, he might assuredly feed himself.

But more than this; the 'Word of God,' the 'Son of the Father,' had given life to all things. All the nourishment which the earth brought forth, all the energies which sustained it were from him. This wilderness, in which he stood, was his handiwork. The trees which grew in it, the stones at his feet, had been made by him. He had but to speak, and they would become bread. Would not this be a proof of his mighty power? Would it not give him assurance and confidence in going forth to exercise it hereafter for the good of men? Would he not be able to declare to men, "I was hungry, and at my bidding the stones became food for me"? Such thoughts the tempter placed before Jesus. And where was the evil of them? And why would our Lord (if he had given heed to them) have yielded to that Spirit whom he came to conquer? Listen, and by God's help, I will tell you.

First. "If thou be the Son of God." It is not then certain that he is the Son of God. That voice from heaven, the seal of his baptism, the descent of the Spirit, were not sufficient to prove him so; He must get some other evidence of it than this. Such is the tempter's language, such is the thought he would force upon our Lord's mind. You see here is distrust. But what is the life of the Son of God? It is the life of faith, the life of trust. That life which he had with the Father before all worlds was a life of love, of confidence, of rest. The life which he came to lead upon earth was the same life, a continued resting upon the love of the unseen Being, a continual listening to his voice that he might utter it forth to men. This was the pledge to him of his Sonship, that when the voice said to him, though clothed in a human body, though humbled to the likeness of a servant, "Thou art my Son," the heart within him answered, "Thou art my Father." In seeking any other evidence than this, he would have given up his character, his very nature. In the act of proving himself to be the Son of God he would have renounced the name.

Secondly. "If thou be the Son of God, *command*." He was to use his power—he was to prove himself a son by showing what he was able to do. But the life of the Son of God was the life of obedience. Proud men cannot understand how He, who is one with the Father, yea, equal to the Father, should yet be obedient to the Father. They do not enter into this mystery of love—they cannot explain in their carnal hearts how the Almighty Father commands because the Son obeys, and the Son obeys because the Father commands; and how there would be no command if there were not obedience, and there would be no obedience if there were not command. And they do not see how the Son came to carry on the same life here on earth which he had in heaven, to show forth this same blessed obedience in his human life and human death. But this is so, whether we understand it or not; and, therefore, by saying, "I command these stones to be made bread," he would have been giving up his privilege and glory as the Son of God; which privilege and glory was in all things to obey—in all things to do his Father's will.

Thirdly. "Command that these stones be made *bread.*" Here was an exhortation to do something for himself, to use the power wherewith he had created the world for the satisfaction of his own wants. But the power of God, the power which goes forth from the Father and the Son, the power which breathed life into all things, is the power of love, the power of diffusing blessedness. This is that power which called everything into being, and which reneweth life in all things at every moment. God created all things for his own glory, because all things are to the glory of love, all things witness of love, and declare the presence of love. But he created nothing for his own glory in the sense that dark and selfish men give to the word; for love delights to shed itself abroad into everything. It is satisfied in itself already, and it would bring all things to its own satisfaction. But if our Lord had used his creating power for himself, he would have been giving up this life of love which he had as the Son of God. Instead of fulfilling the purpose for which he came down from heaven, which was to make men partakers of his own joy and love, he would have been assuming their misery and selfishness—he would have been yielding to the very snare from which he came to deliver them.

Such, and so mysterious, was this temptation. So skilfully was it contrived to meet that state of body into which our Lord's fasting for our sakes had brought him; so well did it seem to honour his character as the Son of God; so completely did it seek to rob him of all the blessedness and truth of that character.

II. And what was the answer? Jesus said, "It is written, Man shall not live by bread alone, but by every word that proceedeth out of the mouth of God." It is so written in Deut. viii. 3. "And thou shalt remember all the way which the Lord thy God led thee these forty years in the wilderness, to humble thee and to prove thee; to know what was in thy heart, whether thou wouldest keep this commandment or no. And he humbled thee and suffered thee to hunger, and fed thee with manna which thou knewest not, neither did thy fathers know; that he might make thee know that man doth not live by bread, but that by every word that proceedeth out of the mouth of God doth man live."

These words were addressed by Moses to the children of Israel, when he was reminding them of all the ways in which God had dealt with them, and renewing to them his commandments and his promises. Was it not strange that our Lord should refer to them as if they had been spoken concerning himself? Was it not strange that he did not use some argument which more immediately applied to his own condition, which showed why he who was above all other men, who was the Son of the living God, would not yield to the voice of the tempter? My brethren, here lay the mystery of this answer. He would not separate himself from the creatures whom he had formed — he would speak as if he were one of them. He says, 'As these Israelites were led through the wilderness forty years, so am I come into this wilderness now to show that I am their King and Captain. As God led them, and proved them, to see what was in their heart, so am I content that he should lead and prove me. I do not wish to decline one of their temptations — I do not wish to escape one evil which they have borne. What is written of them is written of me; I claim no privilege for myself which I do not claim also for them.' All this was implied in his taking those words out of holy Scripture, and using them for his own case. It was as much as saying, 'My glory as the Son of God shall consist, not in the power that I use over these stones to make them bread, but in the power that I have received to go through whatever my people have gone through in all past time, so that men of every age shall own in me one who has perfectly entered into their feelings and undergone their trials, and has cheerfully endured whatever my Father has been pleased to lay upon them.'

But consider a little the words themselves. "Man shall not live by bread alone." He does not say, 'I, the Son of God, have such a high and glorious nature that I scorn to be dependent upon this ordinary food;' he does not say this; he had already given up that power, for at this very moment he was hungering; but he says, "Man," the poor creature that spends his life in toiling for his daily bread—man, made of the dust of the ground—man, who seems as dependent upon the food which he wrings by the sweat of his brow from the ground, as any of the beasts about him, "*Man* shall not live by bread alone, but by every word that proceedeth out of the mouth of God."

In one sense these words had been fulfilled already; in one way they had never yet been fulfilled. They had been fulfilled, for God had given men the most evident tokens that he was watching over them, and caring for them, that it was his mercy which fed them from day to day. But for this they would have had no strength to have obtained their food; but for this, their food, when they had it, would not have nourished them. That gift of manna to the Jews in the wilderness was a proof of this fact which they were never to forget; a part of it was preserved in the tabernacle, that, while they were gathering in their ordinary harvest, and eating ordinary bread, they might feel they were as much supplied with it by God as if they saw it falling from heaven.

So far the words had been fulfilled. But they had not been fulfilled because no man had lived in entire dependence on God's word and promise. No one had felt and understood habitually, It is not by this crust that I am supported, but it is by the power and the word of God, no one had eaten his bread with full joy and singleness of heart, remembering this. Now there stood One, a man with a body such as ours, hungering and thirsting as we do, who did entirely fulfil these words, who could with entire confidence rely upon his Father to give him what he needed for that body which He had bestowed upon him, who felt that he rested upon Him, and not upon meat to sustain him, who could feel that that life was proceeding at every moment fresh from his Father's word. He could say then fully and perfectly, "Man doth not live by bread alone, but by every word that proceedeth out of the mouth of God."

There was still another way in which these words had been partially accomplished. God had been teaching his children that there is a better life within them than the life of their bodies, a life which was sustained by the knowledge of himself. Job felt this life when he said that he had loved God's words more than his necessary food. David felt it when he said, "There be many that say, Who will shew us any good? Lord, lift thou up the light of thy countenance upon us. Thou hast rejoiced my heart more than in the time that their corn, and wine, and oil, increaseth." He felt it again when he said, "Preserve me, O Lord, from the men of this world, the men who have their portion in this life, whose bellies thou fillest with thy hid treasure: as for me, when I awake up after thy likeness, I shall be satisfied with it."

All holy men had at times been possessed with these thoughts, and had seen and understood that thus too, "man doth not live by bread alone, but by every word that proceedeth out of the mouth of God." Yet they had trembled when that bodily life of theirs seemed about to be taken from them, and all had at times, for the sake of that bodily life, been willing to forget for a time their spiritual inheritance. So that here again the words had been fulfilled, yet had not been fulfilled. God had shewn men what the truth was, and what their own wants were, but men had entered very imperfectly into his mind. They had tasted very little of the hidden manna which he would have given them. They had lived as if it were not theirs. But now there was a man who was perfectly fulfilling the words in this meaning also; one who for the joy of communion with his Father — for the sake of drinking from the river of his love, had fasted forty days and nights, and who was beginning on earth a life of constant fellowship with that Father. He was able to say in the fullest power of the words, "Man doth not live by bread alone, but by every word that proceedeth out of the mouth of God."

III. But, brethren, if by this answer our Lord made himself one with us in our humiliation, and claimed for us the privilege of being one with Him in his blessedness, He also teaches that we are partakers in His temptation. These words, "If thou be the Son of God," could in one sense be spoken only to

Him who was the only begotten of the Father; the word "command" had a meaning for Him which it cannot have for any of us; the exhortation to make the stones bread spoke to a power in Him of which we are not conscious as He was. But yet every one of you has heard words like these spoken in his inmost heart, words which you can never understand till you know what they meant when they were spoken to your Lord.

This is strange, but it is true. It is strange, because it is most strange that you and I, creatures of the dust, sinful creatures, should be admitted to claim fellowship with the Son of God; it is true, because he came into the world for this very end, that he might give us this privilege, that he might make us the children of God in him. Therefore as the tempter said to him, "If thou be the Son of God," he says to each of us, "If thou be the child of God." As his first object was to create a doubt in his mind whether that voice which he heard at his baptism was a true voice or no, so his first endeavour is to create in our minds a doubt whether the echo of that voice which we heard in our baptism proclaiming us to be children of God in Him, was a true echo or no. He knows that as the life of the Son of God stood in faith, so the life of us the adopted children of God stands in faith. He knows that if we doubt the witness which God gives us of our adoption, we give up that life just as He would have given up his own amazing life if He had hearkened to that temptation. Believe, brethren, that at every moment the tempter would have you doubting your calling and adoption of God, that he would have you seeking some other evidence of it than the fact that he stamped you his at baptism, and that thus he would rob you of all the fruits of the life which belongs to you as children of God. To some he gives sops, he stupefies them that they may forget their birthright, may never know what it means. To some he gives potions which make them feverish and restless, that they may not be content with God's witness, but may crave for some signs such as the Jews asked of our Lord. But with all his purpose is the same. It is to destroy the life of faith, it is to separate us from the Son, even as he would have separated him from the Father. And secondly, as he would rob us of the life of faith, so he would rob us too of the life of obedience. He would make us think that the privilege which God gives us in making us his children, is that we should have some great power, that we should be higher than our brethren, that we should be able to command. He would take from us the blessed truth (which is the very staff of our being) that our privilege is to submit and to obey, to show forth God's power and not our own power, to be servants, not masters. Understand, brethren, this, and you will have learnt a lesson that it is worth any pain to learn, a lesson that God has brought you here to teach you. It is that when you are laid low, when power is taken from you, power of body, yes, and power of mind, then he would bring you into the condition of his children, then he would be making you like unto his Son, who gave up his body, and poured out his soul unto death, then he would be fitting you for the life of the angels in heaven, who aspire, not to command for themselves, but who "do his commandments, hearkening unto the voice of his words." And be sure that of this blessedness the evil Spirit of pride and selfishness is seeking to rob you, that he is stirring you up to murmur against God, in order that you may not be his willing and obedient children. Lastly, in both these ways the tempter would be taking from you that life of love, that power of helping your brethren, which he wished to take from your Lord and master. While we abide by faith on the Son of God, claiming the portion and inheritance of children in him, while we are content to submit to him, to be commanded and not to command, God useth us for his purpose, God worketh in us to will and to do of his good pleasure. To some he may give one station in his Church, to some another. Some may have a larger part of his vineyard to cultivate, some a smaller; but all are his servants, all are performing his errands, all in their own sphere and vocation, are the ministers of Him who came, not to be ministered unto, but to minister, and to give his life a ransom for many.

My brethren, it is this life of faith, of obedience, of love, which the Son of God would day by day be renewing in you. He calls you to that altar now that he may renew it in you, that he may acknowledge you as his Father's children, that he may give you a heart to serve him, that he may give you power to love your brethren even as yourselves. There he will answer the tempter's suggestions for you as he answered them for himself; there he will perform a greater wonder than that to which the evil Spirit invited him. He will not command stones to be made bread; He will take the bread and say, 'Thou also shalt live by every word which proceedeth out of the mouth of God. Eat, this is my body.'

SERMON XIII.

CAST THYSELF DOWN FROM HENCE.

(Preached at Guy's Hospital.—The Third Sunday in Lent, 1839.)

Then the devil taketh him up into the holy city, and setteth him upon a pinnacle of the Temple, and saith unto him, If thou be the Son of God, cast thyself down; for it is written, He shall give his angels charge concerning thee, and in their hands they shall bear thee up, lest at any time thou dash thy foot against a stone.—MATTHEW iv. 5, 6.

I HAVE explained to you our Lord's first temptation, "If thou be the Son of God, command that these stones be made bread." Let us now, with reverence and fear, enter upon an examination of the second. It is an awful subject, but the Spirit who guided our Lord into the wilderness, himself sets it before us in this season of Lent, and we must not doubt that we shall have his help in considering it.

In his first conflict our Lord felt himself to be in the midst of a wilderness. He saw nothing but the trees around him, and the stones at his feet. He was standing in God's world; but the world of human creatures was shut out from him. There was nothing to remind him that he had come down to dwell among sinful creatures; no sight or sound that brought our pleasures or our sorrows before Him.

The tempter spoke to him there as a solitary being. He reminded him that this earth in which he was standing was his workmanship. He bade him think of himself and his own honour; as by his word he had called these stones into existence let him use them now for his necessity; let him command and they shall become bread. You know how our Lord baffled his suggestion. The tempter would make him think of himself as a solitary being dwelling in his own majesty and power. He refuses so to consider himself. He will not separate himself from those whose nature he has taken. The devil would have him use his power as the Son of God; but he claims fellowship with men. He will use the book which was written for men; he will appropriate the words which were spoken of men, to himself. He is come not mainly to assert his own power as the Son of God, but to make them sons of God. He will not turn stones into bread, he will continue his fast that he may make good for them the promise, "Man shall not live by bread alone, but by every word that proceedeth out of the mouth of God."

See what a victory this was, brethren! Not only over the immediate temptation to satisfy his hunger, but over all the circumstances in which he was placed in that desert. Everything there was withdrawing him from men, and yet, there he maintains his sympathy with men. Everything was teaching him to think of his own greatness, and he takes up his place among the poor members of his flock. Everything was leading him to assert his own dignity for the supply of his own wants, and he will only assert that dignity which he was to maintain for us by the denial and sacrifice of himself. Surely this was defeating the Spirit of evil, this was making mock of him, this was the triumph of the Son of God, not for himself but for the sake of those whom he was not ashamed to call his brethren.

But now it is said that the devil took him and carried him to the holy city, and set him upon a pinnacle of the temple. Our Lord had asserted the dominion of his spirit over his body by his fast. He had maintained that this human body of ours was never meant to be the lord over the motions of the inner man, but to be its servant. And now He proves this to be the case. His body is shown to have that power which all human bodies shall have when they acquire their proper state and become glorified—the power of moving whithersoever the spirit bids them, of beholding whatsoever it calls up before them. But mark, it is not said that he carried himself to the holy city, and placed himself on the temple. No! it is said the devil bore him there. This privilege he did not take to himself as part of his glory; he endured it as part of his temptation. For this was his trial, to see whether he would claim his powers for himself, or hold them for the glory of his unseen Father—whether he would turn them to his own advantage, or only to the good of mankind. So that this wonderful dignity which he had proved himself to possess, even in his humiliation, was itself to become the cause of a fresh conflict.

And where was He carried by virtue of this wonderful power that was in Him? To the holy city. He found himself among those men with whom in the desert He had claimed communion; He was surrounded by the members of that nation to whose fathers the word had come, "Man shall not live by bread alone, but by every word that proceedeth out of the mouth of God." He looked down upon them from a pinnacle of that temple which was the sign of God's presence, whither for so many ages the tribes of the Lord had gone up to worship. It was the holy city; within it dwelt the children of God's covenant, the heirs of His promises, those in whom all the families of the earth were to be blessed. It was the holy temple, than which there was nothing on the earth more glorious, save the body of Him in whom dwelt all the fulness of the Godhead. What a change from that inhospitable desert, what a comfort to feel Himself again amongst these tokens of the divine love, among those for whose sake He had not abhorred the Virgin's womb. But think again, my brethren, what a change from that desert in which He had enjoyed communion with His Father for forty days and forty nights, apart from the confusions and iniquity of men, where He had realized the promise for mankind, as well as for Himself, "Life is not by bread alone, but by every word of God," to a city where men were running hither and thither, intent upon gain, busy in the pursuit of the bread that perisheth, trusting in anything rather than the promise and the word of God. What a sight for His eyes, to behold all the deeds of darkness that were then doing in that city, to see how the holy seed, the seed of Abraham, the seed over which He had watched for so many ages with tender love, were polluting themselves with worse than Gentile abominations. Think how He must have felt as He saw those who were meant to dwell together in unity, to be one people, worshipping their one Lord, tearing and rending each other; here proud, self-righteous men disputing about the law and their forms of worship, and forgetting mercy and truth, and the love of God : here, men, proud of their own wisdom, scoffing at the wisdom of God, priding themselves in their unbelief; there others plotting how they may please Herod, and trick and cajole men with their political inventions and devilries. He saw not only these " blind leaders of the blind " busy in their mischievous toils, but the people, too, ignorant and helpless, wandering about as sheep not having a shepherd. Think of all this passing before the eye and the spirit of Him who had been Himself the unseen guide and watcher over this people for so long, and who was now come down from heaven that He might gather them together in one, and make them indeed a holy people unto the Lord. Think again of all that was passing in the temple on which he was standing, all the false and hypocritical worshippers, the dissemblers with God, the deceivers of their own souls, whom He knew to be there, and then say whether the pain to His body from the hunger He felt in the desert was anything to be compared with the agony which His spirit must have felt at that moment. And this, too, was the tempter's moment, this was the time when the victory which Christ had won by the answer, "It is written, Man shall not live by bread alone, but by every word that proceedeth out of the mouth of God," was to be turned against Himself. "If thou be the Son of God, cast thyself down from hence," said the tempter, "for it is written, He shall give his angels charge over thee to keep thee, lest at any time thou dash thy foot against a stone." 'Thou art right, that it is not the test of the Son of God that he should be willing to seek comfort or ease for himself. No! He should be ready to endure trial and suffering, to do something much more than merely bearing a little hunger. That thou mayest produce an effect upon the people of this city—that thou mayest startle these poor ignorant deluded men, these self-righteous or self-wise or political men, and make them see that God has indeed sent down his Son to disturb them in their vain dreams; for this thou shouldest be ready to do some great and surprising act, which shall prove how thou dependest upon thy Father's care and love. This will not be giving up thy faith—it will be showing the greatest faith. This will not be separating thyself from men—it will be only claiming the promise which was given to them long ago, and of which even sinful men felt they could avail themselves, that God's angels should be continually bearing them up and preserving them from danger. It is written so in the very book to which thou appealest. It would be most distrustful not to rely upon so sure a word.' Such was the temptation — most strange, and deep, and awful—appealing to our Lord's holiness and humility, coming indeed in the form of an angel of light.

And where lay the evil of it? Where the evil of the other temptation lay, where all evil lies. This act would have been an act of self-will. The Son of Man would have been choosing a way for influencing and instructing men. True, it would have been a way of danger to himself. It would not have been the indulgence of any bodily appetite, of any natural inclination; but it would have been the setting up of self still. The Son of God, He who was one with the Father, who could do nothing but what he saw the Father do, would have been separating himself from him. He would have been glorifying his own love to men, not his Father's love, his own wisdom in choosing circumstances for himself, not his Father's in choosing them for him, his own power of bearing danger, not his Father's power of sustaining him in it. Now, brethren, self-will and faith are the two great contraries—self-will must destroy faith, or faith must destroy self-will. Therefore, see how directly this temptation came from the Spirit of lies. 'Choose thine own ways, and trust in the Father to uphold thee in the way that thou hast chosen. Trust in God to support thy self-glorification.' This is faith slaying itself. It is looking up to God to justify the denial of his own being.

And observe how that passage from Scripture was perverted to support this wicked contradiction. You will find it in the ninety-first Psalm. A plague was raging at a certain time in Judea. The Psalmist declares his confidence that God will preserve him in it. He has been set in the midst of this plague, and he doubts not that he who set him in the midst of it, will give his angels charge over him to keep him, so that no real mischief should come to him from it. Here is the case of a man whose ways were appointed for him. Our Lord had used the same argument when he refused to make the stones bread. He had said in effect, if not in words, 'I have been brought into this wilderness by the Spirit of God. I know that by his strength I shall be sustained in it, though my hunger were ten times as keen as it is.' But the spirit of evil says, 'Distrust God's wisdom in fixing thy position, and then trust him to reward thine unbelief.'

Once again, then, we behold the battle of him in whom dwelt all faith, obedience, love, with the spirit of unbelief, disobedience, hatred. The victory was won by these simple words, "It is written again, Thou shalt not tempt the Lord thy God." I have told you already that by these temptations of our Lord we are to understand our own temptation, that we can only know what the spirit of evil is saying to us by knowing what he said to him, that we can only baffle this spirit with his weapons. Let me endeavour, then, with God's help, to apply this history to our own circumstances.

1. You have heard how our Lord was carried from the wilderness to the holy city. Understand by this how all our circumstances in the world may be changed, and yet the tempter be with us still. Hundreds of men have gone out into the desert thinking that in that way they should escape temptation; but it has found them out. The spirit of evil has shown them that they do not escape from him by escaping from men. Then they have run back into the holy city, they have thought that they were exposed to danger because they were away from the ordinances of God. But there, too, they have found there was no security; it has only been a change from "Command these stones to be made bread," into "Cast thyself down from hence." Learn from this, brethren, that your safety is not in your circumstances, but in God—that it is good to be in the desert—good to be in the sick chamber—good to be out of the sight and hearing of men if you are led

thither by the Spirit of God; but that the good is not in being free from danger, but in knowing that in that solitude you have God's presence and God's promises, that you are still one of that race which he has promised shall live by every word which proceedeth out of his mouth. Believe, also, that it is good, yea, a most blessed lot to live in the holy city; to have the living tokens that you are members of God's church about you; to be seeing wherever you turn a token that God *is*, and that he makes himself known to men; to be permitted to join in his praises; to be nourished by the living water, and bread and wine of his sacraments. But neither are these securities against the tempter. They are only pledges, most sure pledges, and most mighty helps (if so you will receive them) against him. And they are pledges and helps in this way, that they bring you into the presence of him who is mightier than that tempter, and who has overcome him.

· 2. But, secondly, consider what was the particular temptation of our Lord when he was brought into the holy city. I have taken the words in their simplest meaning—I have supposed that the evil Spirit actually proposed to him to cast himself from the temple to the ground. For what I wanted to make you understand was the object of the temptation, and the story read in the plainest way makes that evident to us. Yet, I have no doubt that there was a deeper meaning hid under this. I have no doubt that when our Lord was reflecting upon the iniquities of the holy city, the devil suggested to him the thought, ' What avails it to be a Jew, to be a citizen of God's city, a member of the holy nation, when holiness, and purity, and unity have utterly deserted it? " If thou be the Son of God," set an example of throwing away these vain privileges; prove that to be the child of God means something different from what these vain men fancy; teach them as your forerunner taught them, not to say, We have Abraham to our Father, but that God is able of these stones to raise up children unto Abraham.' This would have been casting himself down from the temple in another way than that which I first spoke of; but the spirit which prompted the act would have been the same. Now, brethren, precisely this temptation is presented to us, to all of us, this day. Those words, "What good shall my birthright do to me? What is my baptism good for? What is it to be born in the holy city, to be a member of the church of God, if men can have all these privileges, and yet cozen and lie, and hate one another, just as if they had none of them. Cast thyself down from hence, give up this vain honour: this can have nothing to do with being a child of God, and an heir of his promises;" these words you will hear each of you—they will be spoken to you by your own hearts—they will be spoken to you by other men. I tell you, whoever speaks them, whatever human voice brings them to you, they come from the evil Spirit; it is he, and he only, who in reality is uttering them. I care not what texts of Scripture may be brought to confirm them; I care not what appearance of faith and trust in God they may put on. The temptation is the same, the very same which was addressed to your Lord; the very same which was pressed upon him with a text of Scripture, and was urged upon him as a proof of his faith. "Cast thyself down from hence, for it is written that the angels shall bear thee up, lest at any time thou dash they foot against a stone."

3. Now, under this great temptation to abandon your birthright, to give up that position as children of God, and citizens of the kingdom of heaven, which was confirmed to you, as it was confirmed to our Lord himself, in the waters of baptism, are contained a number of other temptations, all having the same origin, all pointing the same way. Remember, your birthright is union with Christ; the right to call God your Father in him; the privilege of being led by his Spirit. Every time that you are moved to commit any sin, every time that the thought comes into your mind, 'Is it not a little one?' you are urged to cast yourself down from this position, you are urged to renounce your trust upon Christ, and live as if he were not your Lord, to forget that you are a child of the holy God, to resist his Spirit of love. Every time that you are persuaded to think prayer to him an idle or irksome thing, or to forget that your own heart requires to be kept with all diligence, or to separate yourselves from your brethren, and set yourselves up against them, there is a voice, and it is the voice of the evil Spirit, saying, 'Cast thyself down; give up that which God hath given thee to hold.'

4. Understand next from this history of our Lord's second temptation, that we are not to plead love to our brethren as any excuse for going out of God's way, or doing work which he has not set us to do. Our Lord was urged to cast himself down from the temple, that he might convince the Jews of their unbelief. He who urged him to it wished him in that very thing to commit an act of unbelief. Thousands of such acts have been committed by men who thought that they were honouring God and helping their

brethren. They were doing neither. They were not honouring God, for they believed that they loved their brethren better than he did. They were not helping their brethren, for the only way to help them is to follow God's ways, and to give up our own. To be working together with God is our highest honour. When we are not doing this, we cannot be working any good to ourselves or to any other man.

5. Again, brethren, learn the way in which God's word may be used, and the way in which it may be abused. Thou art in sickness, hunger, poverty, which God has brought upon thee; here is his word to comfort and strengthen thee. The privileges of God's children have been given thee; this book, which contains the experience of his children is for thee. Receive the words of it. Believe in God, and take courage. Thou art in some condition in which God has put thee. Some one comes and quotes to you passages from the Scripture to persuade you that this is not the condition in which you ought to be, that some other would be better for you, that you would be pleasing God, and doing an act of faith by changing it. Heed him not; never mind his texts; assure yourself that he does not understand them nor you either; wait till God explains them to you, which he will do in his own time when you want them; meantime be quite sure that you are obeying God in staying where he has placed you, and doing the work he has given you to do, and that you would be obeying the devil if you did otherwise, let him quote Scripture as fast as he will.

6. Finally, learn that faith is the giving up of your own will to God's will; resting in him, because you

cannot rest in yourselves; living in him, because you have no life of your own. Therefore, be sure that all faith which interferes with this—all faith which leads you to think that you are anything—all faith which does not begin in humility, continue in humility, end in humility, is a lie and shall come to nought. Trust in God and be doing good, and verily you shall be fed. But see that you are not casting yourselves down from the temple, for God and his angels will not bear you up.

SERMON XIV.

THE KINGDOMS OF THE WORLD AND THEIR GLORY.

(Preached at Guy's Hospital.—The Fourth Sunday in Lent, 1839.)

> Again, the devil taketh him up into an exceeding high mountain, and sheweth him all the kingdoms of the world, and the glory of them; and saith unto him, All these things will I give thee if thou wilt fall down and worship me. Then saith Jesus unto him, Get thee behind me, Satan; for it is written, Thou shalt worship the Lord thy God, and him only shalt thou serve.—
> MATTHEW vi. 8, 9.

THE prayer which I have just offered up is called, you know, 'The Lord's Prayer,' because he said to his disciples, "After this manner, therefore, pray ye." The Lord's prayer it is, in another sense than this; for whoever has really uttered it has been taught and enabled to utter it by him. But you must not suppose that the petitions in it had never been poured forth from the hearts of faithful men before they were gathered up into this form. Rather believe that these were the very desires with which, in all ages, faithful men had been inspired, though they expressed them differently, according to their different circumstances and the circumstances of the world in which they were living.

They believed in God; they were sure that He

was distinct from all the things and all the persons whom he had made; they wished to keep his name pure and holy, apart from all other names. But the world was full of beautiful things; they met with faces and forms among their fellow-creatures which were lovely to look upon; they met with people who were kind, and gentle, and wise. Could it be wrong to honour and worship this beauty, and loveliness, and gentleness, and wisdom? Must they not be divine? The world did pay homage to a number of such objects. But instead of seeing that which was good, and noble, and pure in them, it degraded them the more it served them. It honoured them chiefly because they seemed capable of doing mischief; it delighted to think of them as capricious and unmerciful, and like itself. Therefore the good men felt, 'Oh! that He in whom is all loveliness, and goodness, and truth, would declare himself. Oh! that he would teach us to distinguish between him and all his creatures, whose excellence has come from him.' They cried in their hearts, whatever their words were, 'Hallowed be thy Name.'

Again, they felt, 'How wonderfully different we men are from the other creatures in the world. They can eat, and drink, and sleep; they can do many great works; multitudes of them are as strong as we; some of them seem almost as clever. But not one of them is able to say, 'I will do this or I will not.' They follow their instincts; they do just what is marked out for them. We can choose for ourselves. A command is given us; but let the power that gives it be as great as it may, we can still refuse to obey it. How wonderful this is! We have wills, but is not this the very cause of our misery? Do we not upset everything because we will have a way of our own?' What, then, they thought, must we do? Shall we ask to have our wills taken away? That is asking to be animals. But surely there are creatures who have wills even as we have, and yet do not use them to their own ruin. There are some who have learnt the blessing of obedience. Might not we become like them? They said, Lord, make us like them; that is to say, they said, "Thy will be done in earth even as it is in heaven."

But I think there was another prayer which we may be more certain would go up from innumerable human hearts than even either of these. It did not require that men should be faithful or true in order to feel what a burden and oppression there was in this world; how little those who ruled it sympathised with those whom they ruled—how little either understood the other; what conflicts and tumults were perpetually going on because this and that man wished to reign; and how few made themselves or others happy by the power which they had. Surely there must be somewhere or other the right government. Surely there must be somewhere one who ought to reign. Oh! that he would appear. Oh! that he would take the great power that belongs to him. Holy men in their chambers and their prisons, the widow and the fatherless in their lonely huts, thousands of desolate and oppressed people, in all corners of the earth, must have cried, "Thy kingdom come."

And now there was one standing in the wilderness of Judea, who had entered into the world that he might glorify the name of God,—that he might do the will of God—and that he might establish the kingdom of God. He had been tempted by the spirit of evil to glorify his own name, and to prove that all the things were subject to him by commanding the stones to be made bread. He had resisted the temptation, and had hallowed his Father's name by claiming for men the promise which had been made to them, that they should not live by bread alone, but by every word which proceedeth out of the mouth of God. He had been tempted to set up his own will—to choose a way for himself by casting himself down from the pinnacle of the temple; and he had resisted, saying, "It is written, Thou shalt not tempt the Lord thy God." One more conflict he must still pass through. He had been tried in the solitude of the desert, whether he would assert his own dominion over the earth which he had made. He had been tried in the Holy City whether he would claim his rights over the flock which he had guided for so many generations. But he had come to redeem, not inanimate things, not the Holy City only, but mankind. He had come to be the ruler over all the nations of the earth. This was to be his especial glory. The Gentiles were to come to the brightness of his rising; the isles were to wait for his law. But he was in the wilderness, the poorest of poor men; his body weak through fasting, his spirit engaged in an awful conflict, all the powers within him humbled and crushed down. In a moment the scene was changed. He was on the summit of a high mountain beholding all the kingdoms of the world and their glory. And he heard a voice saying,

"All these will I give thee if thou wilt fall down and worship me." It was, again, the power within him which enabled him thus to overcome the restraints to which our bodies are subject. And again, the power was part of his trial. It was the devil who carried him to the mountain, not he who placed himself there; the devil who called up this grand vision before him, not he who bade it rise.

But what was it that he saw? There was a picture clear and bright before his actual eye, of people wandering about in their different dresses, at their games, and at their funerals. Emperors, surrounded by their nobles and their armed men; labourers in the fields, slaves in the mines, birth-day feasts, and the plain covered with dead men when the battle was done. All these pictures of human pleasure and woe passed before him evidently, distinctly; no one confused with the other, each person in the group perceived and recognised. But it could not have been so if there had not been another vision as clear and bright before his inward eye; if he had not entered into the meaning of all these things, and into the secret heart of all who were engaged in them. What the kings and wise men were plotting and contriving, what was the source of the peasant's mirth and gladness, what the slave was sighing for, the cause of those battles and their end—all this He knew perfectly, not by guesses or fancies, but as one knows the throbbing in one's own head, or the beatings of the heart. For we must not stop short at the words, 'our Lord knew all these things.' Such knowledge could only come through deepest sympathy. He knew because He felt; all these creatures were dear to Him; they were His own creatures. The bright world in which they were sporting, or fighting, or weeping, was His world; its brightness and beauty which they were striving to enjoy, or to imitate, or to mar, had come from Him. The minds which were laying those schemes of policy, received their thoughts and wisdom from Him. The affections of fear and hope, of joy and sorrow, of indignation and longing, which were coming forth in them, had been imparted by Him: He had made them feel that they could not live apart from each other; He had formed them into families; He had established the bonds of fatherhood and brotherhood, of wife and husband; He had taught them to feel the need of laws, and had given them laws, and had brought them into neighbourhoods and cities, and had set kings over them; He had kindled in kings and subjects an insatiable appetite for glory. And this He had done not once for all on the creation day; but these thoughts and impulses, and charities, as well as all the powers of bodily life and enjoyment, had been going forth fresh every moment from Him in whom is life, and whose life is the light of men.

And wherever He turns, He sees sorrow and confusion, men rending and tearing one another, God's holy order violated, that life which He has set up in families broken by the sins of fathers and children, of wives and husbands; that holy life which he hath set up in nations, broken by the pride of kings, and the rebellion of subjects, by people who think it a misery to obey, and governors who think it a misery to be just and merciful. And He sees the glory of these kingdoms. This is their

glory, to tear each other in pieces, of the powerful
to make slaves of the weaker, of the weaker to
struggle that they may be powerful, in order that
they may make slaves of them; crimes and tyrannies
committed under holy names; law and religion used
to justify and encourage them. All this the Son of
God. beheld; all this confusion and misery passed in
a moment of time before *His* eyes who had seen all
the order of things, and, lo, it was very good. And
then He heard a voice speaking to His inmost heart,
and saying, "All these will I give thee" (for they
are given to me), "if thou wilt fall down and
worship me." Could He doubt the truth of what
the tempter thus said? Were not these the devil's
kingdoms? Was not this the devil's glory? Had
he not a right to say, These are *mine*, I can give
them to whomsoever I will? And what if the Son
of God should consent to receive them? Could
He not answer the prayers, which men had been
pouring forth? Could he not at once make these
kingdoms happy? Could he not at once establish
true glory in them, in place of that lying glory in
which they were now delighting? Should He not
thus at once enter upon that kingdom which had
been promised him? Should He not deliver the
nations in a moment of time from that wretched
yoke under which they might yet have for ages to
groan? And what was to be the price of this
mighty blessing? It was merely that He should do
some act of homage to that power of evil who
seemed to be in truth the possessor of all these
things. Was this too much to give for such an
advantage, not to himself but to mankind? Might

not He who had humbled Himself so far for our sakes, perform this one more act of humiliation? Would it not be righteous, be glorious, to do so? So spake the tempter. When you first read the story of the trial, you may think it was the strangest of all, you may wonder that such a thought as this could ever have been set before our Lord, "Fall down and worship me;" but when we look more into it, we see that there was none more deep and subtle, none that spoke in a more secret and wonderful manner to the holiness and love that were in Him.

And now, brethren, where lay the root of this temptation, and how may we know when this also is addressed to us? The root of it lay in the thought that these kingdoms of the world were the devil's kingdoms, and that it was he who could dispose of them. If our Lord had believed this, if he had acknowledged this claim, he would have been falling down and worshipping the evil spirit, he would have been confessing him to be the Lord. But for all that he beheld this horrible vision of human misery and human crime, for all that he found men actually doing homage to the spirit of evil, actually serving him with their thoughts, and words, and deeds; for all that he saw kings and people choosing the devil's glory, and making it their glory; in spite of all this, he believed and knew that these kingdoms were not the devil's kingdoms, but God's kingdoms. He knew that men's sin began in this, consisted in this, that they thought and believed the devil to be their king when God was their king.

On this occasion, as on the two former, he

answered, "It is written." As if he had said, 'It is not only true that the God of righteousness will be King hereafter when I shall have established my Church upon the earth. It is true now. It has been true always. This book, this record which is preserved in durable letters that it may testify of durable, unchangeable things, this book bears witness to His dominion; I am come to claim it as His, I am come to set aside all Satan's pretensions to be the master of this earth, and of those who inhabit it. So far as this I am come to change the condition of the world. But it will not have a new king. Only He whose right it is will drive all usurpers out of it. Of old it was commanded, "Thou shalt worship the Lord, the Lord merciful and gracious, slow to anger plenteous in goodness and truth." Of old it was said, "Thou, man, shalt worship Him as thy God." Thou shalt look up to Him and believe that He cares for thee, that thou art under his government and protection. Of old it was said, "Him *only* shalt thou serve." His rule is not shared with any other. The Righteous Being has not a half dominion, and thou shalt not pay Him a half service. Thou shalt not think that falsehood has a claim upon some part of thee, that thou mayest render it a share of thy homage and Truth the rest. "Him *only* shalt thou serve." This was the command, and I am come to fulfil it.'

In this instance, then, as in both the others. trust and obedience were proved to be the pillars of our Lord's life, and his defence against the tempter. In this, as in both the other cases, He maintained his position as the Son of God by an act of submission and humiliation; in this, as in both the other cases,

He took his place among men, submitted to the law which had been made for men, and claimed for men the privileges which He asserted for Himself. Let us consider what blessing He has hereby won for us.

1. That vision of all the kingdoms of the earth and the glory of them is one which no eye, perhaps, could bear to receive, but his to whom it was shewn in the wilderness. It would be sufficiently appalling for us to behold some tiny portion of that world which he beheld at once and altogether. If we could see only what is going on in this England, or in any one county of it, that would be enough to frighten us, and to make us think that the devil speaks true when he says, This is mine. And yet this, on the whole, may be, as we boast it is, the best and most favoured portion of the earth. If we went on farther and thought of all the rest of the Christian world, its divisions, its idolatries, its miseries, we should be still more inclined to think it was the property of an evil spirit. And if we sent our minds abroad still farther and remembered how large a part of the universe has never belonged to the Church, or has broken loose from it, nearly all doubt would vanish from our minds, and we should say, 'There may be some exceptions to this rule, there may be a few here and there who are still standing out against it, but, if God's word be true, if wickedness and injustice are contrary to his nature, this world, which we inhabit, must belong to some other than to him.' So hundreds of men have said, many in words, more in their thoughts, and they have fancied they were saying what was right and pleasing to God. But though they might not know it, or

mean it, they were admitting a blasphemous doctrine into their minds, they were doing that very homage to the spirit of evil which he requires of us.

If there be one man in any county of England who declares that the Lord is his God, who says, 'I was baptized into his name, I am taken to be his child, and his Spirit dwells with me,' that man says what is true of him and true of all the men and women in that county, and true of all members of Christ's Church, in every part of the world. If they do not think so, that is their misery. If they make the spirit of evil their Lord and God, that is their lie. But though every man be a liar the thing is true; we have been taken to be God's children, and He is our father. And as every true man in the Church is a witness of what every other man in the Church has been made, so the Church itself is a witness to all mankind of what God has done for them, and what they really are, created in Christ, and redeemed by Christ, and capable, but for their disbelieving this truth, and not taking their position as members of his body, of shewing forth his character and his glory. We have no right to speak of ourselves as belonging to an evil spirit, nor of any human creature, nor of any one insect, or flower, which God has made as belonging to it. The evil spirit never has created anything, never can create anything. He is simply the destroyer, death is his only handiwork, and Christ has taken that from him. Lay fast hold of this truth. The kingdoms of the earth are God's, and the glory of them. You are his by every title of creation and redemption, and adoption. And you are to tell your children and your neighbours, and all that have to do with you, the same thing. You are to say to them all, The God of Truth, and righteousness, and love, the God and Father of our Lord Jesus Christ is your God, and there is none other, you owe no homage to any other, you are not under the power of any other except by your own choice and pleasure: Him and him only must thou serve.

2. It is a hard thing to believe this, brethren, when there are so many things that seem to contradict it, but believe it we must, if we would be honest men, if we would not practise a hundred cheats and rogueries even when we fancy we are doing what is most right. Holy men have been betrayed into sins which make one weep and blush when one reads the history of Christ's church, because they have thought that falsehood and evil were the lords of the world, and that if they were to overcome the world they must do it by entering into some bargain or compromise with these masters of it. They thought they might practise frauds, and utter lies for the honour of God, they thought they might now and then do a base or a cruel action provided it was done for the sake of God's honour and of charity. The devil was saying to them, These are mine, and I give them to whomsoever I will. They believed him. He asked this token of homage from them, and they paid it. They are, I trust, forgiven by One who knows that their hearts were right in the main, that they loved truth, really, though they could not trust it at all times. But the mischiefs that have followed from every such faithless act, have been more than I can tell you of, and though they are no warrant for us for condemning others, they are most terrible warnings to ourselves. If ever we

who are the ministers of God, are guilty of deceiving you, or saying something which we do not really believe, for the sake of leading you to do something we wish you to do, we are mocking God, and shewing that we do not really own him for our only master; that we think we may sometimes serve his enemy as well as him.

3. But, remember, that though this sin is greatest in us, you may fall into it, too. When the thought comes into your mind, as it has come into the minds of you all, and will come again, how by a little dishonesty, by a little unfair dealing, you will better your chances in the world, and be more likely to succeed than you would if you did the simple, right thing; then be sure the devil is saying to you, Fall down and worship me. To one the temptation may come in this way, and to one in that. The hungry man will be tempted to steal, the seller to hide some bad quality in his goods, the man who has done wrong to equivocate for the sake of keeping it hidden. And sometimes there is a sort of desperation which leads a poor man to say, All is going so badly with me, there is no help; I may as well give up struggling to do right; I will drown my thoughts in drinking; I will do just whatever the lusts within me urge me to do. These, I am sure, are very great and sore trials, of which none can know the force fully whose course of life leads him into another kind of difficulties. But remember that He who was tempted in the wilderness of Judea knows the force of them, and is as much concerned that you should overcome in them, as that any great apostle or martyr should triumph over his enemies. And remember that these temptations of yours can

only be resisted, as the enemies of saints and martyrs were resisted, by the might of him who said, 'Get thee behind me, Satan.'

In one sense the conflict in which He engaged in the desert is over, the issue of it is decided. We know who is the mightier, and that he will be shown to be mightier at last. In another sense the conflict is still going on in the heart of every living man. And when one conflict is over, another must begin, even as in our Lord's case the temptation to make the stones bread, was followed by the temptation to cast himself down, and that by the call to worship the Evil Spirit. And when this call has been repelled by us for ourselves, it is only that we may fight with it again in our brethren, even as the entire temptation of our Lord was only the beginning of his warfare with the sensuality of the people, the pride of the Pharisees, the desire of greatness in his own disciples. And if Satan leave us for a season we must expect that he will return in some other hour, even as the conflict in Lent was only a foretaste of our Lord's more terrible agony in the Passion-week. But it will be true of us, also, as it was of Him, that when in his strength we have, at any time, overcome our foe, angels will come and minister to us. There will be a peace within the heart following and rewarding its struggles, and secret tidings will be brought us of a time when the last struggle will be over, and no power shall any longer dispute that Christ is the King of kings, and Lord of lords.

SERMON XV.

THE ALABASTER BOX OF OINTMENT.

(Preached at Ely Chapel, Holborn, May, 1840, for the Repairs of the Chapel.)

Now when Jesus was in Bethany in the house of Simon the leper,
There came unto him a woman having an alabaster box of very precious ointment, and poured it on his head, as he sat at meat.
But when his disciples saw it, they had indignation, saying, To what purpose is this waste?
For this ointment might have been sold for much, and given to the poor.
When Jesus understood it, he said unto them, Why trouble ye the woman? for she hath wrought a good work upon me,
For ye have the poor always with you; but me ye have not always.
For in that she hath poured this ointment on my body, she did it for my burial.
Verily, I say unto you, Wheresoever this Gospel shall be preached in the whole world, there shall also this, that this woman hath done, be told for a memorial of her.—MATTHEW xxvi. 6—13.

THERE is a difference, you may remember, between the report of this transaction which is given by St. John, and those which we find in the Gospels of St. Matthew and St. Mark. The complaint against the woman is attributed by the one to Judas, by the others to the disciples generally, or to some who sat at meat. I believe that the variations of this kind which occur in the different evangelists, are worthy of very diligent study. Those who wish to have an inward and real knowledge of our Lord's life, would be sorry to obtain traditions of his words and acts which we do not possess by the sacrifice of those various records of the same transactions which have been given to us. For one act devoutly considered, may often lead us into a more deep acquaintance with the life which it reveals as well as with the characters and circumstances of the bystanders, than a long history; and there is no greater help in the study of any act than to look at it in the different lights in which it presented itself to several witnesses or contemporaries. In the present case a very important moral is suggested, I think, by a comparison of the narratives. The words, St. John says, were spoken by Judas Iscariot. The feeling expressed in them, we may conclude from St. Matthew, was exhibited by the Apostles generally. It was evident from their countenances or their language, that they thought his objection a reasonable one. A thoroughly hard-hearted and selfish man was thus the spokesman and interpreter for a number of honest, earnest, and affectionate men. That which was in him an utterance of mere heartlessness, seemed to them a just and benevolent sentiment. It would not have seemed so if their hearts and minds' had been perfectly clear; if there had been no mixture in them of that guile which predominated in him. It would not have seemed so if they had been watchfully cultivating those better thoughts and affections, which distinguished them from him. But so it was, and so it has been in all ages of the Church. Good men have repeated the plausible sayings of evil men; have made cold and vulgar thoughts respectable by adopting them; have checked, so far as they could, the designs and inspirations of humbler and purer spirits; under pretence of serving the poor, have forbidden acts of devotion and of homage to Christ; and have found at last that none had so much cause to complain of their wisdom, as those whom they had intended to benefit by it.

We shall lose the effect of this warning, my brethren, if we do not observe how very plausible the complaint of the disciples was. They had lived three years with their Master; they had never known him to do one act to indulge or to glorify himself; they had seen him disclaim the honours which the people would have put upon him; they had been commanded to gather the fragments after the feast of the five thousand, that nothing might be lost; they had been taught to husband every saving for the poor; his whole life had been one of devotion to the poor. Was it wonderful they should think with themselves, 'This woman is merely obeying a foolish thoughtless impulse; she fancies she will please our Lord by this service, but we know better; we know she is doing what will be most offensive to him. He does not require homage to himself, he desires to be helping and blessing the poor creatures around him. Surely then he would desire that this ointment should be sold for three hundred pence, rather than that it should be wasted upon his head.' It would be difficult, I think, to find any flaw in this calculation. If the spirit of calculation is to govern us, Judas was right.

But our Lord came into the world that men might

be governed by another spirit than the spirit of calculation, namely, by the spirit of love. He knew that Mary was actuated by this spirit, and he wished his disciples to understand, that it was a much deeper, more far-seeing spirit, than that to which they were yielding. "Why trouble ye the woman?" he said, "she hath wrought a good work upon me." A good work—a work springing from a deep root, and therefore which will bear fruit hereafter. "For ye have the poor always with you, but me ye have not always." As if he had said, 'You would have wished her to bestow some act of kindness upon the suffering people that are before your eyes; but she has seen more into the meaning of things; she has seen that I am the Lord and Prince of these poor men; that I am come for a little while into the world to shew myself to them and that then I shall go away. She is pouring out her tokens of faith and confidence upon one who is himself the poorest of the poor; she is performing, not merely a common act of love, but is come to do reverence to the source of love. "She is come to anoint my body before to the burying." Her act has a meaning in it. You do not understand it now, but you will understand it hereafter, and therefore, hereafter, wherever my cross or my tomb shall be spoken of among men, wherever it shall be told and believed that the Son of God died and was buried, that he entered into fellowship with sufferings of men, and that he rose again to be their King and their Priest; there shall this which this woman has done—this simple, genuine, uncalculating act of love, be told for a memorial of her. The deed of hers shall be connected with my life and death.'

It was not then by refuting the reasoning of His disciples that our Lord rebuked them; it was by telling them that there was a higher principle of action than all such reasonings, a principle which, though it may seem rash and reckless of consequences, has really more wisdom in it, and leads to greater consequences, than all plans and contrivances whatsoever. Only consider this. Suppose that ointment had been sold for three hundred pence, and distributed among a few poor people, who were living at Jerusalem at that time, what hundreds of thousands of poor people who have lived in all countries of the world, from that time to the present, would have been cheated of this history of Mary's act of love and devotion—cheated of the witness which it bears to His willingness to receive and honour every mite that is given as a proof of affection to Him—cheated of an example—cheated of a comfort that has perhaps gone with them to their death-beds. It is easy to measure the effects of three hundred pence, or of thirty thousand talents; but how utterly impossible it is to measure the effects of one good thought, or feeling, or desire communicated to the spirit of a man, of one strong conviction implanted in his heart that he does not belong to this earth, but is a citizen of another kingdom, of one settled persuasion that he has an invisible friend and Father. And then, if we think of such feelings and hopes communicated to hundreds of minds from generation to generation, we may form some estimate (and still but an imperfect one) of the difference between the worth of the box of ointment which was poured upon our Lord's head, and of the three hundred pence which might have been given to the poor. Who can calculate how many hundreds of thousands of pence may have been given with a heartiness and tenderness which were far more precious than the gift, in consequence of the feelings of affection and devotion which this record had been the means of inspiring?

The applications which have been made of Judas's remark in different periods of the Church, and the applications which may be made of our Lord's answer to it, are innumerable. Every page in the history of past times, and certainly in the history of our own, suggests them.

I shall refer this morning to but one, which is connected with the demand that I am to make upon your charity. It has been said again and again by persons who have looked at the pains which have been bestowed upon churches and cathedrals to make them goodly and beautiful, "To what purpose is this waste? All this might have been sold and given to the poor." Sometimes I know the language takes a stronger form. It is affirmed that simplicity should be the great characteristic of the worship of God, and that all such attempts to honour him must be hateful in his eyes. Of this complaint I shall say but little. If by simplicity is meant the absence of all tawdriness, all conceits and affectations which so constantly defile the works of man, and from which the works of God are so free, no words can be spoken too strongly in praise of it. What we most lament in those modern buildings, which have been raised since men began to act so much upon mere principles of calculation, is that everything in them seems contrived for outward display and effect, that they have no singleness of purpose, that they are artificial, not natural. But if by simplicity be meant the absence of beauty, and richness, and harmony, of all outward tokens and symbols that there is a wonder and a mystery within, from what part of God's universe, I would ask, is this simplicity copied or derived? The endless varieties of hill, and wood, and waterfall, the leaves of spring, the fruits of autumn, surely do not testify that God has left all things bare and naked, that this is the way in which he would build a temple to his own glory.

But the other argument has undoubtedly most weight. How can it have been right we are asked in times when there must have been poor men wanting common bread, as well as the bread of life, to raise great and noble edifices? How can it be right to preserve or restore them now? The question is as I have stated it. It is not whether we should attempt to raise such buildings in our own day; possibly we are not at present called upon to do so; possibly we have not among us the ability to do so. But it is whether our ancestors were doing a right or wrong thing in bequeathing us such buildings, and whether the bequest is of any value to us in this day. Now these inquiries I think our Lord has answered by anticipation. The same spirit of love, unconscious of any object except that of doing homage to Him which He attributed to Mary, when He said, "She hath wrought a good work upon me;" the same real care for the poor under an apparent forgetfulness of them which He appears to have recognised in her act, when He said, "The poor ye have always with you, but me ye have not always;" the same foresight of future sorrow which is acknowledged in the words, "She hath anointed me for my burial;" were exhibited by those who, in our cities and in our country, in rich neighbourhoods and in poor, in open squares or narrow courts, dedicated churches to God.

1. They did what they could. They believed that Christ was the king of the world, and they came to own Him as the king; they brought their alabaster box of ointment as a confession that from Him came all the wealth or honours that they had; all power to serve Him, all the desires which made that power effectual. They set up these tokens in the midst of the land, and they believed it was no waste to squander upon them either their outward or their inward resources, either the riches or the genius which God had bestowed upon them. They thought it no waste of time to be years in raising these buildings to Him; if it were centuries, yet it was to One who is the same yesterday, to-day, and for ever, that they were rendering their homage, and it signified nothing whether they should see the completion of their work, for because He lived, they would live also, and they trusted that He would be the refuge of their children from generation to generation, as He had been theirs.

2. And in this way, brethren, I say they were providing for the poor, as they could not have done if they had husbanded all their pence to give to them. For they were testifying to all the poor men who lived about them that a kingdom of righteousness and peace was set up in the midst of them, and that He who preached the Gospel to the poor, and died for the poor, was at the head of it; and every poor man, as he went forth to his work in the morning, or returned from it in the evening, though he might not be able to

read the book which is the charter of his inheritance, yet might look up to some of these spires that pointed towards heaven, and might say to himself, 'Here are tokens that I am a fellow citizen with the saints, and of the household of God—here is that which reminds me that I am baptized into the name of the Father, the Son, and the Holy Ghost—here is that which says that durable riches are provided for me—here is encouragement to bear the toil and drudgery of life, as my Lord bore it before me, in the hope that I may one day overcome, and sit down with Him upon His throne, even as he has overcome and is set down with his Father upon His throne.' And the more pains were bestowed upon the construction of these buildings, the more elaborately they were contrived to outshine all the costly houses and castles of the earth, the more might the poor man feel and be assured, 'That fellowship to which I am admitted, and of which these buildings are a witness, is a greater and more glorious fellowship than that from which I am excluded, and will last when it is no more.'

3. But there is yet another effect of these buildings, which seems to connect them directly with the act of Mary. There have been periods in the history of the world—we have every reason to suppose that there will be such periods again—when faith and hope seem utterly to perish out of the hearts of men, when nothing is felt to be real but what is visible, when every action is judged by its immediate results, when there is no vision in the land, when Mammon alone is worshipped. These may be called the times of the Church's burial. Her life is safe, for it is hid with Christ in God; her body is safe, too, preserved

from all decay, watched over by the angels; but she is, as it were, gone into the grave, men are rejoicing that she ceases to vex them any longer, only a few Maries are still weeping beside the tomb, and thinking of the third day. But these buildings have been provided against this time of burial; they stand as solemn witnesses of what was: they confront the eyes of those who can see only with their outward eyes; they insult the worshippers of Mammon with tokens that there has been another worship in the world; they scare them in their dreams with the prophecy of a time when there shall be another worship again. The humble see them, and are glad; they speak of permanence when everything seems changeable and perishing; they are signs of Him who has been, and is, and will be; they testify that the man of the earth shall not always oppress, but that the Lord will awake as one out of sleep, and will put His enemies to a perpetual shame, and will make His Church the praise and glory of the whole earth.

4. And, therefore, it is true, that wherever this gospel is preached in the whole world, there shall also that which these builders of churches have done be told for a memorial of them. Wherever men shall hear and shall believe the glorious tidings that God has sent His Son into the world, to make men His children; wherever any shall bring their children to claim that glorious state in the waters of baptism; wherever any shall come to be confirmed with new grace before they enter upon the conflict of the world; wherever any shall come to feed upon the flesh of their Lord, and to drink his blood, there

shall be a witness and memorial of those who in ages past laboured that the stones of this earth might be consecrated to these blessed purposes, that outward temples might be the symbols of that which hath foundations, whose builder and maker was God. The memorial of these men, my brethren, is among you at this day; here, in this little nook of this huge city, they left this house of prayer, as a sign that there is something better to live for than gain, and that the treasures of the earth may be fitly bestowed upon even the smallest building which testifies that God is in the midst of us. Here some of the holiest and greatest men of the English Church have offered up sacrifices to God, and have declared his name to their brethren. Till the day in which all things shall be revealed, it will never be known what may have been done here to stay the hand of the destroying angel from the marts and towers of London, to preserve a seed which, in days of blasphemy and cruelty, may still hallow the name of God and preserve brotherly love. Do not think that you are asked to do a vain or useless thing when we ask you to preserve those houses which your forefathers raised. The work that cometh of love was honoured in them, and will be honoured in you. He who read the heart of Mary when she poured the alabaster box of ointment on His head, and of the poor widow who gave all that she had to the treasury of the temple, will see in your gifts to-day a pledge that you honour His name and His Church, that what you do not give directly to the poor, you give to Him, and through Him to them; and though your names may never be heard, that which you have done will be a memorial for the times to come. He will own that you have done what you could that the blessings of the past might not be wasted upon us, that the acts of the fathers might be made known to the children.*

* In the private devotions of Bishop Andrews there is a prayer for the worshippers in Ely Chapel, as being a place in which he had for a long time ministered.

SERMON XVI.

THE PRINCE OF SUFFERERS.

(Preached at Guy's Hospital.—Good Friday Morning, 1840.)

> Then came Jesus forth, wearing the crown of thorns, and the purple robe. And Pilate said unto them, Behold the man!—JOHN xix. 5.

My brethren, on such days as this, our minds are often very much confused. We feel that there is something wonderful for us to think of, but we know not where our thoughts upon it are to begin, or how we may carry them on. We feel as if there were a kind of weight upon us which we cannot throw off and we cannot lift. The day is full of such strange recollections, so much deeper than any man or angel can take in, and yet it seems as if every one of us was meant to take them in. Therefore it is that many wish to get rid of these days altogether, just as they would be glad to get rid of Sunday altogether out of the week. They say they like to have thoughts as they rise up naturally in their minds, they do not wish to have thoughts forced and pressed upon them. They say this obligation hinders them from feeling freely about such subjects, it frets and torments them instead of making them quiet and happy.

Now I can quite well understand what they mean

by this, and can feel something of it as well as they. But, my brethren, I would earnestly exhort you, and myself, to beware of this. Do not let us fancy that when we have a natural disinclination to a thing, it is therefore unsuitable for us, or not likely to do us good. These natural inclinations and disinclinations which some persons lay so much stress upon and think that they are to follow and obey, are not our true masters. They pretend that everything which opposes them is an enemy and a tyrant, but surely they are themselves our greatest enemies and tyrants. These natural tastes and inclinations lead us to indulge ourselves. Sometimes they say, Indulge in eating and drinking, sometimes they say, Indulge pleasant and pretty thoughts; but any how they bid us please ourselves. It is not what we ought to do, but what at any moment we like to do, that they would have us think of. Now if we do this, every hour that we live takes away some of the strength which God gave us, and makes us more poor and helpless creatures. The man who thinks as he wakes in the morning 'What will it be pleasantest for me to do to-day?' instead of saying 'What am I meant to do to-day?' is a poorer creature to-day than he was yesterday, and will be a poorer creature to-morrow than he is to-day. He is at the mercy of all accidental things which move him hither and thither, a feather floating about whichever way the wind carries him. There is no man so utterly unhappy as he is, for he is plotting to attain something which he never will attain; the things which he calls pleasant clog and disappoint him, all painful things worry and distress him to the utmost.

You see, then, how idle it is to make this the rule of our lives, that we should do things or think of things, just when they take our fancy. And, surely, it would be the strangest thing of all if we set up such a rule about such a subject as that which this day brings before us. For to what end do you think that Christ came into the world? I believe it was that he might redeem us. That is to say, that he might set these spirits of ours free from this yoke of our own inclinations which has been so burdensome; that he might make us free to serve God, which is a service of love, and not to serve ourselves, which is a service of hard compulsion. And for what end do you think it was that Christ died? Was it not that he might destroy selfishness? Did he not give up himself for us all, that so we might be reconciled to the God of love and to each other, and that we might not be self-willed separate creatures? But if it be so what can be more foolish than to say, 'I will think of him who came to raise me above this inclination of mine, just when my inclination leads me to do so. I will meditate on his death, who died to destroy selfishness, just when I find it quite agreeable to my selfishness'? Let us not be so vain in our imaginations. But let each one of us say, 'Thanks be to God for every voice of his by which he calls me to rise up and resist these inclinations and be a man. Thanks be to God for giving me the encouragement to say, Now I will think of him who came to set my will free; let the flesh, and the devil, check me as they list. Now I will draw nigh to him who gave up himself, that I might give up myself; let this self smart and struggle, and claim to be my master as it may. Thanks be to God for this Good Friday which comes round year after year, speaking to me and saying, Man, rise up and behold him who for thy sake wore the purple robe and the crown of thorns; come and behold The Man.'

I could not have spoken to you with any comfort upon the mysteries of this day, without saying this to you, beforehand. For, brethren, it is no play-house spectacle which we are called to behold. Think not, I pray you, that you are to weep over the sufferings of our Lord, as you might over the sufferings of some one who chanced to move your compassion by a sad tale. They are far too real and awful for any such tears as these. Neither do I wish you to think that you are come to find out something about your own particular sins. At other times, I may be ready enough to tell you how each of you may obtain freedom and deliverance for his own conscience; and something of that knowledge you may gain now. But it is not the main purpose of Good Friday to give it us. 'We beseech thee' (says the Church) 'mercifully to behold this thy *family*.' 'Almighty God' (it prays again) 'by whom the whole *body* of the Church is governed and sanctified, have mercy upon all estates of men in thy holy Church.' And then, not only upon those, but 'upon all Jews, Turks, Infidels, and Hereticks.' So that Good Friday is not to lead us to dwell upon ourselves, and upon our own necessities, but to carry us out of ourselves, to teach us that we are brothers of a family, members of a body, yea, connected with the whole race of man. We do not receive the right benefit from it unless we make this use of it. It is not a solitary day, it is a day of reconciliation and union. It is a day which tells us that we have a common Lord, one in whom rich and poor, high and low, have an equal interest. Therefore, they who would rob us of this day, pretending that we can think well enough of such matters each by himself, are seeking to separate us from one another, to take from us the witness of our blessed fellowship in Christ. Let us determine to prize the day the more, because our fleshly hearts would turn away from it, and that we may prize it truly let us ask for God's help, that we may enter into the meaning of my text.

"And Jesus came forth wearing the crown of thorns and the purple robe." As you have attended all the services of this week, I need not speak to you of the history of our Lord's betrayal and of his trial. The Gospels have been chosen day after day that you might have a complete history of his passion, as it is set forth by all of the four Evangelists. These will have told you that on the night before his crucifixion, He kept the feast with his disciples; that after He had instituted the sacrament of his body and blood, by giving the bread and wine to his Apostles, He went out with them, into the garden of Gethsemane, and that He there endured his agony, and that after he had prayed the third time, "Father, if it be possible, let this cup pass from me," the band of men, with Judas the betrayer, came to him, and apprehended him. They took him to Annas, the father-in-law of the high priest, and to Caiaphas, the high priest. By them he was examined and pronounced guilty of blasphemy. He was then brought before the Roman governor, and accused at his judgment-seat, not of calling himself the Son of God, which was the crime the Jews thought blasphemy, but of making himself a King, and so setting himself up against the Roman emperor, to whom the Jews were in subjection. Pilate, the Roman governor, thought the charge a foolish one. He could not see how a poor humble man, such as now stood before him, should ever be able to persuade men that he was a King. He suffered his soldiers, therefore, to mock him for this pretension. They put on him a crown of thorns, and a robe of the same colour with that which the Roman emperors wore; they gave him a reed for a sceptre, and pretended to do him homage, saying, "Hail, King of the Jews." Pilate, if he had not commanded this to be done, yet encouraged them in it. And that he might make the Jews feel how weak a person they had been reverencing, and at the same time might teach them how little he feared his opposition to Cæsar, he brought him forth wearing the purple robe and the crown of thorns, and said, "Behold, the man."

1. You will see at once what Pilate himself must have meant by these words. He wished to release Jesus. That he might persuade the Jews it was better to release him, he wished to exhibit him to them in as contemptible a light as possible. ·He as much as said to the priests and rulers, 'How can you be jealous of such a man as this? How can you fear anything from him? See in what a condition he stands before you. The very meanest soldiers taking leave to mock him. Is this the man

you tell me is threatening the empire of the Romans? Behold the Man.' Well, brethren, and we shall not enter into the mystery of this day, unless we understand that he really was what Pilate thought him. He had come into the lowest state to which a man could be reduced. Do not confuse yourselves by thinking of the glory that belonged to him before the worlds were, or of the glory which really belonged to him now. All these thoughts are true, as I shall show you presently. But whatever else he was, he was this which he appeared to the multitude, and to the Roman Governor who saw him then. He was really, and not apparently, the poor suffering man. He had not seemed to become like the poorest of you. He had become so. Think of the poorest, saddest state in which you have been—think of the poorest, saddest creature you have ever conversed with, and say, 'Christ was poorer and sadder than I or than that man.' And do not, for an instant, fancy that, in his mind within him, there was some compensation for his outward contempt and humiliation. Do not think that he could say in himself, 'All this is nothing; it will last but a few days; then triumph will follow.' No! he poured out his *soul* unto death. He gave up the power of having such thoughts as these, they were crushed by his agony. The contempt which was poured upon him was felt within; down in the very depths of his being. When a poor man is despised and trampled upon by a powerful man, or a number of powerful men, he may feel the insults very bitterly; they may sting him to the quick; but there is a pride in him which throws them back; he can, in some measure, despise those who are afflicting him. Our Lord, I speak it reverently, could not do this. There was no pride in him. He was the meek and lowly of heart, in whom resentment for wrong had no place. And yet the bitterest, intensest feeling of the wrong was in him. He knew what it was; he could measure the length and depth of the sin; but he measured it by feeling it; the whole sense and anguish of it passed into him. There was nothing in him which could say, 'It is their sin and not mine.' He felt it as his own, for everything that belonged to man, and was causing grief to men, and was separating man from God, He felt as his own; and yet he felt it as most contrary to himself; it was that which was *the* hateful and horrible thing to him. Do you find it very hard to take in the thought of such a conflict? It is most hard; yea, impossible; because it is impossible for creatures such as we are, to understand the anguish of a perfect Being. But we know that if he was perfect, this must have been his anguish; it could not have been less. All that is less than this, comes of that wherein we are unlike him; of our selfishness, of our pride, of our wanting that perfect sympathy with men, and that perfect hatred of evil which was in him. And therefore, my brethren, though we cannot comprehend what he felt, and what he was, each according to his own measure and circumstances may behold Him. Do not think that any of you are shut out by your ignorance, or your poverty, or your pain, from that power and privilege. The very words I have been speaking to you, show that you are not. This ignorance, and poverty, and pain, bring you nigh to him. Such a Being as this is the only one you could behold; the only one who you could feel was really sympathizing with you. You may well say, 'I cannot understand those fine words,' 'I cannot tell what is meant by that doctrine:' but you cannot say, 'I am too weak to look up to a person who made himself as weak, I am too much crushed to trust in one who was mocked, and scorned, and spitted on; who was poured out like water, who cried out, My God, why hast thou forsaken me?'

And yet I would here again remind you of what I said to you just now, that though this faith is meant for men suffering on sick beds their solitary anguish, yet it is not meant to keep us solitary or to make us brood on our own woes. The wonder of our Lord's humiliation is, that it brought Him into contact with every creature, that, while he felt the deepest loneliness of spirit, he was really sharing the griefs of all those whom he had made. As we behold him in his human sorrow, we shall rise out of ourselves, we shall feel that he is *the* man who is to bind us together as men; we shall pray that all may know him as the one who has suffered with them and for them.

2. For remember next that when Pilate said, "Behold the man," our Lord was crowned with thorns, and clad with a purple robe, and had a reed in his hand for his sceptre. By these signs the Roman governor and the soldiers mocked at his pretensions to be a king. By these signs we claim him as our King. We say that the Prince of sufferers is he who is worthy to be the King of Kings and Lord of Lords; that he who could bear

a crown of thorns, has shown that all the crowns of the earth are his; that he who wore the purple robe, has poured mockery and contempt upon all human pride and grandeur. While then I would have you recollect to-day that Christ was the man of sorrows, I would have you think of him also as a Sovereign. I would have you bind these two thoughts together, and by no means let any one put them asunder in your minds. Behold the man not only who stooped to your low estate, but to whom you, and all creatures in heaven and earth, owe homage. Behold him who was a King when the soldiers were setting him at nought, who is a King now, who will be shown to be a King in that day when he shall come again in the glory of his Father and of the holy angels. It is a mighty thing to you and all men to believe that there has been One in the world who has felt for every one of you; but it is a mightier to know that this is really the Lord of heaven and earth; that it was by suffering, he shewed what he was; by suffering, he made it manifest that he was different from all who had ever come before or shall come after him; by suffering, he overcame and received that name which is above every name. To his kingdom every other kingdom is subject. Those which acknowledge the subjection, those which rebel against it, will alike be shown to be its servants. By declaring this truth we testify against all cruelty and oppression in high places; we testify on behalf of the poor man. And there is no other truth which can do this, if the truth of Good Friday be taken away; if it be not a true declaration that He who wore the crown of thorns and the purple robe, is really and actually the Lord of the earth, then there is no refuge for the needy and the suffering; they are at the mercy of every strong man; and they will find what that mercy is, when men have learnt to deny that the greatest strength which was ever seen in the world, was shewn forth in the most utter weakness. But if what I say be true, my poor, and sick, and dying brethren, then in God's name, act as if it were true. Believe that he who died on the cross is the Lord of your hearts and spirits; give them up to its government; ask him day and day to purify them, and to fit you for beholding him in his death and resurrection, in his agony and his triumph.

3. I have shown to you our Lord, first, as a sufferer, next as a King; first, as sharing men's griefs; then, as having a right to their obedience. But I told you that he was arraigned before the council of the Jews not as a King, but as one who called himself the Son of God. That is, a higher title than this of King; and it may seem to you at first, still more remote from that of sufferer. Not so; it is that which interprets both the other words, which shows how they could both belong to Christ, and which makes them a blessing to us. For the sufferings of Christ were so unfathomable, because the being who suffered was perfect love; How dare we speak of perfect love as being in any but God? His kingdom is one which stands not in power only, but in right, which has been proved to be his by conflict with all that opposed him, and where shall that Right and that Power be united but in God? Believe that he who suffered for you is the

Son of God, one with the Father, and you believe God to be love; otherwise, a man has given us a proof of love which God has not given. Believe that he who you feel has a claim upon the entire services of your heart and lives is the Son of God, one with the Father, or you withdraw these services from God to bestow them on a creature. Believe that he is the Son of God, or you have no power to sympathise in his sufferings, or to do his will. For he proved to you by everything he taught, and did, and endured, that man, apart from God, is weak, helpless, incapable of affection or obedience. If you are to behold him or be like him, it is because he came down to make you the sons of God in him, and has ascended on high, that he might bestow on you the Spirit of the Father and the Son.

Doubt not, brethren, but earnestly believe that the Spirit has been given to you, and will be renewed to you to-day; so will you be able to keep Good Friday, and to ask blessings on behalf of all the family for which Christ was content to die.

SERMON XVII.

THE UNIVERSAL PRAYER.

(Preached at Guy's Hospital.—Good Friday Afternoon, 1839.)

For there is one God, and one Mediator between God and man, the man Christ Jesus, who gave himself a ransom for all, to be testified in due time.—1 TIMOTHY ii. 5, 6.

You may remember that this morning* I was explaining to you how the death of Christ is especially the death of the head of a family. I showed you how he entered into the sufferings of all those whose nature he had taken, so that the very words in which they described their sorrows were not completely fulfilled till he had accomplished his. I showed you that in this way he proved that we are one family, that we have a common life, and a common death — that his death was expressly for the purpose of making us truly a family, not united by bonds of nature or of place, but simply by our relation to the One Lord who had sacrificed himself for us. I showed you that this family was held together by his death, that we are baptized into his death, that we are sustained by his death in the Holy Communion; that all our acts upon earth derive their value from his death, and are good just as far as we

---

* These words, of course, do not refer to the preceding sermon.

enter into the spirit of it; just as far as we die to ourselves, and live to God. I told you that this family was actually established, that Christ, by his own death, has broken down every barrier that separates men from God, or from each other; and that if they choose to live without God in the world, and to be indifferent to each other, it is because they renounce the privileges which Christ, by his sacrifice, has obtained for them. All these thoughts were brought home to us by the first and the second Collect for this day, wherein we pray that God will be pleased to bless the family for which Christ died, and that he will enable us, as members of the family, truly and godly to serve him in the different stations to which he has appointed us. But I said that there was a third Collect which took a still wider view of the purpose and end of Christ's death; a view not inconsistent with that of which we have spoken already, but closely connected with it, and growing out of it. In this Collect we pray God, who "has made all men, and hateth nothing that he hath made, to have mercy upon all Jews, Turks, Infidels, and Hereticks; to take from them all blindness and hardness of heart, and so to fetch them home to his flock that they may be saved with the remnant of the true Israelites."

You see this is a larger prayer than the other. That was for Christ's Church, and this is for those who will not belong to it. By using the first, we declare that we believe Christ's death to be the bond of a great family; by the other, we declare that we do not believe its blessing to be confined to those who are members of his family now; we believe it to be a testimony of God's universal love of his creatures; a proof as clear as daylight that "He hateth nothing which he has made."

Now, when you first hear such words as these you may begin to ask yourselves, Why then do we deplore the condition of these Turks, and Infidels, and Heretics? why do we pray that God will make them different from what they are? If his love be over them all, if Christ's death be declared to be for them as well as for us, what need that we should wish to bring them into our family? why not leave them where they are, and rejoice in the thought that God may have purposes of good for them as well as for ourselves? Many persons have had these thoughts, and have them still. They think God is so good to all, and has made his goodness so manifest by the death of his Son, that we may entertain the most comfortable thoughts about all men; that we need not molest ourselves to improve their condition, for, perhaps, it may be as well as it is. God, they say, will have mercy upon all, and save all in his own mercy; let us trust them to him.

My brethren, let me show you what truth there is in that which these persons say, and then I shall be able to show you what lies they have mingled with their truth.

It is true, as I said just now, that God hath proved his love to all men everywhere, by the death of his Son. This was the message which the Apostles went forth declaring to all the nations upon earth. They said, The Son of God has taken the nature of man upon him; he has gone through the sufferings and death of a man; he has made himself one, not with Jews only, but with Gentiles; and he who hath done this is the Son of God, the perfect image of the Father; the love that shone forth in him was God's love—"Whoso hath seen him hath seen the Father." They declared that by his death our Lord "made reconciliation for the transgressors;" that in him God was perfectly well pleased with all his creatures; that by giving up himself he had "taken away the sins of the world;" and that now a perfect communion existed between Heaven and earth.

This love was shown not to the Jews, who were in God's covenant, only, but to the Gentiles, who were out of his covenant. Any one who could say, I am a man, could come and enter into this fellowship, and draw nigh to God on the faith of those words: "There is one mediator between God and man, who gave himself a ransom for all, to be testified in due time." This language, then, is true language; we must not alter or weaken it, because any may contradict it, or any pervert it. Again, it is true that when we look upon Christ as the Saviour of all men, and see God's love revealed in his death, we must have cheerful and comfortable thoughts about the condition of our brethren, whoever they are, wherever they may dwell, whatever their state now may be. We see that God means them well; we must hope that he will, in his own time, do them good; that, whatever evils and dangers surround them, whatever darkness and death may hang over the world, he will at last set it free, and make it a happy world, a kingdom of himself and of his Christ. Not to think this is treason against our Father in Heaven, treason against him who died for us and rose again, and treason which it were a double guilt to commit upon such a day as this.

But now, brethren, consider in what the love of God towards us has made itself manifest. Is it not in bringing us into a family? Is it not in making us his children, and declaring that he is our Father? Is it not in receiving us into communion with himself, through him in whom he is perfectly well pleased? Is it not in making him the head of us all, who was willing to die for all? Supposing, then, there should be any who will not believe that they are members of a family, who will not meet as members of a family, who will not acknowledge him in whom alone we are bound together, and without whom we must all be separate, who will not receive his death as their deliverance from their selfish and miserable condition, and their admission into fellowship with God and fellowship with each other; do you not see that to them that blessed and perfect love of God is defeated of its purpose? It is about them, round them, but they are not dwelling in it. It belongs to them, but they have it not. And what, then, are the cheerful and comfortable thoughts that we may have of them? what are the hopes that we may entertain from God's tender love to them? Must they not be these? That he will not let them go on for ever shutting themselves out of his family; that he will bring them to feel at last that he does love them, and that he has sent his Son into the world to seek and to save them. Is not this the good hope that this day is to keep alive in us? Is it not despair under the name of hope to have any other feeling than this?—Is it not cruelty under the name of love to talk of leaving men to themselves?

You see, then, I trust, something of the mind of the Church, when she prays to God as one who hateth nothing that he hath made, that "He will have mercy on Jews, Turks, Infidels, and Hereticks, and will fetch them into his fold." You see she has as large a view of God's mercy and love as those pretend to have who would say that we are to let the world alone; but her confidence in God's love is, that he will not let it alone—he will not leave it in a state which we believe and know to be a miserable state. She looks upon the Jew, wandering about homeless and heartless, although sprung from the noblest ancestors, the most miserable and degraded being upon earth, though to him belong the law and the covenant and the promises,—though "of his race, as concerning the flesh, Christ came." She sees him with a soul given up to the god of this world, worshipping mammon only, and she does not say, 'Father of mercies, because thou art so good to all—because thou hast sent thy Son to die for all—leave this man in his misery and degradation,—let him have his own way, and be a groveller for ever,' but she remembers this Jew is one of a race who thought it too mean and low a thing to have a crucified Lord and Saviour, who thought the man of Nazareth too mean a being to be their king, who wanted greatness and power in a Saviour;—she sees in him one of a race which refused to have a universal Saviour, a Saviour who would bring all men into his family, because he would not give up his own privileges. She sees in this pride the cause of his degradation, and she asks of God in his mercy, because he is so merciful, and because he has redeemed the world by his Son, to take away this pride out of the heart of the Jew, that he may save him from his degradation, and restore him to the number of those faithful Israelites who are worshipping God day and night in the heavenly Jerusalem. She sees the Turk in miserable slavery to men, because he is in miserable slavery to his own lusts, and she remembers that he too has thought the crucified Jesus not a sufficient prophet for his wants, that he sought a great leader of armies to be his head, a destroyer, not a Saviour, and that, therefore, because he has not stooped to the cross, he has no notion of what the heavenly crown is, because he would not be the servant of all, has no notion of what it is to be free; and she does not say, 'Father, because thou art so merciful,—because thou hatest nothing that thou hast made,—because thou hast redeemed all men by the death of thy Son,—give these men up for ever to their ignorance and sensuality and slavery.' She says, 'Make them free, bring them into thy family, save them with thy children.' She sees an infidel looking into the heaven above and the earth beneath, and unable to find a God anywhere, and yet hearing in his own heart the voice of God, the voice of conscience,—telling him that he is not far from him, urging him to cast away his pride, and to feel himself one with his poor brethren, and to behold in Jesus of Nazareth his Saviour and their Saviour, his God and their God. And she does not say, 'Father, because thou art merciful, because thou hatest nothing that thou hast made, let this man dwell apart in his solitude and his wretchedness,—let him strive against his conscience for ever,—let this earth speak to him with all her thousand voices, and yet never tell him of a Father.' But she says, 'Because thou art so good and loving, break down that barrier of pride which hinders him from falling before the cross, and seeing in Jesus one to unite him to his Father, and with all his brethren.'

She sees the heretic, for the sake of a notion, an opinion of his own mind, separating himself from God's holy family, denying that one holy blessed Spirit is given to bind us all together; denying that that Spirit is the bond between the Father and the Son, and that the Father and the Son, and the Spirit, the one God of love, is to be worshipped and glorified for ever. She sees that he is breaking down the principle on which the whole family rests and is united, is destroying peace and unity in the world, and all this that he may glorify his own judgment and wisdom, and she does not say, 'Father, because thou art so merciful, let these heresies which are separating him from his brethren, from his Father, from himself, continue to possess him wholly;' but she says, 'Destroy them, tear these grave clothes from thy child—from our brother whom thou hast redeemed—that he may be thy child and our brother indeed, and feel the joyful freedom of thy family, and covet no more the miserable freedom of being his own guide and teacher.'

Such, dear brethren, is the Church's prayer for the world, on this Good Friday. And now an awful question remains, which in humility we must ask, and to which without impeaching that love of God which is our only hope for ourselves and for all our brethren, we can resolve—why has this prayer not been answered? Why have the inhabitants of the earth not fallen before the banner of the Cross? Let God be true and every man a liar. The sin is *ours,* we are to confess it this day before God. God hath called us to be workers together with him, to make known to man the privileges and the glory of belonging to his family. We were to live as a family of love amongst ourselves, serving each other, washing each other's feet; remembering how it is that he said that all men should know that we were his disciples; and, being such a family, he bade us go forth in the name of him who has all power in heaven, and in earth, and preach the Gospel to every creature, baptizing them into the name of the Father, and the Son, and the Holy Ghost, teaching them to observe all his commandments, and He said that He would be with us even to the end of the world. We have not chosen to be such a family; we have not chosen to live as those who are united in a crucified Saviour; we have been tearing and rending each other in pieces; we have mocked our own words when we would call upon men to become members with us of a united Church. The words of life and power, from our lips, have been like the utterances of men in their dreams. There has been a spot in our feasts of charity. We have met at the table of our Lord, and gone away to quarrel and debate with each other. There has been pride and contention in the Church, therefore has there been infidelity and hardness of heart in the world. O then let us pray that first prayer of the Church, that God would be pleased to look upon His family. Let us beseech him to take from us our hardness of heart, that we may be able to carry his message of peace and deliverance to others; and that the earth may indeed, according to his promise, be filled with the glory of the Lord as the waters cover the sea.

SERMON XVIII.

THE RESURRECTION OF THE SPIRIT.

(Preached at Guy's Hospital.—Easter-day Morning, 1842.)

> Therefore we are buried with Him by baptism unto death, that, like as Christ was raised up from the dead by the glory of the Father, we also should walk in newness of life.—ROMANS vi. 4.

ON Good Friday I spoke to you of Christ's being lifted up on the cross, that he might draw all men unto him. The death of Christ was a spectacle to angels and to men. It was so at the time to the Jewish multitude, and to the priests, and to the Roman centurions and soldiers, and to the disciples and women who stood beside the cross. It is so now to those in all parts of the universe who will believe that the Son of Man and the Son of God really gave himself up that he might make all one in him, with God, and with each other.

But yesterday we were hearing of our Lord's burial. That was altogether different. It was no spectacle for numbers to behold. He was wrapt in the linen cloth, and laid in the new tomb hewed out of the rock, in which no man had lain before. There he was left unseen and unknown, while the Jews and his disciples were keeping the Sabbath-day. No visible sign remained that such an one had ever been upon the earth.

Consider what a confounding thought this must have been to his disciples. Not only our friend is gone, but the Son of Man is gone, we know not where. He may be in some unknown region, he may be alive there doing it good. But us he has left altogether; the light is quenched, this tomb is the last witness that it ever shone upon the earth. And we must not lose this thought. No, brethren, though we speak to-day of Christ's being risen, we must not forget that dark solitude of his tomb; we must not forget that all seemed to have passed away which his chosen friends had looked upon and loved; we must not forget that, in one sense, it had actually passed away. It was an actual death which he died, it was an actual grave into which he went. His body and his soul were both poured out unto death. Neither his body nor his soul had in itself any power to resist death, or to overcome it.

I. I wish you to understand what I mean, because much depends upon it. This death and burial of our Lord were but the fulfilment of his purpose when he took our flesh in the womb of the Virgin. He was in that grave before he appeared in this world. He appeared in this world that he might descend into the grave again. Every hour that he dwelt here he was giving up his body and soul, confessing that there was no life of their own in them. Every hour was one of weakness and humiliation, so far as he himself was concerned, though he was exercising the mighty powers which he received at his baptism for the good of others. His last day upon earth was the greatest of his sorrow, but all the rest were, in their degree, like to it.

But how, then, could he say, "I have power to lay down my life, and I have power to take it again"? Does not this seem as if there was something in that body and soul of his which could enter into the last conflict, and could win the victory? St. Paul tells you the answer in my text to-day. Christ was raised from the dead by the glory of the Father. That body and soul were, indeed, his—his most truly and literally. But who was he himself? He was the Son of the living God, one with the Father. It pleased the Father that in him should all fulness dwell. He was actually God manifest in human flesh, and it was this other life, this divine life, which came forth in him in every act that he did upon earth. By this he commanded the winds and the waves; by this he healed the sick of the palsy; by this he raised Lazarus out of the grave. And yet these were only the more apparent and glaring signs of his divinity. His love, and his gentleness, and his meekness, his eating with publicans and sinners, his long suffering with the ignorance of his disciples, his endurance of contempt and scorn, his going about doing good, these were surer tokens still; these were the complete manifestations of God. These did not come forth in him because he had a human soul, but they glorified his human soul; they shewed it forth in the beauty it was meant to have, the beauty which belongs to it, because it is made after the image of God. They did not come from his human body, but they glorified that human body. They enabled it to bear hunger and pain, and to shew forth the brightness and sweetness which it has by reason of the brightness and sweetness of that which is within. And as Christ said again and again that he could take no glory to himself for his acts of power and mercy, but ascribed all the glory to his being one with the Father, so in his death and burial, by a still more awful proof, he made the same truth good. He gave up himself. He let it be seen what utter weakness there was in his body and in his soul except as they were upheld by the mighty power of his Godhead. He cried in the bitterness of his agony, he felt himself forsaken of the Father, and yet he could say, " Father, into thy hands I commend my spirit," and so yielded up the ghost.

The mystery of Easter-day, then, like the mystery of Good Friday and Easter-eve, is but a part of the mystery of our Lord's whole life. The glory of the Father had gone with him through every hour of his earthly pilgrimage, raising up his body and soul, and enabling them to fulfil the work which had been given him to do. The glory of the Father was with him on the cross when it seemed to have departed from him, making his sufferings and death, the humiliation and extinction of all that belonged to him as a man, the very means of perfectly setting forth the divine love and power. The glory of the Father went with him into the grave, and it brought him back in that human soul and body unhurt by death, unweakened by his conflict with the powers of darkness, to shew forth the might of his heavenly life, and to be the means through which it should be bestowed upon those for whom he died.

II. And thus, brethren, you will be able to enter

into the other part of the text, "We are buried with him by baptism unto death, that like as Christ was raised from the dead by the glory of the Father, we also should walk in newness of life."

In the early Church, Easter-eve, the time when we remember our Lord's burial, was the great time for baptizing those who had been converted from among the heathen to the faith of Christ. This practice answered to St. Paul's words; both were meant to teach the same truth. Christ went down into the waters of baptism to signify that his life was not in his human body or soul, but that it was in his union with the Father, and the Holy Spirit came upon him, to testify of this union, to show that he was the Son of God, and give him divine power for the work which he had undertaken. Each of us is baptized as a sign that his life is not in himself but in Christ, and Christ gives us his Holy Spirit in baptism to testify that we are united to him, and are the sons of God in him, and have power to do the work he gives us to do. Christ's baptism was a burial; it was giving up his body and soul to death and the grave; it was 'declaring life is not in them but in thee.' Our baptism is a burial; it is a giving up of our body and soul, and 'declaring life is not in them but in thee.' All through his stay upon earth Christ was renewing this confession; all through our stay upon earth we are to be renewing it; we are to be saying every day and hour, 'In us is no righteousness, no good thing, no strength, we hold it all from thee.' By prayers we say this, by sacraments we say it, in every act of our lives we ought to be saying it. We are not making a pretence when we say it, we are not uttering a fine phrase, we are not being great saints—we are merely speaking the truth, the truth which God is teaching us and forcing upon us continually, if we would but learn it. When St. Paul says, "I die daily," it sounds a great thing, and so it is a great thing, that a man should be brought willingly and cheerfully to give up himself, and confess that he has no strength of his own. But yet the dullest and most backward of us might use these words honestly and truly. God teaches the ministers and stewards of his mysteries how ignorant and stupid they are, how incapable of understanding the truths they are to make known to others, how disinclined to practise the things which they exhort others to practise; he makes them feel that they have no power in themselves to sympathise with their brethren, or to bear their burdens, or to help them and comfort them, no power and no will; he makes them feel that they have no power in themselves to resist paltry temptations, no power to perform the common daily tasks which he has set them; and he teaches you the like lesson as to your bodies, that you have no life in them, no strength to do or to suffer, that they carry about death in them at every hour. Yes, brethren, willingly or unwillingly, we must die daily; we have the seal of the grave set upon all we do, all we think, all we are. The great thing is to be content that it should be so, not to wish that it should be otherwise; the great thing is willingly, cheerfully, to enter into the meaning of our baptism, and say, 'We know we have this death written and stampt upon us—we know we have this seal of the grave, confirming and attesting the writing: so be it; we do not rebel.' For we believe and are sure that as we have this death in us, so we have also a life in us, not our own, but a better—not a human life, but a divine. As Christ was raised up from the dead by the glory of the Father, so we have his glory with us to raise us from our grave, to enable us to think what of ourselves we cannot think, to speak what of ourselves we cannot speak, to do what of ourselves we cannot do. Now, brethren, this belief is just as true as the other. This is no high privilege for some great-soul, it is for you and me, for every baptized man. We are even now walking about in our grave-clothes and shroud, we are even now carrying about with us the power of that eternal life by which Christ was raised from the grave, and which the spirits of just men made perfect are enjoying before the throne of God. The thing is true, and the decree is certain according to the law which does not change. This life is given to us. It is not dependent upon the weakness of our bodies or of our souls. It is assured to us by a promise which cannot be broken. It is stored up for us in One who cannot die. What remains for us is to say whether we will walk in this new life or no, whether we will act as if it belonged to us, or as if we merely lay under a sentence of death struggling to be free and finding the curse too strong for us. This, brethren, is a question for our choice. It is not in our choice whether the sentence of death shall go forth against us; it has gone forth against every man. It is not in our choice whether another and better state shall be conferred upon us; it has been conferred upon us, Easter-day and our baptism testify that it has. But that state is one of continual dependence and trust in another. By this trust we overcome our enemies, by this trust we possess that union with our risen Lord without which, as he says himself, we can do nothing. God has justified us by raising Him from the dead. He has declared that we are not merely under a law of death, we are under a law of union with the Lord of life. We may disbelieve what he tells us; alas! by far the greater number of us do, by far the greater number of us seem to say, We are unworthy of this eternal life, and when it is given to us we will not have it, we prefer death to it. We had rather not be spiritual beings. We had rather look upon the grave than the conqueror of the grave as our master. Brethren, let it not be so with us. The signs of death are all around us, and there at that table are the signs that death itself has been taken out of the hands of him who had the power of it, and has been made into a pledge and instrument of resurrection. Oh! let us go to it remembering how deep is our weakness, and that there is the assurance of all strength; remembering that our bodies and souls are both alike dead in themselves, and that there is the witness of life and immortality for both. And let us leave that table assured that Christ has accepted the service which by his own command we have presented to him there, that he has given us his own Presence, that he has renewed in us his own Spirit, that we can return to our daily task and our appointed sufferings in the strength of that meat, trusting that he who was with us there will be with us in all times of our tribulation, in all times of our wealth, in the hour of our separation from the body, and in the day of judgment.

SERMON XIX.

THE RESURRECTION OF THE BODY.

(Preached at Guy's Hospital.—Easter-day Afternoon, 1840.)

O death, where is thy sting? O grave, where is thy victory?
The sting of death is sin; and the strength of sin is the law.
But thanks be unto God, which giveth us the victory through our
    Lord Jesus Christ.—1 CORINTHIANS xv. 55—57.

EASTER-DAY, as I told you this morning, says to all men generally what our Baptism says to each of us particularly. Easter-day saith, God hath justified mankind in Christ. Our Baptism says, God hath justified thee in Christ. Easter-day declares that mankind live in Christ, and in no other way. Baptism declares that I live in Christ, and that I have no life apart from him. Thus this day is connected with the first event of our lives. But it is also connected with the last. As it enables us to see in every new-born infant a witness of Christ's redeeming power, so it enables us to see in the corpse of every departed man a witness of Christ's redeeming power. Easter-day testifies of that infant which has yet given no tokens of having more than a bodily life, that it has a spirit by virtue of its union with its Lord—Easter-day testifies of that departed man, whose body all of life seems to have forsaken, that he nevertheless hath a glorified body provided for him, by virtue of his union with the same Lord. This is another part of the mystery of Easter-day, which is set forth in the fifteenth chapter of the Epistle to the Corinthians—the chapter which the Church commands us to read at the funeral of our brethren who depart hence in her faith and fellowship.

I have chosen one of the last verses for my discourse this afternoon. It is one which will help me, by God's grace, to show you how the two mysteries of Easter-day are connected together; how the justification of our spirits, which is assured to us in the waters of Baptism, becomes the ground of that justification and redemption of our bodies, which we look for when we commit all that is visible of our friends to the grave, "Earth to earth, ashes to ashes, dust to dust."

St. Paul, in the beginning of this chapter, had been answering some who said that the resurrection was past already. These persons had mistaken what he and the other Apostles had told them about our being risen with Christ, having a new life in him, being born again to a glorious inheritance in him. They saw that these blessings were in a manner conferred at once, though men might be very slow in entering into the apprehension of them, and therefore they concluded that the whole of their resurrection was completed, that they had nothing further to look for or desire.

St. Paul answers this notion of theirs in this way. He says that Christ actually brought his body from the grave, that he was actually seen in that body by five hundred brethren, yea that he had actually been seen in that body after he had ascended by St. Paul himself. Now he says, this could not be if the dead are not to rise with their bodies, for Christ hath made himself so entirely one with us, He is so completely the head of our race, that whatever befel him must befal us. If then men were not to rise from the dead, all that they had been told about Christ's resurrection was a fable. He had never risen at all, and then what became of that justification of their spirits which they were talking of, and which they were setting up against the resurrection of their bodies? If Christ had not risen, they had no justification at all, they were yet in their sins. He goes on to ask them what the meaning of their Baptism was, if they were not to rise again from the dead? In their Baptism they were accounted dead men, dead as to their bodies; but did not their Baptism declare also that all which was in them should come to life, that they should partake of Christ's resurrection, as they partook of his death? Or again, if there were no resurrection, what had become of all those who had died already? The life of these men was over, we were never to see them again, never to be united to them again.

Again, he says, Why am I fighting and toiling all my life long, if so be that my resurrection is past already, if so be that this life contains all the blessedness which I am to look for? Verily, he adds, if this were the case, we should be "of all men the most miserable." These are strong words, and, perhaps, they may make us wonder. For St. Paul tells us in another place, that in spite of all his hardships and tribulations he was always rejoicing; that the delight he had in being one with his Lord, and in doing his work, infinitely overpaid him for all that he suffered. But then you must consider that this notion of there being no resurrection after death would have robbed him even of the consolation which he had at present. For he could not believe that Christ had begun his work, if he did not believe that he was to finish it; he could not believe that Christ had redeemed his spirit, or that he had any portion in him, if he believed that He meant to leave him for ever shut up in his prison-house, in his body of death. Therefore, he maintains, this was no proof of their holding a very fine and spiritual faith, that they did not like to think about this resurrection of the body. It is a proof that their faith was very weak and likely to perish; "evil communications had corrupted their good manners, they must awake to righteousness and sin not;" for this want of hope as to their bodies, proved that they had not the knowledge of God in their spirits.

He then goes on to answer the questions which arise in men's hearts when they think of this subject. Such as this. But what body shall I have? I have seen the bodies of my friends crumbling to dust, and becoming the food of worms, and I know the like will happen to me and to all. Foolish man, he says, and what kind of body do you expect that the seed will have which you put into the ground? Does it look anything like the ear that comes in harvest time? And yet are not the two connected? Could there be the ear without the seed? Consider then that if God gives a growth to that seed, and makes it turn to an ear, he will make the seed of life, which he has put into thy body, produce a body such as he pleases. It may be very unlike that which thou wearest here in this world of death, as different as the seed is from the fruit or the flower: but it will be *thy* body still. Then he proceeds to explain what the difference shall be between the bodies of our humiliation and the bodies of our glory. One, he says, is an Adam body, the other is a Christ body. One is a body that contains a soul within it, a seed of life within it. The other will be a spiritual body, inspired, actuated in all its movements by a living Spirit. Christ, the quickening Spirit, who hath quickened our souls, will also quicken our bodies; and this, he says, is connected with that promise of the Father, that "He shall reign till all his enemies be made his footstool." He is the great conqueror and champion for his Father here upon earth, and not one of the enemies who have stood up against God, and have enslaved man, but shall be led away in triumph by him. Death, the last of these enemies, shall be vanquished, shall have no power over any part of God's creation, shall not have dominion over the body any more than over the spirit; for that over which it hath had power, that which hath been "sown in corruption, shall be raised in incorruption," that which had been "sown in weakness shall be raised in power," that which had been "sown in dishonour shall be raised in glory." The resurrection of our spirits hath indeed been accomplished for all who believe and are baptized; the resurrection of the body hath not been accomplished, but it shall be when the "trumpet sounds, and the dead are raised, and we are changed."

Then, he says, shall be brought to pass the full meaning of that which is written in the Prophet Isaiah, "Death is swallowed up in victory." It was accomplished partially when he overcame the hosts of the enemies of Israel, and delivered his own people. There was joy and triumph, and thanksgiving to God, not only among those who were alive, but even those who were in their graves felt the victory and gave thanks for it. It was accomplished still more when Christ arose from the dead, and became the first fruits of them which slept;—when the Great Captain of the hosts of the Lord walked with dry feet through Jordan, and entered into the promised land. It is accomplished in part in the baptism of every child who is received into Christ's Kingdom, out of the kingdom of death. But it shall not be accomplished completely till every member of the flock enters into the rest which Christ hath gone to prepare for him. And because he is sure that this will come to pass—that "He will accomplish the number of his elect," and establish his kingdom—because in what he has already done he sees the pledges and foretastes of his future triumphs—he bursts out into that cry, "O death, where is thy sting? O grave, where is thy victory? The sting of death is sin, the strength of sin is the law; but thanks be to God, which giveth us the victory through our Lord Jesus Christ."

You see he answers both his own questions; to the first, "O death, where is thy sting?" he answers, "The sting of death is sin."—To the question, "O grave, where is thy victory?" he answers, "The strength of sin is the law;" and then he goes on to say, that sin and the law are overcome by Christ, and that therefore death and the grave are overcome by Christ, who giveth us the victory.

I. "The sting of death is sin." I explained to you the meaning of this in the morning when I was speaking from the words, "He was delivered for our offences, and raised again for our justification." I showed you that there was a conscience in men which showed that they were separate from God, and that this separation was their guilt and crime. And I showed you that that death which happens to all men, was that which brought the feeling of this sin or separation continually before them; which seemed to them the continual proof that they had offended the living God, and that they would be yet more completely cut off from him. Death, I said, and sin were twin sisters, which they could never divide in their minds from each other. It was this feeling, 'We have separated ourselves from God, we *are* separate from him,' which put such blackness and hideousness into the face of death, and made it impossible for men not to tremble at his approach.

II. But he goes on: "The strength of sin is the law." These are harder words. At first they seem very hard indeed. Can they mean that the law of God, the law which was made against sin, gave strength to sin? St. Paul tells us how this is, in the 7th chapter of the Epistle to the Romans. He says that he had done wrong actions for a time without feeling that his whole mind and heart were wrong; without understanding that he himself was separate from God. He had desired, for instance, his neighbour's goods, without any very strong feeling that in doing so he was rebelling against God. But when the law, "Thou shalt not covet," came home to his heart, then he felt in himself all manner of corruption; he knew what the mind of God was, and he knew that his own mind was opposed to it. The like was the case with other men. The law bred a more terrible fear in their minds than it had before they knew it. Once they thought of death as the great end and misery of man; now they began to think of something after death, of the grave, of the unseen world. All the horrible shapes they had ever seen on earth, or ever imagined, must, they thought, fill that region—it was the place of darkness, and of more than of darkness, of horror and of anguish. This was the victory of the grave—and in this way did the law by adding strength to sin teach them to look upon the grave as more terrible than death itself. But St. Paul says, "Thanks be to God which giveth us the victory through our Lord Jesus Christ." Thanks be to God, who taketh the sting out of death, who separated those twin sisters which had never been separated before. For when Christ, the sinless One, walked through death, then were those two divided, never to be united again; Christ is now the Lord of death as well as of life. He has the keys of both. Yea, and he has the keys of the grave, and of hell too—for he has taken away the strength of the law, the strength which the law gave to sin. By uniting us to himself, he hath redeemed us from under the law; he hath brought us into his kingdom of grace. Now the law may thunder at each of us, and say, 'Thou hast sinned; thy mind has been separated from God's mind.' But thou canst answer bravely, 'No; I am united to Christ; in my spirit I serve him; in my spirit I cleave to him; nought but my flesh serves the law of death, and that flesh death may have, I willingly give it up to him. Thanks be to God, then, which giveth us the victory over the grave, as well as death; for now, that dim and invisible world hath no more terrors than death hath terrors; Christ hath been in both; he that was crucified under Pontius Pilate, also went down into hell; and I, being united to him, need fear neither of these; I must fear being separated from Him; I must fear not to trust Him, not to cleave to Him, but, over death and hell, he hath gotten the victory, not for himself only, but for me.'

And this victory he won not only for his own spirit but also for his own body. The body which he gave to death, he redeemed from death; the body which he gave to the grave, he redeemed from the grave. And what he did for himself he will do for those who trust in Him. Their bodies, also, he will "fashion like unto his glorious body, by that mighty working whereby he is able to subdue all things to himself." Therefore, my beloved brethren, heirs of death, heirs of life; partakers of Christ's sufferings, partakers, if you will, of his resurrection, sharers in the body of his humiliation now, sharers, if you will, in the body of his glory hereafter; "Be ye patient, immoveable, always abounding in the work of the Lord, forasmuch as ye know your labour is not in vain in the Lord."

SERMON XX.

THE RESPONSIBILITIES OF MEDICAL STUDENTS.

(Preached at Guy's Hospital, to the Pupils of the Medical School.— Sunday Evening, March 4th, 1838.)

Now there are diversities of gifts, but the same Spirit. And there are differences of administrations, but the same Lord. And there are diversities of operations, but it is the same God which worketh all in all.—1 CORINTHIANS xii. 4, 5, 6.

ALMOST the first reflection which strikes us when we look out upon the natural world is, that everything lives for the good of something else. When we say the sun shines, we mean that all the world about us is the brighter and warmer for his presence. The fragrance of every flower goes forth to enrich the air and impart fragrance. The song of the birds we feel to be joyous, because it makes those who hear it joyous. When a thing has no more power to affect any other thing—when it has gone away into itself—then we say of it, 'it is dead.' Something of it may still exist; there may be the dry relic of the flower or the tree, that once gave out odours or bare fruits, but the meaning of it is gone. This word 'dead' is the only one that we can find for it.

If we look upon the world of human creatures, it would seem as if all this were exactly reversed. The commonest saying among those who have lived long in society, and boast of understanding it, is that each man is living for his own sake; that he is making use of his fellow-creatures only to serve his own ends. Experienced persons tell us that we are merely cheating ourselves, if we suppose a man to have any other purpose in his life than this. 'He may talk much about his fellow-creatures; he may even fancy that he has their interest at heart, but secretly he has himself in view in all that he does. It makes him happy to get their praise, to be accounted generous and benevolent; and, therefore, he does many things for them: or, perhaps, he has been taught by religious men, that if he puts himself to some suffering here, he shall have more enjoyment hereafter; but, any way, the same motive governs him. It is himself that he is seeking to make happy; and he would rather that all creatures should perish, than that he should be disappointed of this aim.' Such is the opinion which you have often heard, and it is one which could not be uttered with so much confidence by clever and sagacious men, if it had not some foundation.

We all feel that it has a foundation. Every man knows that there is something within him which says, 'Please thyself, live for thyself, be thine own God.' Every man knows that he has obeyed this voice, that he is tempted to obey it continually. But he knows also that no man has been able to obey it fully. He may have made it the purpose and maxim of his life to regard himself first—his neighbours only for his own sake; but he has found it impossible to act according to this rule. Is it not impossible? It is not in our power to choose that others shall not profit by our work. The man who spends money, must spend it upon others; the man who uses his hands, must use them for others. The lawyer, if he acts as a lawyer at all, must act for his clients; the physician, if he acts as a physician at all, must act for his patients. And when we see any person who is not doing anything—who is not exerting any power for any other creature—we feel about him as we felt about the plant which had ceased to give out odours: 'there is no meaning in him, he is as good as dead.'

Thus much then seems to be clear, that if any man is pursuing selfish ends, he is pursuing them not in conformity with the order in which he is placed, but in defiance of it. And if this be the case, and if men have these selfish inclinations, it becomes a most interesting and important point to ascertain what this order is which so thwarts and contradicts the tendencies of the persons for whom it is formed? What is it, and who established it? May we expect that it will at last yield to us, and permit us to be as selfish as we please; or, on the other hand, are there any means whereby we may be brought into accordance with it? In the chapter from which my text is taken, St. Paul is making answer to these questions—the only answer that ever has been, or ever can be given to them. He tells us what this order is, who set it up, by what means the heart of every man upon earth may be brought into consent and harmony with it. He tells us that there are not as many centres in the world as there are men, and each man his own centre; but that there is one centre round which all are meant to revolve, from which all derive their light and heat. He says we are all created to be members of one body,

with one head; that, as in the natural body, there are
many limbs related to each other, each affected by
the movements and the sufferings of the other; so
every single man in this world is related to his fellow
man; so the acts and sufferings of every man shall
affect those who surround him, those at a distance
from him, yea, those who shall live generations after
him. He says that all the parts of this body are
contrived with wonderful skill, so that each shall supply
life, and health, and strength to all the other parts.
He says that no one member of this body, let it labour
as hard as it will, can separate itself from the rest,
or refuse the services of the rest; that the foot cannot say to the hand, 'I have no need of thee,' that
the hand cannot say to the foot, 'I have no need of
thee.' He says that the Eternal God has created this
order, and upholds it; that Jesus Christ is the head of
this body, and gives it its proportions, its coherency,
its comeliness. He says that the Spirit of the Father
and the Son, the Spirit of love, and peace, and order,
is intended to dwell with men, to bring their hearts
into conformity with this divine scheme and order; to
teach them what is their own position in regard to it.
He says, moreover, that all gifts and endowments, be
they of what kind they may, which are intended for
the benefit of mankind, are the gifts of this Spirit. He
says that all professions, offices, orders, existing in
society, which are for the good of mankind, are administered and superintended by the Lord of this body.
He says, that he who ordained this whole wonderful
system, works on the minds and spirits of those who will
submit to it, that all the gifts which he has bestowed
may be applied in those directions, may be con-

secrated to those purposes for which they were intended. "For there are diversities of gifts, but the same Spirit; and there are differences of administrations, but the same Lord; and there are diversities of operations, but it is the same God which worketh all in all."

It may strike you, perhaps, when you read this chapter, that I have unwarrantably extended the meaning of it. You may think that St. Paul is especially and exclusively referring to certain powers, which were conferred upon certain persons in his day, and that it is impossible to deduce from his words any principle which can govern our circumstances or conduct. And, unquestionably, this Epistle, like every other, does refer to the conditions of the times in which it was written. It would be far less interesting and useful to us than it is, if it did not. As you would be sorry that any case in medical practice should be recorded without the most minute and peculiar circumstances relating to it, as it would be far less useful to you in other cases, if it were stripped of these particulars, so the books of the New Testament are left encompassed with all the characteristic incidents of the period in which they were composed, on purpose that they may serve for the more practical guidance of all future periods. Thus it is here. St. Paul had been asked by some members of the Church at Corinth, to enlighten them as to the use of those gifts and powers which were entrusted to the first apostles at the day of Pentecost, and afterwards, in different degrees and measures, to different Christian congregations. He had heard of incorrect and disorderly practices which prevailed at

Corinth, in reference to these gifts; he had observed that a very undue importance was attached to them, merely because they had been conferred in a sudden and remarkable manner. To answer these questions, and to correct these errors of practice and opinion, St. Paul explained to them their whole position, as members of the Church of Christ. Because all were members of one body, all cared for by its head; therefore he had invested certain persons with certain faculties and endowments for the good of the rest. At first these endowments were conferred upon those who were to be the witnesses and preachers of Christ's word. Such an arrangement was necessary, in order that the source of these powers, and their object, might be the more immediately understood and recognised. Again, they had been given at first with signs and wonders, which should arrest the attention of men, and compel them to feel that God was indeed interesting himself in the thoughts and feelings of his creatures. These peculiarities would not last. The powers of healing would belong to a distinct class; the powers of language would be cultivated by slow and painful processes, not descend upon men in the likeness of cloven tongues, or amidst the sound of a rushing wind. But the truths which these signs had demonstrated would remain. These powers, in whomsoever they might dwell—in whatever manner they might be exercised, must still be regarded as trusts from God, to be used for the benefit of men, under a solemn sense of responsibility to Him, under a comfortable assurance that He will himself direct the employment of them.

Thus, St. Paul's words supply us with the ground

upon which all addresses to the members of any profession, or to persons preparing for any profession, respecting their duties and responsibilities, must be built. There are but two principles upon which any persons can be addressed. The one is that selfish principle which confuses everything, darkens everything, and, at last, most completely defeats itself. The other is that lofty, humane principle which St. Paul brings forward in this Epistle to the Corinthians, a principle which does not wage war with the order of things in which we are placed, but explains it, conspires with it; a principle which wages war against nothing, but against that which makes us at war with God and man. It is the principle of speaking to men as members of one body, one family redeemed out of the position of selfish separate creatures, permitted, if they will, to consider themselves "members of Christ, children of God, heirs of the kingdom of heaven." To men having such titles, and they appertain to every member of Christ's Church, we can speak cheerfully of duties and responsibilities, because we can tell them how the duty arises, to whom they are responsible, what strength they have to fulfil the duty, to meet the responsibility. I shall arrange what I have to say, respecting those which particularly appertain to medical students under three heads, which the words of St. Paul suggest. He speaks of gifts of different kinds; this will offer me an occasion for speaking of the duties and responsibilities connected with your peculiar *Studies*. He speaks of different administrations or offices: this will offer me an occasion for speaking of the duties and responsibilities connected with the *Practice* of your profession. He speaks of Divine operations; this will lead me to speak of the means whereby you are to gain continual help for fulfilling these and all other works which God may appoint for you.

I. The chapter from which the text is taken, is concerned with all offices and occupations existing among men, which it is not disgraceful for a man to be engaged in. All these, it speaks of as ordained by God; all these as having gifts appropriated to them by God. The most sublime of the writers in the Old Testament does not scruple to say, when he is talking of the different labours of the ploughman in the different seasons of the year, "For his God doth instruct him to discretion, and doth teach him." All the ancient nations believed this: they could not understand how the arts of tillage could ever have been imparted to man, but by some Divine communication, how they could be practised and improved without fresh supplies of Divine illumination. And it is a most vulgar wisdom which sets aside this faith of all people, and affects to ridicule it. It is a most vulgar religion which pretends to consider such notions as suggesting thoughts unworthy of God. Wherever there has been any great work done in the world, any great discovery made, there must have been strange thoughts and processes of thought preceding that work and that discovery. And if God ordains the acts and movements of the meanest insect that he has formed, do you think it can be beneath him to interest himself in these thoughts and processes of thought, to superintend them, to guide them to their issue? A man must feel little what a wonderful thing this thinking is, what an awful thing it is, if he believes it was suitable to the greatness of God, to create the earth, and all the animals that people it, and yet that it is beneath him to care for that which is transacted within the breast of a living man. It is the business then of every one, be the work which is assigned him as insignificant as it may, to consider that work, what it means, and how it may be accomplished, and to believe, that in all these thoughts and meditations, he has an invisible guide and teacher and friend present with him. But especially does it become those to entertain this belief, who are called students, whose very business it is to think and to reflect, who know that whether they shall be useful or mischievous hereafter, depends upon their thinking wisely or unwisely now. And the duty and responsibility of students to assure themselves continually that this is the case, that they are not alone in their studies, but that there is one near them, who is able and willing to give them right habits of thinking, to make them earnest and reasonable men, is increased in proportion to the importance and dignity of the subjects upon which they are called to reflect. Now, surely there are not more than one or two classes of men at the most, who have higher and nobler themes to engage their attention than the medical student. A whole world of wonders and mysteries is daily brought under his notice. He must contemplate the strangest piece of mechanism in the world, one compared with which every other that men have ever looked upon, or shall look upon, is like a mere child's toy. If he sets about examining any one, the smallest portion of this machine, he is lost amidst the multitude of springs and valves, which seem necessary to its movements; and each of these portions is connected with each other portion, and new relations and affinities between the parts are continually unfolding themselves to him, and the whole which they form is more wonderful than all these parts. He has constant opportunities of observing this machinery, and taking it to pieces; and then, when he has done so, a new marvel is presented to him; he finds that all its nice contrivances, all its intricacies and complications, can serve no purpose whatever, unless there be something else present there, which he has no instruments for taking to pieces. There was that which set all this machinery in motion, there were powers within it, which enabled it to act and suffer; to receive from other things a portion of themselves, to give to other things a portion of itself. He learns to feel the difference—the greatest it is possible to express in human language—the difference between life and death. I ask you whether it is not a solemn duty and responsibility for one who is brought into contact with such facts as these, to cherish a humble, reverent, wondering spirit? The more he wonders, the more he will desire, and delight to inquire: —Again, the more he inquires, the more he will wonder. He will find that there are some truths which cannot be explained, because they themselves explain all other things. He will find that he must either go on without understanding the things which he was meant to understand, or be content to acknowledge these truths which pass his understanding. Thus, he will find it necessary to get rid of all shallow vain conceits and pretences of wisdom, in order that he may be really wise. And seeing that he cannot purge his heart of such vanities, by any efforts of his own; seeing that new broods of them will be ever starting into life, when a former brood has been destroyed; he must be continually seeking for the aid of that Teacher who has endowed him with all his powers, and who has promised, that they shall be blessings and not curses to him.

But besides these inquiries respecting the mechanism and powers of the human body, the medical student has to inquire into the causes of their derangement and decay. Here again, a new region of wonders opens upon him. To the unhappy empiric, indeed, who, for the sake of pelf, trifles with the lives of God's creatures, there is no wonder at all in the origin or growth of a disease; he thinks what occurs so frequently must be very plain; that a few chance observations of a few outward symptoms, are all that a man has need of, before he presumes to suggest remedies. For him, I say, there is no wonder. But the man who, with sincere purpose to discover the secret source of that which causes so much evident misery, and with good hope of benefiting not only his immediate patients, but many that are yet unborn, travels through the same region, must feel continually that he is going further and further away from mere shows and appearances. How often when we describe to you some local suffering, you ask about other feelings which seemed to us most entirely unconcerned with it, and refer both to some secret derangement of the powers of life. I would beseech you to feel the great responsibility which is laid upon you, by being permitted to engage in studies possessing this character, and involving this necessity. Of all men you ought to be the least imposed upon, by the shapes and outsides of things. Of all men you ought the least to fancy that what is unseen, must be unreal. Of all men you ought the least to fancy that what is unseen can be accounted for by what is seen. Of all men you should be most ready to admit, that of everything concerning which our senses report to us, there is a deep hidden ground, of which they take no cognizance. And if you feel it difficult, as indeed in a world where men are pursuing shadows and phantoms, and taking them for substances and realities, it is most difficult, to derive this benefit from your studies—then remember, that for the sake of those studies—if, for no higher reason—it is most needful that you should submit your minds to the guidance of Him who has formed both these, and that which they are to investigate; and has promised to lead them into the secret fountains of knowledge and truth.

There is a most interesting branch of your studies, which leads you to investigate the properties of different animal and vegetable and mineral substances, and the services they may render to man. If we heard for the first time that a connection existed between the life that is in us and that which is in plants and flowers, that this connection has been established since the creation,—that it is possible for man to trace it out, how we should be amazed! What new and delightful trains of thought such an announcement would suggest to us! But it is your privilege and your duty, as students, to renew this delight in your hearts every day. It is not necessary that the fountain of wonder and pleasure should be dried up, because you are employed in following out a multitude of streams that flow from it: the fact which rejoices the first discoverer, remains fresh and living for every one who succeeds him, if he will not close his heart against it. But I pass over this and many other interesting topics, that I may allude to one which must very often be brought under the notice of those who are preparing for any branch of your profession. I spoke of the powers of life being deranged; but in popular language—and I suppose, also, in medical language—we sometimes use that word—*deranged*—in another and more awful sense. We apply it not to the functions of the man, but to the man himself. We say, He is deranged, his being is subverted. I would beseech you to think deeply of these words. The facts to which they point are in themselves so appalling, that for a moment they may absorb all your attention. But if, when you have a moment's leisure from the contemplation of the mere signs and symptoms of a mind overthrown, you ask yourselves what is implied in the very possibility of such a disaster, you will find that an amazing deep opens upon you. Insanity could not be, if there did not dwell in that mysterious body with which your studies are occupied, a mysterious person who calls it his, who rules it, who needs himself to be ruled. Such a person there must be in you and in me; what he is your science does not tell us; what he is we must in some way or other learn. For this person must have all capacities of happiness and misery in him; what he is, not what his circumstances are, must be the great question. To whom may he look up in his strength, and say, "Thou gavest me this strength"? To whom may he cry in his weakness,

"Do thou uphold me"? To whom may he call, when he feels himself broken and maimed, "Do thou restore me"? "The depth saith, It is not in me; the sea, It is not with me." All nature declares that it can do something to compose or rearrange the outward circumstances,—the dress of the man,—nothing to alter, or regenerate the man himself. All the things that surround him, are beneath him; less grand, less wonderful than himself. But he needs one more mighty, more wonderful. These things are incapable of sympathising with him. But he cannot be content, unless he can find some one to care for him, to feel with him, as well as to superintend him. All these things are incapable of imparting to him any portion of their own life, or happiness. But he needs one, whom he may not only confess as a superior, and trust in as a friend; but who is willing to confide in him, and communicate with him. Now the declaration of such a being, unto whom this man within us may look up, who has sympathised with him in his low estate, who makes him a partaker of his own spirit; this is the Gospel of Jesus Christ. The Holy name into which you are baptized, is the name of this Being. The possession of that mighty Teacher who is with us, to guide us in all our commonest thoughts and pursuits, but with us, most of all, to interpret those deeper feelings which concern our own inmost being, with us to breathe into us a new life, to renew us, after the image of Him who created us — this is the mighty consequence of being brought nigh to this God in his blessed Son. See then, how your studies, by that which they teach you respecting other things, and by that which they teach you respecting yourselves, by the proofs which they give you of your power and of your weakness, by leading you into depths you cannot fathom, by making you feel that the profoundest deep of all, is that in which you yourselves are living and moving, and having your being—see how they bring you at last into contact with those mysteries of which you have heard since you were children, and which you must receive as little children, if you would enter into their meaning and their blessedness.

II. But it is more than time, that I should speak of the responsibilities connected, not with the studies, but with the practice of your profession.

It is a great and striking advantage which belongs to you, that these can scarcely be separated, even in thought. Your studies are a practice, your practice is a study. In order to make that comparison which I spoke of just now, between the living and the dead subject, you must have attended to the operations of life in actual men. In order to understand anything concerning diseases, you must have attended to the sufferings of actual men. In order to enter at all into that most awful calamity, to which I last alluded, you must have seen men, whose minds were temporarily or permanently deranged. Nevertheless, it must not be forgotten, that the position which you occupy now is different, in many important respects, from that which you are destined to occupy hereafter. Now you are visiting sick and dying men, mainly, that you may improve in knowledge; by and by you must learn to feel, that all your improvements in knowledge are chiefly precious, as they enable you the more usefully to visit sick and dying men. You are not dishonouring your fellow-creatures in the first case; you are not dishonouring science in the second. To understand the truth of things, to know the meaning of God in creation, especially in that most splendid creation, the human body, is a worthy object, to which the very highest pursuits may be content to minister; to confer the slightest benefit on a man—the child of God—is an object which the knowledge of an angel would not be degraded in promoting. But these two pursuits, each in itself so noble, each so necessary to the other, have their distinct privileges, their distinct responsibilities.

When I use language of this kind, and when I speak as I did before, of selfishness, as an utterly ineffectual, as well as an intrinsically bad principle; you may fancy, perhaps, that I am urging you to disregard the outward and tangible advantages which result from the fulfilment of your vocation. Nothing is farther from my thoughts. I hope I should never impose a rule upon your profession, which I do not think applicable to my own; for, undoubtedly, we ought to set the example of whatever disinterestedness we recommend to others. But as selfishness is a much deeper thing than the mere wish for money, so disinterestedness is a much deeper thing than the mere contempt or disregard of it. A man may be thoroughly selfish, selfish at heart, who is utterly indifferent about wealth; a man may be thoroughly disinterested who thankfully receives it as a gift, though a perilous gift, from God. What I should wish you to feel is this: By the order and design of God, we are placed in certain vocations for the good of mankind and for His glory. To the fulfilment of this vocation, certain outward and material blessings are attached. If we faithfully depend upon Him, these will come to us at such times and in such measures as are best for us; if we keep them constantly before us as an object, we shall be restless and dissatisfied, incapable of pursuing one of those duties rightly, of which they are meant to be not so much the rewards as the needful supports and appliances.

This is the habit of feeling which the members of a profession are especially bound to cultivate, which it is their especial privilege that they are able to cultivate. In ordinary trades, though in themselves most honourable, and though they may be pursued in a most honourable spirit, for the most honourable ends, it is very difficult not to measure the labour done by its direct results. The profit from an article is so exactly proportionate to the quantity of time and work bestowed upon it, or if this be not the case the change is produced so entirely by some temporary fashion or caprice, that persons constantly engaged in trade, must, unless they are very careful in observing their hearts, insensibly acquire the habit of trying the worth of everything by its market value. But who can ever ascertain the pecuniary equivalent for that kind of labour which your profession calls upon you to put forth? Who can say, what amount of the wealth of this world is to be weighed against so much of silent meditation, and minute watching, and anxious fear, and patient kindness? The attempt is impossible; no schemes are so utterly preposterous as those which pretend, in such cases, to adjust the quantity of reward to the quantity of labour. We may no doubt complain of this as a calamity. We may murmur at the great inequalities in the circumstances of different men not distinguished from each other, so far as we can perceive, by their intellectual or moral qualities; but we may also, and I believe if we are reasonable men, we shall, hail this condition of things as one of our highest blessings and privileges. It instructs us continually that the highest qualities must have higher blessings attached to them than any which our fellow-creatures can bestow: cases of wise and benevolent men struggling on in poverty and not losing their zeal and hope; cases of successful imposture and quackery; cases of true science and real industry acquiring dignity and reputation; all contain this lesson. The poor man had something better than wealth to support him; the impostor had thoughts of reckless murders to torment him for which no wealth could compensate; the man of prosperous honesty obtained money because he had sought what is higher.

But, after all, the best school for learning the real value of those rewards, for which some are content to sacrifice themselves and God, is that into which your practice itself introduces you. It is one thing to be told from a pulpit, that 'the rich man fadeth away in his ways;' that the soul of a man, who has lived in things which he can see and handle, is left in dreary vacancy when he thinks that he is about to see and handle no longer, that then he confesses his need of something else—though what that is, it is now too late to ask; it is quite another thing, to have these words realised continually before your eyes, to witness the very spectacles which they feebly strive to describe. Oh, consider the responsibility which the sight of them brings with it! It is not a light thing to see a fellow-creature looking into your face, and asking in unutterable agony, whether you cannot give him a week, a day more of life; whether he must leave all that he has delighted in; whether he may not at least have a little while for considering where now he is to transfer all his thoughts and desires and affections. Such looks should not depart out of the memory, at least not out of the heart, for assuredly they will meet us again on our own death-beds, and at the day of revelation. Assuredly, we are permitted to see them, that each man may consider deeply with himself, 'This man is not of another race from myself; whither he is going, I must go; what he cannot carry with him, will leave me; if there be something which he is crying after, from the lowest depths of his being, to appease its wants, that is something which I too must have, or, be wretched for ever.'

If the words of the preacher, when he talks of death, carry but a dull and drowsy sound to the ears of most men, how much feebler is the echo of his voice, when he speaks of *sin*. The first men own to be a reality, though it is one which they choose not to contemplate, the other seems to most of them a mere abstraction. But you will see the effects of this abstraction, of this imaginary thing; you will see what it can do with forms and countenances, which the eye loved to look upon; you will see the decay and corruption of that which was most beautiful; and you will hear words which will tell you, that the misery without is only the sign of a deeper misery within. You will read, written with the finger of God himself, upon his own exquisite workmanship—"The end of these things is death." My brethren, is there no responsibility in being called to such scenes as these? Will you rid yourselves of this responsibility, by a few words of passing compassion to the sufferers, or by calling them the victims of miserable circumstances? Their circumstances were, no doubt, most calamitous; for they encountered persons, who had yielded to the evil in their own hearts, and were eager to call out evil in all other hearts. But we lie to our own consciences, if we do not own that the evil itself was within, that the root of bitterness was there, and that all outward occasions and accidents did but assist it to send forth buds and blossoms, and fruit. We lie to our own consciences, if we do not acknowledge that the same evil is within us, and is incapable of being permanently controlled, far less really extirpated, by any calculations of expediency, or fear of consequences. We lie to our own consciences, if we do not ask how we may make the tree good, that the fruit may be good; how we may purify the heart, so that it shall send forth streams not of corruption, but of health and life.

The responsibilities of which I have spoken, arise from the consideration that the persons whom you visit are of the same flesh and blood with yourselves, that you are sharers in their propensities and temptations. But this is not all which even such cases teach you. The poor worldly man who feels that death must tear from him all that was precious to him, feels that he had a right to a possession, with which he need not have parted; the poor creature who feels that sin has the dominion over her body and spirit, feels that she had another Master, to whom she was bound, and whom she might have obeyed. You cannot doubt the language in which these feelings are expressed. It is not taught language, cant language; it is the sincere utterance of a heart compelled by death and despair to speak out the true thing which it has long hidden and kept down within it. Here, then, are testimonies issuing from the very lowest pit into which humanity can sink, of its grandeur and glory. Yes! you will see your fellow-creatures stripped of all the disguises in which they have showed themselves off in the world; exhibiting themselves to you as they actually are; you will see them in the furiousness of passion, in the depth of pride and pettiness; and yet I tell you that you shall never see a man or woman who does not exhibit some token of belonging to a race which God created in his own image.

How many will you meet with, who would give worlds to believe that they are not immortal; and yet the truth, the certainty of immortality comes upon them in that hour with an appalling evidence, before which all sophisms of the intellect, all feelings of indifference, all habits of scorn are scattered to the winds. How many will you see, who actually persuade themselves that they can in some way or other give a sop to death, that they can hold him at a distance with their shrivelled arms. It is a melancholy and ignominious delusion, yet it shows how deep the assurance is in man, that death is not meant to be his lord, that he ought to be able to trample upon it.

How many will you see to whom the thought of God is the most frightful and overwhelming of all thoughts, which they would give worlds to banish from them; and yet if you ask why the vision of Him is so terrific, you will find that it is because a voice within them proclaims him to be a God of Love, with whom they can have no sympathy because they are utterly unloving.

My brethren, here is a high responsibility indeed. To learn that you carry about with you a corrupt nature, which is leading you continually to deeper degradation—this is most important. But to learn in this strange manner, from these unexpected and indubitable witnesses, that you come of a royal parentage, that you are connected with an Almighty friend—that you are meant to enjoy an eternal life in the knowledge of Him—this is more wonderful and precious still. When your hear us speaking of a flesh that is not subject to the law of God, neither indeed can be—and of an inner man who delights in the law of God, but feels weak and incapable of conforming to it; when we tell you, that Jesus Christ came into the world to claim fellowship with this inner man— when we tell you that he being in flesh of man, suffered death, and that he rose again, and that he permits us by baptism to claim union with him, as our risen Head, and enables us by faith to put off the old man with its affections and lusts, and to put on the new man, which is made after God in righteousness, and pure holiness—when we use such words as these, they seem at first like strange riddles, incomprehensible dreams. But are they not rather the solution of those practical riddles, those inexplicable dreams, with which your daily experience brings you acquainted? Are not they the only key to those mysteries, which you are compelled to observe in your intercourse with others, and which, if you look earnestly, you find to be only the counterparts of mysteries as great within yourselves?

I may seem to have wandered from the purpose which I proposed to myself, in this part of my discourse. I may seem to have been speaking rather of the good which you yourselves may derive from the practice of your profession, than of the services which you owe to your fellow-men. But, in leading you to reflect upon the bonds which connect you with them, upon the evil tendencies which you share with them, upon the glorious privileges and hopes which you share with them, upon the certainty that the first will predominate in every man who depends upon himself, upon the certainty that the other will be realised by every one who claims fellowship with the Lord of men, I have, in fact, been laying the only safe foundation for an appeal to you respecting your professional duties. I might have spoken to you of the dreadful obligation which you contract to God, by taking upon you the office of watching over the lives of his creatures. I might have endeavoured to awaken you to sympathy with the miseries which you must every day witness. But though I could not exaggerate the awfulness of that obligation, I might very easily lead you into an exaggerated, unprofitable state of mind with respect to it. The man who carries about with him no other thought but this—'There is a debt which he owes, and which he must discharge,' will soon become dissatisfied in himself—cold and heartless towards others. He will try to pay his debt, but it will be in mere outward services, which carry with them no real blessing, which obtain no gratitude; for that which men really crave after, the gentleness, the kindliness, the sympathy, is utterly wanting. It is almost impossible again to think too deeply of the calamities under which men are groaning, in this world of death. But it is quite possible to call forth a sentiment of compassion for these sufferings, which would be too delicate for use while it lasted, and would be quite unable to sustain itself against the hardening effects of familiarity with the scenes that awakened it. If you would unite all that is wholesome in both these feelings—if you would convert them into calm, settled habits of mind, understand and embrace the truth, which St. Paul is expounding in my text. Believe that an administration is committed to you by the Lord of men for the good of men; believe that every creature with whom you are brought into contact, is connected with Him by the same bond that unites Him to you; believe that to make us conscious of that bond, to deliver us out of our misery and ignorance, that Lord thought it not too great an ignominy to bear our flesh, to die our death; believe that He would now use you as His instruments, to awaken in His creatures the feeling, that there is a care and tenderness exercised in their behalf, of which they never dreamed; believe that, in proportion as you show kindness, and care, and tenderness to them yourselves—in proportion as you deal honestly with them, making them feel that you dare not lie to them because they are members of the same body with you —you will be the means of inspiring this conviction, and by inspiring it, of lifting your brethren out of selfishness and despair into confidence and hope, into respect for themselves, into an acknowledgment of God; believe that for this end you need not become preachers, (though on many occasions, doubtless, you will be led to speak words in the ears of sick and dying men, which will strike the more deeply, because they were not expected from you), but that while you are acting out your own peculiar and appointed task, you will be following Christ, and benefiting the souls as well as bodies of your fellow-men, far more than if you assumed to yourself any function which he has not assigned you; believe that, if his life upon earth was meant as a guide or pattern to us, who are sent with a message of peace to the hearts and consciences of our brethren, it was not less meant as a pattern to you, who are commissioned to heal their bodies; believe that, when he assumed a dominion over the secret powers of human life, when he staunched the fountains of human disease, when he quelled the fury of the madman, he was as much honouring and hallowing the work of the physician, as he was honouring and hallowing the work of the Evangelist, when he opened his lips and said,— "Blessed are the poor in spirit, for theirs is the kingdom of heaven."

III. You will acknowledge, I think, that hitherto I have not been enforcing upon you any duties which are not directly connected with the practice and the studies of your profession; I have been merely urging you to reflect upon the nature of those studies and that practice. If certain truths, which you have been wont to call theological, have been thrust upon your notice, you will allow that they seem to be suggested by the facts which occupy you in your chambers, by the scenes which you witness in the sick-room; and instead of accusing me of leading you into an unprofessional line of thought, you will begin to ask yourselves whether the voice of the preacher and the words of the Inspired Book are not guide-posts to principles which lie at the foundation of all that you think, and speak, and do. And if, at the conclusion of this discourse, I address you upon a set of duties different in kind from any to which I have yet alluded, I am still not withdrawing you a step from those which your science and your patients require of you; I am only showing you how you may obtain the energy and the freedom necessary for performing them.

Men engaged in active labours for the good of their fellow-creatures, often find it exceedingly difficult to understand the grounds upon which we urge them to cultivate those habits, and attend to those services, which are technically, perhaps not very happily, distinguished as religious. They ask whether God has not given them an important work to perform, and whether they are not likely to please Him better, by discharging it faithfully, than by occupying themselves in acts of devotion to Him? They ask, whether it is not acting more in the spirit of Christ's commands, more in imitation of his example, to be doing deeds of mercy, than to be offering sacrifices? I do not think these questions are always fairly met by those to whom they are addressed. I fear, that we are sometimes guilty of confusing men's minds respecting the nature of their obligations to God, and even of converting religion, which should be the great instrument for overthrowing selfishness, into a means of encouraging it. But, I think, that the remarks which I made just now, respecting the kind of blessings which it is your privilege and your duty to impart to those whom you visit, may, perhaps, assist in extricating you from the difficulty. If to attend the bed-side of a patient were merely a mechanical act, or if nothing more were required of you than that you should give sound advice, I do not know that I could establish any very clear connexion between your ordinary tasks and those exercises of which I am now speaking. But it is degrading the dignity of your profession to think this. Your consciences tell you, that more, much more than this is required of those who are brought into constant experience of the woes of humanity: you feel that the kindness and sympathy, and sincerity, of which I was discoursing, under my last head, are as much demanded of you as scientific knowledge itself; and you feel that these qualities cannot be acquired at the moment,—cannot be got up for exhibition at the bed-side; you feel that the man who merely presents counterfeits of them, is an impostor and hypocrite, far less to be esteemed than he who honestly shows forth the indifference or unkindness that are in him. It is necessary then, that these should form the very substance of your characters, that they should be worked into your very selves. But now consider how this can come to pass. Can you trust to the ordinary influences of society to do it? Do not you know perfectly, that these influences are adverse to the cultivation of such a character; that they tend to form in us habits of confirmed selfishness? Can you trust to the mere sight of pain and suffering to do it? Have we not said already, that the repetition of these sights deadens the impression which they at first produced? Can you trust, then, to your belief and recognition of the principles which I have been endeavouring to assert, to your conviction that the Spirit of God has indeed endowed you with all your gifts and powers; that the Lord of man has appointed you to administer these gifts for the good of men? But do you not feel that commerce with the world is continually corroding these convictions, changing them from practical realities into mere formal phrases, and that if they be honestly held, they must imply something more, they must imply the desire and necessity of seeking continual help from that Spirit, of holding intercourse with that Lord? Do you not feel that all gifts, all administrations, must be profitless, unless there were also operations of God to renew our minds and characters, and form them into the likeness of his own?

But you wonder that God should require of you acts of prayer and praise. My brethren, ask your own hearts if they do not require these acts. I cannot think of a fellow-creature merely as the author of certain gifts and blessings to me; I cannot think of him merely as making certain provisions and arrangements for me. The moment I believe he is the source of these blessings, the author of these arrangements, that moment I desire to know what he is, I desire to think of him as a person in himself; I desire to commune with him, to contemplate his character, to enter into the feelings in which these kind acts to me originated. Unless I can do this, I feel that I shall never really preserve a recollection of his benefits; I shall never feel any relationship to him; I shall never connect him with others as well as myself; I shall care for him only for my own sake. This is the case with us in reference to our fellow-men; and is it not still more emphatically the case with us in reference to the Most High God? If we believe Him to be the source of every blessing to us, the Ordainer of every scheme of life for us, we must carry our thoughts beyond these gifts, beyond that scheme of life, to Himself. We must desire to enter into holy and awful intercourse with him. We must desire to think of him, and to utter our thoughts to him as a distinct Being. We must desire to adore, and wonder, and worship.

Here, then, is the meaning of the offices and ordinances of Christianity. All these ordinances are built upon the idea, that an actual communion has been established between God and man; that it is possible for man to express his sorrows and his wants to God; that it is possible for God to communicate his own life, his own character to men. This is the meaning of prayer, this is the meaning of the teachings of the commissioned minister of Christ, this, above all, is the meaning of the sacrament of the Lord's Supper. Of the deep mystery which is involved in all these ordinances, and especially in the last, I will say no more than this, that, were there no mystery, every reasonable man would feel that it was not the thing he was seeking after, the thing he was wanting. He wants something which shall bring him into intercourse and fellowship with the invisible and eternal God, and the man who says that there is no mystery in such a fellowship, is not worth listening to; he is mocking and deceiving us, because he has first delighted to mock and deceive himself. You cannot be staggered at mysteries in this highest region; you are encountered with them at every turn in the region of your own experience. You will only ask, 'Would any other than this suffice me? Can I live without this?' Can there be any other way into the presence of Him who is perfect love, but through Him with whom he is perfectly well pleased? Will anything less than a participation of his substance, of his life, of that love which overcame death and sin and selfishness, enable me to do his meanest work here on earth, enable me to behold his glory in heaven?

Do not suppose that I am limiting the operations of God on the hearts and minds of men to these ordinances; I am urging you to take the privileges which they offer you, because I am sure, they interpret to us all His other operations, because they enable us to feel His presence, to hear His voice in all the common events and accidents of life; in sickness and in health, in the daily pleasures and the daily crosses of life; in the wonders of nature, in the wonders of our own frame, in the sufferings of our fellow-men, in the acts which we are permitted to do for the relief of them. The persons whom I ordinarily address from this place, are men who have neither science nor a profession; they have this only, they are men carrying about with them the signs of Adam's curse, the marks of suffering and death. Yet I am bound to look upon them as the objects of God's love, I am bound to tell them, that all the privileges of the kingdom of Christ are theirs, I am bound to believe that they are as able to enter into the deepest mysteries as the wisest man upon earth; I am certain that they may, if they will, know God and love Him, and dwell with Him for ever. In these ordinances, you will learn to feel yourselves one with these poor creatures; you will learn to feel that what you possess in common with them is more precious and permanent than that which separates you from them; you will learn that you and they and all God's creatures, have desires, which nothing but God can satisfy; you will learn to love them and to care for them, as sharers of the same glory with yourselves; you will rejoice to meet them in the last day, when all other voices shall be silent, but when this one shall be heard, by every true and faithful man, "*Inasmuch as ye have done it to one of the least of these my brethren, ye have done it unto me.*"

SERMON XXI.

HUMAN SORROW THE BEST EVIDENCE OF CHRISTIANITY.

(Preached at Guy's Hospital, to the Students connected with the Hospital.—The Evening of the Sunday before Easter, 1840.)

Surely he hath borne our griefs and carried our sorrows.

ISAIAH liii. 4.

THE chapter from which this text is taken has been the occasion of much controversy between Jews and Christians. The latter, in general, believe that it contains a direct prophecy of our Lord; the former say, that it describes the humiliation and sufferings and final triumph of their nation. A third interpretation of it has been suggested, and has obtained some supporters. It has been said that the words refer to Isaiah himself, whose report none would believe, who was living in the midst of a godless people, who wept over their sins, and felt their miseries as his own.

Now, when we hear such different meanings affixed to the same passage, and that passage the one in which Christians have discovered a more clear announcement of the great act of human redemption than in almost any other which the Old Testament contains, the thought may perhaps occur to us,

'Surely this must have been a most imperfect guide to the Jewish people in determining the character and person of their Messiah. Even supposing it were meant, as you think it was, to record His sufferings, and the glory that should follow, those among whom he dwelt may have been very excusable for not detecting the allusion; the words admitted of more than one other very plausible signification. Can it be right to blame them for not acknowledging this application of their own prophecies, when, after eighteen hundred years, with all the advantages of Christian prepossessions, you have some difficulty in making it good?' Such difficulties as these, if they are not started in a captious spirit, which makes an answer to them useless and unintelligible, should be frankly and fairly met.

Unquestionably it is no work of ours to make out a case of sin and rebellion against the Jews, who rejected our Lord. They have another Judge —another, and happily a wiser and a truer one, who knows the whole history of the life of each man, knows what opportunities of knowledge he has wanted, and what he has rejected, knows how far the light has shone upon him, and how far through an evil will he has closed his eyes against it. Into such awful mysteries no one will dare to penetrate who has any reverence, no one will wish to penetrate who has any faith. We may be sure that our judgment in such a case must be full of ignorance and confusion, and that God's judgment will be according to truth. We have enough evidence, if we believe there is a divine order in the world, that some signal act of crime and apostasy must have been committed by a nation which for so many centuries has been a homeless wanderer upon the earth. We have sufficient motives to compassion when we see that people in their present forlorn condition. We have sufficient grounds of hope, that they will recover more than they have lost. With anything beyond this we have no concern, except so far as we can draw from it lessons of fear and warning for ourselves.

It is for the sake of such a lesson then, and not for the purpose of bringing home any peculiar guilt to the Jews, that I would show you why the charge against them of rejecting the testimony which their history and prophecies bore to Jesus of Nazareth is not affected by the interpretation which they put upon this or upon any similar passage. Supposing the modern Jews to be right — supposing their fathers did not see in this passage any prophecy of the Messiah whom they expected, but only an account of their own national woes, the question then presents itself—'Was this head and king of your nation to be one who should participate in the sorrows of those over whom he came to rule, or one who should stand aloof from them, satisfied with his solitary grandeur, known to his subjects only by the contrast which his splendour offered to their misery? You have here, according to your own showing, a striking and awful picture of human sorrow and desolation. You expect some one who shall come to deliver you out of this condition; what manner of being do you think—what does your past history teach you to expect that he should be?' The champion who delivered their fathers out of

Egypt, their divine lawgiver, spent forty years of exile in the land of Midian. Afterwards, when he had been permitted to bring his countrymen out of the house of bondage, his toil and suffering only increased. In all the affliction of the people whom he led, he was afflicted; he shared their privations, ate the same manna, drank the same water with them; he had to endure the weight of their murmurings, to complain that they would stone him, to cry to God that He would cut him off. At last he was to see the land promised to his nation, and himself to die in the wilderness. It was not otherwise with the king, to whom the Israelites looked as the pattern of the future glory which their country was to attain. David was first the shepherd boy, then the fugitive and outlaw; then when, after a hard struggle he had won his kingdom, great only by reason of sympathy with the poorest of his people, and when he violated that sympathy, punished by the ingratitude of his children, by persecutions and sufferings which none of his subjects had ever experienced. Thus, to say nothing of all other instances from the lives of their prophets, who endured one continual fight of afflictions from the opposition and ingratitude of their countrymen, the Jews had been taught, in the persons of their two greatest teachers—of those two whom all their scriptures and all their traditions taught them to regard as God's most favoured servants, and most resembling the future Deliverer — that the fullest participation in the sorrow which his subjects endured was the test and criterion of the highest and divinest ruler. One who wanted this characteristic would have wanted the chief of the signs by which they were to distinguish a true from a false leader — him who should represent the mind of the God of Israel from him who should come like one of the Gentile kings whose power they were to break in pieces.

Still it may appear to some that to take this view of the lessons contained in their past history, and in the books recording it, required some capacity of judging and comparing, which might be expected of laborious teachers, but which it would be unreasonable to look for in the ordinary members of the nation. In them, surely, it was natural to associate the idea of a great king and deliverer with something of outward show and magnificence. It was harmless in them to think of the Christ as shining forth in the glory of Solomon, rather than stooping to the first estate of David. Again, let us admit that this *was* natural, that all such notions are very natural to the mind of man; nay, that in this case they did conceal an actual truth, though one held ignorantly and imperfectly. But, at the same time, I wish you to feel that the idea of a man of sorrows and acquainted with grief, was not one which had need to be extracted by slow and painful processes from the history of God's dealings with men: that it was not one which presented itself the most vividly and prominently to a person who was learned in the letter of the Scriptures; but that the true interpretation of it lay in the actual sufferings and sorrows of those to whom the word of God came. A man who had felt nothing in himself or seen nothing in others of sorrow and wretchedness, would read the histories of Moses and David, and would be able to discover in them some traces, perhaps, of divine power and wisdom. But this peculiarity of these men, that they felt with those whose guides and leaders they were, that they were distinguished from them, not by suffering less but more than all the rest, this would escape him altogether, or, at all events, would be coldly and feebly recognised. These were real facts speaking straight to the hearts of real men. If there was a heart to receive them, a heart oppressed with its own wants, or deeply entering into the wants of other men, there was that which responded to these records, acknowledging them as true and divine, confessing that those who the most willingly shared in the miseries of men were those who brought with them the surest token that they came from God. It became the teacher to unfold this great principle to his hearers, to show how every act of God towards man had been an act of condescension, a stooping to meet his ignorance and satisfy his wants; to show how every one of his messengers had been permitted to exhibit more of the divine character the more he identified himself with the poorest and most wretched of God's creatures. The teacher was to do this, the really inspired teacher did it, and in this way prepared the chosen nation to expect that any one who perfectly manifested the divine character, must be one who more completely and wonderfully than all who had preceded him entered into the depths of human grief. But those who heard these words did not need any deep understanding and foresight in order to entertain them. They commended themselves to the conscience within, and if they did not penetrate there, the prophet could say confidently that the heart of the people was waxed gross, that their ears were dull of hearing, and their eyes they had closed. It was not the misfortune of their circumstances, but their moral corruption which made them inapprehensive and stupid.

See now whether the accounts given in the Evangelist are not consistent with these remarks. Actual poverty and suffering were not hindrances to any one in owning Jesus as the Christ. One would say that they helped men to believe he was so. The paralytic, the leper, the blind man, the centurion whose servant was sick, the woman whose daughter was grievously tormented, these could believe that He who was called the carpenter's son had the mighty power of God. And it was not that Christ's miracles carried with them an overwhelming demonstration which no one could resist. Hundreds and thousands saw these and went away surprised, but with no settled conviction, nay, perhaps, if they were obliged to acknowledge some power at work, believing it to be an evil one. It was that which these miracles betokened; that he who cured infirmities and sicknesses was himself bearing them, that he was entering into the very inmost suffering which he relieved; it was this which compelled those on whom a moral compulsion could operate to say, 'Here is the son of David;' yes, and to add, however difficult it might be to reconcile the thoughts together, 'Here is the Son of God.' This, in fact, was the reconciliation: the glory of divine sympathy and love which shone forth through the human sorrow and suffering, and most perfectly when these were most intense, carried men above themselves, and made them feel it not impossible, but most necessary, that he who had presented himself to them as the object of their love, should also be the object of their adoration; that he who had entered into all the wants of their hearts should be the Being who created them; that he who was perfect Man should be perfect God. And it was because the Scribes and Pharisees had for the most part no similar feeling, no consciousness of any deep hollow in themselves which it needed the love and mercy of another to fill up—no sympathy with the sorrows of others, no feeling of a general human misery which had need to be redressed —that they could not look upon their expected Ruler otherwise than as a rich and powerful prince, who would have the means of rewarding those who succeeded in winning his favour, and of subduing those who resisted him. For precisely the same reason all their conceptions of the divine character were dark but not awful. They looked upon him as an absolute Power rather than an absolute Truth and Goodness. Though they could understand how he should condemn and punish sin, they could not understand how he should desire to deliver men out of it. Therefore, rather than own Jesus for their King, they cry, "We have no king but Cæsar;" rather than own him for the Son of God, they will say, "We have a law, and by that law he ought to die, for he has spoken blasphemy." To look upon the man of sorrows as having either of these characters seemed to them impossible, and it was as the man of sorrows that he himself claimed to unite them both.

I do not think then that the interpretation of this fifty-third chapter of Isaiah, which connects it with the fortunes of the Israelitish people, or that which connects it with the feelings and sorrows of the Prophet himself, would have hindered the Jews from believing that this and all their other Scriptures had their fulfilment in Jesus of Nazareth. I think that if there had only been in them the heart to understand God's mercy and their own necessities, either of these explanations might have led them to the truth rather than have drawn them away from it.

Nay, I can believe, if it be lawful to speculate on such a subject, that when our Lord himself, after his resurrection, met two of his disciples on their way to Emmaus, and opened to them in all the Scriptures the things concerning himself, this may have been the very revelation which made their hearts burn within them; that everything which referred to his Church, toiling and striving here upon earth, had its perfect meaning and fulfilment only in Him who came to bind together the members of the body in one, to unite the hearts of the fathers to the children, and to connect the glories of the old Jerusalem, which was established upon earth, with those of the new Jerusalem, which was coming down out of heaven. I can conceive that it was by going through the history of every saint of God suffering here upon earth, and looking forward to a glory which should be revealed, that he expounded the words, 'Ought not Christ, the King of all these Saints, to have suffered these things, and to enter into his glory?' And to speak of an occasion somewhat less solemn, but still profoundly interesting, of that meeting, I mean, which the deacon Philip had with the treasurer of the Ethiopian Queen, as he sat in his chariot, and read the words of this prophecy, I can conceive that the teacher answered the question, "Speaketh the prophet this of himself, or of some other man?" by showing that if he did speak them first of himself, he must speak them also of another; that if he suffered and sorrowed for the sins of his nation, there must be one greater sufferer—one who in a more deep and real sense bore all griefs and carried all sorrows, and that it was to this argument the convert replied in the memorable words, "I believe that Jesus Christ is the Son of God."

The question, then, whether the Jews should or should not believe that he who died on Calvary was their Prince and Saviour, did not turn upon any doubtful explanations of Scripture. If they took it only in the lowest commonest sense which could be given to it, provided they did but connect that sense with their own calamities, and the calamities of the brethren, his incarnation and passion would have seemed to them most deep and wonderful mysteries indeed, but mysteries without which everything they had ever read of in times past, everything they saw around them, everything in the future, was incoherent and unintelligible. And here, my brethren, lies the lesson for the sake of which I am referring to the Jews. You may have fancied, perhaps, that the language in which you hear the death and passion of Christ spoken of in pulpits, and in the forms of the Church, belongs to a high and mysterious theology —that it has been derived from texts of scripture admitting perhaps of more than one explanation, and that you who are destined to a practical life, and have other and most important duties with which the laborious study of religious controversies would very mischievously interfere, may safely pass it over—

either taking it for granted as something which you are to acknowledge, but in which you have no concern, or treating it as the dark utterance of priests, who found that they could best preserve their power by enforcing upon their disciples some strange dogmas which they had not time to examine or courage to deny. Now, my brethren, I do not come to tell you that the fact which is declared daily in our creed, and which this Passion-week brings before us, is not a mysterious fact. I do not come with any easy, natural, interpretation of it, which may remove all the wonder and the perplexity with which you have hitherto regarded it. I would earnestly desire that your wonder at it might increase; I would earnestly pray that all the ingenious contrivances by which men have darkened this awful fact, under pretence of explaining it, might be swept from the earth. But I do come to tell you that this fact, mysterious and profound as it is, belongs to you; that you want it, that it does not stand apart from those toils and studies with which you, as members of a profession devoted to the removal of human sorrows, are concerned; that it has the most close and inseparable connexion with them; that you have not to turn away from your daily works, in order that you may feel the importance and solemnity of it; that these works are the very best witnesses of its importance and solemnity. I come to say to you, that so far as you are brought into contact with real life and real suffering, just so far have you an evidence of the truth which we preach: we ask for no other. We announce to you certain things as true—we believe we have commission to announce them; the proof of them is in your hearts, and consciences, and daily experience. If you believe them, the world with which you are conversing, the living and dying beings whom you see before you, and whom you hope to relieve, will become intelligible to you; you will be able to meet suffering with clear, honest eyes, not flinching from the sight of it, nor yet thinking it a light thing, but understanding the measure and the greatness of it; you will be able to connect the sufferings of others with your own; you will be able to pass through the world as men pass through it who know that they have something to do in it, and that their lives are not to be spent in dreaming. If you disbelieve these words which we as God's commissioned ministers speak upon the warrant of his word, then we say, the universe will be to you a medley of strange fantastic shapes, which you can bring into no order; the honourable work to which you have given yourselves up, will seem to you nothing but a weary hopeless fight against an intolerable destiny; you will not see what you and your fellow-men have to do with each other, or why you were sent here, or what is behind you or before you. You dare not, as brave and thoughtful men should do, question this life and death with which you are busy every hour, what they mean and what we have to do with them. You may try to fashion some theory about these matters—you may keep it so long as you are away from actual things—so long as you can avoid the sight of sick beds or preserve yourselves from one; but ask your theory to help you in any emergency; ask it to tell you how to act and live; ask it to make you calm in the fret and worry of life; ask it to make you simple, true-hearted, warm-hearted men; and you will find that it is good for nothing—a cheat and delusion, which you have adopted perhaps, for the very sake of avoiding cheats and delusions, and which has no good in it but what it has borrowed from the truths that you have bartered for it.

My brethren, I know that this language may sound strange to many of you. Those who, from a devout reverence for the instructions of their parents, have been led to persevere from their youth upwards in religious duties and services, may have felt the influence of these upon their daily life and conduct, but they may still have been induced to look upon them as very little connected with the business and duties of their profession. They have rather thought, perhaps, that while seeking for instruction respecting things unseen, or while strengthening their faith in them, they were making a sacrifice, desirable and necessary, but still a sacrifice, of time which the studies of their profession partly demanded. Others there may be who have been roused by the admonitions of some friend, or by some startling illness, into the feeling that there was a spirit within them of which they had taken no heed. These may be inclined even more than those I spoke of first, to think that the truths respecting their immortal being which are now for the first time breaking in upon them and overwhelming them with a sense of their importance, are altogether disconnected with anything in which they had been previously engaged, and can scarcely without profaneness be associated with the routine of what they call their common and earthly duties. There may be some again who do not positively reject those principles which were announced to them from the lips of their mothers, but who have never taken the pains to ground them in their hearts, have never been strongly impressed with the need of them, and therefore of course look upon all the knowledge and wisdom that they have acquired as men as the most remote possible from this childish lore. Again, it may be that there are those who have actually cast away the doctrines of their catechism as the tales of nurses which are contradicted or at all events superseded by the lessons which they have acquired from more enlightened teachers. Once more, there may be some (I would hope a very few) who regard professional studies and moral teachings with equal indifference, whose only object is to get through the world and kill time as they can, not recollecting that the medical man who kills time now is likely to commit other and worse murders hereafter. Yet to one and all of these classes I would address myself, confident that though in some there may be a readier ear than in others, there is an ear in all to which truth may find access, while I endeavour to shew you how much the truth which is set forth in my text does appertain to your professional life, and what a worse than blank it would be if this faith were banished from men, that Christ himself bore our griefs and carried our sorrows.

I can quite believe that instances of men struggling under a heavy sense of shame and guilt do not present themselves to medical men in the course of their practice nearly so often as persons in my profession are apt to imagine. That you will meet with cases of men who cannot conceal the secret grief which is preying upon them, I am certain. But it may be that far the majority of those who are suffering this oppression will reserve the utterance of it for other ears than yours. I will therefore speak only in a passing way of this subject. I will speak mainly of that misery with which you are directly concerned, from which the patient hopes that you will be able to deliver him. Now there are two ways in which that misery will force itself upon your notice. You will consider it as that which is weighing down each particular individual to whom you are summoned. You will consider it as it affects the whole of our species. You cannot by any possibility turn away from either of these considerations. You are called to the sick bed of a particular man. His disease may be in no sense a peculiar one. You may have seen hundreds before who were in the same or nearly the same condition. But if you are able to classify the disease ever so accurately and satisfactorily, there lies this one man groaning under it. To him it is nothing at all that numbers have felt that very same pain in all ages which he is feeling. He does feel it as actually and really as if there were no other creature in the universe beside him nor ever had been. It is his pain, his torment, it absorbs him just as much as if it were some newly devised calamity which had been sent singly to him. And so it will be with each man you meet. You may complain justly and reasonably enough that each of these persons attaches so much importance to that sorrow under which he is labouring, but you cannot make it otherwise by your complainings. Each man will feel his own heart's bitterness. Each will utter his own groan, and will not be stopped because tens of thousands have uttered the like groan before. Now I beseech you reflect upon this fact. It is a very common-place one assuredly. You may be inclined to pass it over as something too plain and obvious to be worth considering. But it is worth considering for all that, and the more because it is an ordinary every-day fact which encounters each of us. Marvellous events that happen once in a century we may talk about, but it is not these which it much signifies to us to explain. Those which each day brings forth, deserve our examination far more. What answer, then, can be given when each man is crying out for himself, Why is it thus with me? Why is this grief which I cannot share with any one sent to me? You try to give a practical answer by curing the man of his sickness, and assuredly he who can do this has a wonderful gift, and one cannot wonder that in barbarous nations he should be regarded almost as a god. But you know well enough the limits of your power, how often it will not be effectual, how certain it is that some new sorrow will assail the man when an old one has left him, how surely there is one disease to which all are subject that admits of no cure. There must be some other answer than these efforts of yours, however honourable and successful, an answer which you want yourselves as much as those with whom you deal. We say that an answer has been given by Him who alone could give it, by Him who created each man and sent him into the world. We say it is this: "Himself bore our griefs and carried our sorrows." The being who made you, and of whom you are demanding, Why hast thou made me thus? takes your nature upon him, becomes a man even as you are, different from you in this that he is more suffering, more sorrowing than any of you. He does not take this nature under some singular and happy circumstances exempt from the accidents to which it is in other persons liable. He takes it in its lowest possible condition. He takes it under all its curses and penalties, the penalty of poverty, of infirmity, of desertion, of death. Do you want him to explain further whether the suffering you are experiencing was inflicted upon you by some cruel design of his? do you want him to tell you by any other evidence than this whether he created his children to be miserable? Or do you want any other proof than this furnishes that that misery must have come from some other source, that it must have arisen not from his will, but from some dreadful rebellion against his will? Not from our being in the state in which he made us, but from our having departed from that state.

And here we begin to feel how that misery of which I said that you were appointed to take cognizance becomes connected with that other deeper misery which the sick man reveals to us. He is enduring a pain which may or may not have been caused by his own fault. But whether it has or has not, this pain awakens in his mind the sense of an evil which none inflicted upon him, which he inflicted upon himself. As his bodily suffering took him apart from all other creatures and made him feel alone in the world, so it is with this more inward suffering. His conscience says to him, 'Thou hast sinned. Myriads of beings may have been around thee doing the same acts, feeling the same feelings. But they do not affect thee. Thou art thyself responsible. Thou art arraigned. Thou must answer at the judgment-seat of the universe alone, unsupported, though all the world were to confess the same evil or could prove itself free from it.' In what way do those tidings, Himself bore our griefs and carried our sorrows, come in here? In this way. They tell this self-accused man that there is a Being of perfect goodness and love, that this evil of which his conscience speaks can arise from nothing else but from his having separated himself from that goodness and love, refusing to be in submission to it. They tell him that this Being of perfect goodness has come down from heaven that he may reconcile those who were wandering from Him to Himself. They tell him that as the loss of belief in that goodness, and so of submission to it, was the cause of his misery, so it must be by turning to that goodness, trusting to it, submitting to it, that he obtains peace. They tell him, lastly, that all bodily pain and suffering, those outward evils under which each man groans, have been converted into remedial processes in the hands of him who himself bore those griefs and carried those sorrows by which he brings men to feel their separation from him and the necessity and the possibility of a reconciliation. I ask you again, How, if this faith were taken away from the world, if there were no longer any dream in it that the Creator of mankind had himself borne their griefs and carried their sorrows, it would be possible that the demand in each man's heart why he suffers, and what his suffering is for, and what is the end of it could be satisfied? Being convinced of this truth, we can satisfy it, and therefore we say that it is one in which you who are brought into contact with all the distinct forms of human misery are most interested.

But I spoke of another way in which the pains and sorrows you meet with must present themselves to you. You have to deal with individual cases; you see each particular man enduring his own calamity; but you are obliged also to look upon it as belonging to the human race. These diseases, which seem to take men so much apart, and separate them from each other, you are taught to look upon as the common inheritance of the different tribes of the earth. You know under what circumstances such and such a disease is likely to assail, not a few scattered persons merely, but whole neighbourhoods or countries. You read the history of these diseases in past times; you are told how the individual symptoms are only varieties of some common species. You know, above all (we all of us know) that death, the great divider, he who takes every man by himself, and admits no partnership, is at the same time the great uniter—the common symbol of all creatures.

This too is a strange fact—strange in itself—most strange, when one connects it with the other, that the very power which seems to tear us from one another, is in another sense the link that connects us with each other. Do not let this truth pass you by till you have grappled with it and made it tell you something of what it means. And when you have thought long and wearily, I believe these old nursery words will come in as the best and completest solution of the difficulty, turning a feeling of the most oppressive sadness into one of peace and joy, 'Himself bore our griefs and carried our sorrows.' This sorrow and death, which divide men from one another, are indeed meant to be bonds of the closest fellowship between us; for the Creator of the world hath come down and suffered the sorrow and died the death of all. Being thus lifted up, he does, as he said he would, draw all men unto him. His death becomes the one centre of the world, to which all eyes may turn and find there the meaning of their own death, the beginning of their own life. The world has been a great contradiction, because it has been a selfish world, each man setting up himself, while yet he confesses by every act he does that he is of one flesh and blood with his neighbours, and cannot live without them. Christ is without selfishness. His death is the great denial of all self; it is a voluntary giving up of a life and glory which belonged to him—a voluntary identification of himself with all his creatures. And therefore this death becomes the true uniting bond of all creatures— the true and only foundation of a universal society among men.

Every society in the world has had to fight with this principle of selfishness, to keep it down by laws, to counteract it by encouraging family affections. Christ comes as the true fulfiller of all laws and all relationships, because he comes as the destroyer of selfishness, because he proclaims to us that in him we were all created, that in him we are redeemed; that being taken into covenant with him by baptism, we become one with him, and one with our brethren; and that it is in the power of every man who claims that union to live not to himself, but to him that loved him, and gave himself for him.

In this way, then, the mystery of Christ's death, as it is set forth in the catechism and creed which you learnt in your infancy, becomes the greatest interpreter of the strange marvels and contradictions which present themselves to you in your manhood. Men who live in their closets may try, if they can, to get rid of this great fact, or to make out that it is only a story invented to teach us some lessons about God's mercy and goodness. But you cannot be content with this; you have to meet with actual human wretchedness—to meet with it as it is in human beings—not as it seems when it is put into books; you must have something real to meet these realities : that which is not as good for the beggar as for the scholar, carries a stamp of falsehood upon it which you must recognise. Here is a truth which does meet men as men, which meets them as individuals, which meets them as those who feel that they have a common life, common sufferings, and a common death. It has stood the opposition of all the folly and wisdom of eighteen centuries; it is as fresh now as it was when it was first uttered as a prophecy by Isaiah, or proclaimed as an accomplished fact by the apostles in Jerusalem; 'The Creator of the world hath himself borne our griefs and carried our sorrows.'

But, my brethren, if what I said just now be true, this cannot be all. I have appealed to the facts which will meet you in your professional career as the evidence for this truth, and I said that I wanted no other. But if this fact be indeed the key to all the puzzles of our life, it must too be the foundation of all the acts of our life. To what extent it has actually become the foundation of our social progress, of the wisdom and science which have existed in Christendom, I believe few are aware. I could shew you, I think, by well attested facts, reported by travellers in countries where the name of Christ is not known, that the acknowledgment, however inconsistent, however resisted in practice by human selfishness, of him who died for all as our Lord and King, has been the great reason why men have cared for each other, why they have felt that they had a common humanity, and that the feeling of our being redeemed creatures possessing a body which shall one day be glorified, has been the great motive to all earnest study of men's physical circumstances and condition. Do not think that this progress will go on, that we shall retain what we have got, yea, that we shall be preserved from a worse than barbarous state, if this truth be taken from us.

But how shall we avoid its being taken from us when all influences without and within, the canker worm of luxury which is destroying nations, the canker worm of selfishness which is preying upon our own hearts, are alike conspiring against it? Only by the determination formed by each man in the strength of God, that he will make this truth the one which governs his own character and being. Only by each one saying, 'He who bore men's griefs and carried their sorrows is he to whom I was bound in infancy by the solemn sacrament of Baptism, who took me then to be a member of his body, who bestowed upon me his Spirit; therefore will I hold that the griefs and sorrows of my brethren belong to me, that I am interested in them. Feeling this I will give thanks to God that he has called me to be a member of a profession in which I can administer relief to those griefs and sorrows. I will count it my highest privilege, that by these preparatory studies I am acquiring the power of doing so. I will account it a sin in the sight of man and of God, that I should dare to waste the opportunities here given me of acquiring that knowledge which hereafter I cannot acquire, or acquire only by an experience the most fatal to the lives of those who are committed to me. I will believe that every act which is against the law of God, every corrupt habit of mind, is just as inconsistent with the office to which I am called, as those acts and habits which are felt by every one to be unprofessional and disgraceful. I will confess such acts and habits before God, and will ask him to deliver me from the guilt and power of them. I will look upon it as part of my professional duty, to strengthen that faith within me by which I am brought into fellowship with the members of God's family in earth and in heaven. I will feel that to be a faithful and true physician, I must, above all things, be a faithful and true man, and that I can be this only when I claim communion with the great Head of men. I believe that it is by weak instruments, even by men like myself, that he utters his word and will to us, even as it is by weak instruments, by men also, that he communicates bodily restoration to his creatures. I will therefore receive that word from those who I believe are appointed to deliver it, looking to him to quicken it. I believe that it is by the earthly things which he sanctifies and glorifies, that the souls and spirits of men are healed and nourished, even as it is by earthly herbs and minerals that their physical natures are sustained and purified. I will therefore with thankfulness and wonder receive that sacrament by which he promises that I shall become partaker of his death, and of his resurrection. I believe that by the fellowship and ordinances of his Church below, he is training us for a higher fellowship and more glorious ministries above. I will therefore seek him in those ordinances, not doubting, that by them he will strengthen me to labour for my brethren on earth, whose sorrows and infirmities he bore, and will fit me to meet them in a world from which sorrow and infirmity shall be banished for ever.'

SERMON XXII.

THE TRUE REST AND HOPE OF MAN.

(*Preached at Guy's Hospital.—Quinquagesima Sunday Evening, 1841. The day after the funeral of Sir Astley Cooper.*)

I am the resurrection and the life ; he that believeth in me, though he were dead, yet shall he live, and whosoever liveth and believeth in me shall never die. Believest thou this ?—JOHN xi. 25, 26.

THESE words were spoken eighteen hundred years ago to a poor woman, the dweller in a little village of Judea. They were spoken by one, who, in outward appearance, was not greater than she herself was, and who was threatened with death by his countrymen. This woman had lost her brother. The person to whom she was speaking had loved him. She wondered that he had not been with him when he died. She had a strange feeling of his power, despised as he was. She said, "Lord, if thou hadst been here, my brother had not died." The answer was, "Thy brother shall rise again." This was no new doctrine to her. The most popular of the Jewish teachers believed it, and inculcated it. She therefore replied at once, "I know that he shall rise at the resurrection, at the last day." Then spake Jesus, "I am the resurrection and the life, he that believeth in me, though he were dead, yet shall he live."

Since these words were first uttered, generations have passed away, empires have been subverted, the land of Mary and Martha has sunk into degradation and misery, this island has been raised from insignificance and barbarism to greatness. Everything in the world seems to have undergone alteration. But these words remain; within this twelvemonth, they have been spoken here in England—yes, within this week they have been spoken here in this parish, at the graves of rich men and poor men, of ignorant men and learned, of men dying amidst all kind offices, and men dying without a kinsman or a friend to weep for them, of some whose names may be remembered for generations, and of some whose names were scarcely enough known to be registered on their coffins. As that which remained of each of these was laid in the earth, a voice was heard saying, "I am the resurrection and the life, he that believeth in me, though he were dead, yet shall he live, and whosoever liveth and believeth in me shall never die." Nor is it merely that the words have been adopted from the book which records the conversation of Jesus Christ with Martha. The meaning is the same now as it was then; we mean that the Person who spoke these words then is He to whom they apply now. We mean that he is death's enemy and death's conqueror, that by him only does any creature obtain life and resurrection, and that in Him every creature may claim them.

My brethren, our Lord added to these words certain others. He said to Martha, "Believest thou this?" The minister who reads the service at the grave does not ask this question. He goes on to say, "I know that my Redeemer liveth, and that he shall stand at the latter day upon the earth." He declares that he believes this truth himself, he assumes that those who are about him believe it; for he knows that if they do not, the service which they are witnessing must seem to them the idlest of ceremonies. Yea, that not only the solemnity of committing a body to the earth, " Dust to dust, earth to earth, in sure and certain hope of the resurrection to eternal life;" but that all other religious acts and offices,—the Baptism by which we are admitted members of Christ, the prayers which we offer in his name—must seem to them tricks and mockeries. He cannot stop at such a season to consider whether those about him do or do not recognise the force of the mighty language he is using. But yet this question is asked, though not aloud. It is spoken to each man in his own conscience. The coffin speaks it, the vault speaks it, God's word speaks it. He speaks it, who addressed it to Martha when He was going to the tomb of Lazarus. He says to each one who is seeing the dust of his brother committed to its native earth, 'Thou, even thou, who art looking on here to-day, art engaged in the same struggle which has just closed for him. Thou art standing between life and death, they are wrestling which shall have thee, and this conflict thou must carry on alone in the secret depths of thy own being, none can share it with thee. Death will take thee apart from all other creatures when he comes to hold debate with thee. There is but one friend from whom he cannot divide thee, one who has proved himself mightier than he is. "I am the resurrection and the life. Believest thou this?"'

And therefore it seems to me that this is the use

which it behoves me to make of the scene which you witnessed yesterday, and of which this chapel will be a standing memorial to you. It may suggest many other thoughts to you, thoughts both sad and encouraging, on which it may be very profitable for you to dwell. You will consider, doubtless,—your wisest friends will impress the recollection on your mind,—how much a course of honourable and patient industry is better than one of temporary pleasure, and excitement; how disgraceful it is to throw away means of acquiring knowledge, which, when rightly used, have enabled men to be benefactors to hundreds of their fellow-men. You will think of the steady, earnest, humble temper, in which the distinguished members of your profession, and he whom you are now mourning especially, must have applied themselves to the search after truth, before they could be rewarded with the discoveries of which you and we receive the benefit; and you will remind yourselves how far such a temper is removed from that haste and self-conceit which are natural to us all, and which young men sometimes encourage in themselves as marks of ability. You will hear of the affectionate esteem with which the eminent person whom we have lost was honoured by the members of his own class, and you will not forget to reflect upon the meanness and paltriness of spite and jealousy among those who should be labouring together for the advancement of knowledge, and for the good of their race. All these are reflections which belong not merely to your position as members of a profession, but as men; they belong not to a low, but to a very high morality, and if you determine not merely to adopt them as fine sentiments, but to act upon them in your lives, you will find that you need helps and assistances of the highest kind. And along with them, I have no doubt there will be other recollections which appeal even more directly to your feelings, and therefore may in one sense be of even more value. If you have not many of you looked up to the departed with the personal affection and piety which are due to a teacher and a friend, you will at least have received the tradition of his wisdom through others who did regard him in that character, towards whom you now feel as they felt towards him, and in whose affection and sorrow you have a right to participate. The meditation into which I would lead you to-night is not alien from any of these thoughts. You may find hereafter that it has very much to do with them. Still it is of a more universal character. After you have thought of all the circumstances by which one man is marked out from another, the deepest, most wonderful thought remains—that he was a man. There is no quality for which we feel that we ought so much to admire any one as for his humanity. That is to say, for his not setting himself up as if he had nothing to do with his fellow-creatures, but for feeling himself one of them. Even the genius of a man we respect, not because it lifts him above others, but because it enables him to understand more perfectly some of the relations which exist between him and others, something more of that which is common to him and them. Thus we testify unconsciously when we seem most to be making distinctions, that what belongs to us generally overtops them all. Instead of it being any disparagement to the wisest or the greatest of human beings that we should draw lessons from his tomb, which concern the humblest as well as him, I believe there is no better way of shewing our respect for his memory; none which, if he could speak, he would so entirely approve. And I think you will see the advantage in your particular case of such a practice. You are so familiarized with death in all the forms in which it can present itself, that it would be strange indeed if it did not lose a great part of its wonder, and become to you, even more than to others, a trite common place. Neither the suddenness of any particular instance of it, nor the way in which it occurs, can be likely to surprise you. Instances of the kind have been so carefully reported in your books, or registered in your memories, that they will not strike you, or if they do, they will strike you merely as professional novelties and exceptions, not as suggesting any thoughts respecting the condition of men universally; it is only either some circumstance which occurs in your own particular families, or one which occurs to some illustrious member of your profession, that can be expected to make you pause and remember that what is happening at every moment is really new to each person; that death, though six thousand years old, is the greatest of miracles now. It must then be right to take advantage of such an event for the purpose of bringing this thought home to you.

I. It is, however, of death only as it is connected with and interpreted by life and resurrection, that my text bids me speak. That recollection suggests to me the propriety of pointing out to you first of all the emptiness and futility of the language which men sometimes use respecting death, as if it were a blessing instead of a curse, a friend instead of an enemy, the mere end of toil and commencement of repose. That all such expressions as these point to a very deep truth, I am willing and anxious to acknowledge. We do want repose—we long for it, and the silent smiling look which a corpse sometimes wears for a day or two after the breath is departed, is an image and shadow to us of that which we desire. It seems as if we beheld all that we had seen of goodness and gentleness in him who is gone, without the fever and the restlessness which we observed while he was still mingling with us; we are sure that restlessness is the thing we want to be rid of, that to be calm and even would be the highest blessing which could be bestowed upon us; and we say to ourselves, 'Surely nothing but life is the cause of this restlessness, death terminates it.' But these are thoughts in which the mind cannot for more than a few moments find relief and comfort. They are not sound—they are not real; they indicate to us something that we want, but they do not shew us where we may procure it. And when sickness and suffering come, which are the preludes and foretastes of death, these feelings and imaginations desert us; we do not find that death is the thing that we need—the thing that is to do us any good. Our minds get back into their natural tone,—death seems to them a dark and hideous thing; it has lost its prettiness and softness; it comes before us in the aspect which it wore to men in earlier and simpler times, as a foe and a destroyer, which may be too strong for us, but which we would contend with and shake off if we could. Do not fancy that this is not so, because you have sometimes heard persons in great agony crying out for death to deliver them. You know well how strong pain is able to disorder our faculties, and to give us the most confused notions of the things which we mean and desire. I do not say that it may not drive men at times to cry out that God will send them death, as it may tempt men actually to seek death by their own hands; but then it is because their minds are out of joint, either through positive insanity or through some unhappy ignorance and delusion which acts in the same way as insanity. And if you set off against these instances, all that you have seen of men clinging to life, even in the midst of the greatest suffering, and deeming anything better than that end of it which appears to be at hand, you will agree with me, I think, that the verdict of mankind is not in favour of the notion which some sentimentalists seek to encourage; that men everywhere, when in their right senses, are seeking for some deliverance from death, not looking to death as if it were itself a deliverer.

II. I would observe next, that the notion of the soul being freed from the prison-house of the body when the breath leaves it, is not one which has been found of much more worth than the one we have last considered. Here, again, I would carefully distinguish. This language was used by some of the better men who lived before the coming of our Lord, I believe, with a most important and excellent meaning. With the souls or spirits within them, they had longed after truth and righteousness; these had been their aims through life, and they had pursued them, inconsistently indeed, but still with a fervent love, resisting the inclinations of the body which hindered them from conversing with the invisible things they knew to be most precious. Such persons spoke of being controlled by their animal natures while they dwelt on earth, and of wishing to escape from them that they might attain what here, under great disadvantages, they had hungered after. Their words were, I think, not always well chosen; at all events, they were imperfect; but I doubt not they were seeking the right end, and that what they sought they found.

Most persons, however, when they speak of the soul being disengaged from the body, have a vague and confused notion that somehow or other their intellects will become brighter after death than they were before; that they shall mix with minds as noble as their own; that they shall no longer be disturbed by the intrusion of narrow and vulgar people; that they shall obtain a reverence, and a dominion, which are denied them here, nay, which are bestowed upon many whom they despise. Now, such thoughts as these will not, I am sure, stand a man in any great stead, nor enable him with a really brave spirit to contemplate the change which awaits him. He fancies his faculties will be brighter and clearer in the new condition of things. What evidence has he of it? Do the faculties generally become clearer during the days and months which precede the passing into that condition? There have been, doubtless, examples of such an improvement; among good and humble men, whose powers have been depressed by circumstances during their stay on earth, they are not rare. But assuredly this is not the common experience, and perhaps the fewest examples of such excepted cases are to be found among men of high gifts and reputation. The melancholy words, "Non eadem est ætas, non mens," have with them become almost a proverbial complaint, when they are comparing their later with their earlier years. It is no reproach to them that it should be so; God has ordained it, and those who cheerfully submit to his will, present, it seems to me, as beautiful and interesting, and even cheering a spectacle, as they would do if they had been permitted to retain their vigour to the last. But surely this decay and second childishness on the eve of dissolution are not in themselves a warrant to expect that the intellect will be the better for its actual occurrence. If there be such a warrant, and I fully believe there is, we must seek it from some other source.

Still less do I believe that the expectation of a requital for the little favour or honour which wise men receive in this world, can ever sustain one who is looking death in the face. The moments in which a neglected sage has tried to comfort himself with that faith, have not been the best in his life. They have been, unless I am greatly mistaken, times of chagrin and fretfulness, when he was much overrating his services to the world, and judging most hardly of the treatment he had received from it. Such thoughts will only occur to him on his deathbed, as reasons for sorrow and humiliation; he will regard them as bitter fruits of that pride and self-glorification which, seen by the light of an opening eternity, appear the most wretched littleness and baseness. They will come to him with recollections of talents given and wasted; of sins committed; of the worship he has rendered to fame and to himself. He will find that these are not sins to which he was compelled by his circumstances or his body; that they are sins of that very soul which he expects to dwell in such freedom and sovereignty; he will feel that in whatever state the soul be, of corruption or purity, when it leaves the world, in that state must it awake in the new circumstances which are prepared for it. Surely, then, the thought of *this* emancipation is not one which can give us satisfaction, even if we be content (and I do not think any of us can be content) to believe that the body, with all its wonderful machinery and its inward life, is only bestowed on us for a few years, and is then to be cast off as a burden for ever.

III. Once more, the mere belief in a general resurrection of the just and the unjust, seems to me a very inadequate source of consolation to any one who has been either separated from dear friends, or who is expecting his own departure.

You will not suppose that I wish to throw any doubt upon this doctrine, because I say that it will not of itself be sufficient to sustain us in life or death. You may know from the history of your own science, that a principle of the greatest truth and importance may need some other principle to support and explain it; may be almost without value, nay, may actually mislead, till that other is discovered and asserted. So, I believe, it is in this case. The idea of a general resurrection is most precious, because it gives us the sense of our being members of a family, every one connected by innumerable links with every other, influencing each other continually for good or for evil, responsible, therefore, for our conduct one towards another, incapable of possessing a felicity which we do not share. And yet this very doctrine, as it was held by the Pharisees in our Lord's time, seems only to have increased their selfish spirit by making them calculate upon the ways of winning rewards or averting judgments at the last day. That Love, without which, as the Church teaches us to-day, all services, and all doctrines, are worthless, did not inform their faith or prompt their obedience; and, therefore, whether they were looking forward to another state, or arranging their conduct in this, they were equally mistaken themselves and equally indifferent guides to others. Martha had evidently learnt nothing from their teaching which enabled her to bear the loss of a brother: but then she had learnt to revere and trust in one who had loved her brother, and who she believed had power to save him from death. And when she spoke to that friend of her brother rising at the resurrection in the last day, he answered, "I am the resurrection and the life."

This is the point to which my observations have been tending; I wish to show you how that repose, which we cannot find in the thought of death—that promise of deliverance, which we cannot find in the mere belief that the soul will escape from the body—that assurance of fellowship and communion with those who have gone before us or may follow us, together with that feeling of a just and righteous judgment, which we cannot get from the mere belief of a general resurrection, are all contained in these words of our Lord, and may be drawn out of them, if we will, by each of us.

I. Why is it that men become drunkards? Why is it that they plunge into a course of reckless dissipation? It is that they may forget themselves. The preacher tells those who are pursuing this object, that their conduct is most ignominious; that for a man to try to destroy the consciousness of his being, of his own responsibility, is the more base, the more highly we deem of what we are, and what we are meant to be; that every man should desire to cultivate to the uttermost, and for the highest ends, all the energies which God has given him. You cannot doubt that he says true; your consciences tell you that he does; you cannot think that we were meant to sleep away existence. And yet, I am sure, that there *is* a meaning in that wish to forget ourselves. It could not have been felt through the whole heart of our human kind, in all periods and in all circumstances, if there had not been a reality in it. The longing is too deep, too inward, in each of us, not to have some reasonable ground and some right satisfaction. While we speak, at one time, of an 'abandoned man,' as if he were the worst of his species, we speak at another of self-abandonment, as if it were one of the highest and noblest qualities. While we try to rouse people to a consciousness of their life and their powers, we denounce a person who is self-conscious, who is always thinking what he is, and what shall happen to him, as artificial and morally offensive. The words unconsciousness and self-forgetfulness are identified in our minds with the beautiful simplicity of childhood, with the highest perfection of manhood. And, therefore, it is that while we think of death as in any sense connected with the ceasing to be conscious of ourselves, we cannot, in spite of our better judgments, refuse to regard it with a certain degree of affectionate wonder.

In spite of our better judgments, for they bear witness, as I have said already, that this sleep is not intended for us, and, that if it were, death would not bring it to us. As our great poet has said, with such wonderful wisdom and truth, this death-sleep may have dreams in it. No one has ever thought of it seriously, without believing that it will be peopled with dreams, that it will bring with it a flood of recollections, that it will withdraw us from the confused rattle of the world, that it will take from us those objects in which we have contrived to drown thought, and concentrate us more entirely in ourselves. It is not here, then, we can look for escape from that spectre which has been pursuing us all our way through the world,—it is not here we can find deliverance from the pains of consciousness or the stings of conscience. Death, nakedly considered, is nothing but the being left *by* ourselves and *to* ourselves.

But where, then, is the fulfilment of that wish so deeply seated in all our hearts ? How may it be realised, and realised in such a way, that we need not be ashamed of it—that we need not feel we have parted with anything to attain the accomplishment of it? The experience of our lives here on earth seems to answer the question. The true rest of man's spirit is in love. When it can find an object that it can really embrace and delight in, then it may indeed forget itself —then it may lose the miserable restlessness of consciousness, and yet live only the more for doing so. And, therefore, this is what men want, and that only can be a gospel or 'good news' to man which shows him how this want is supplied. If there be not some person to whom each man may feel he is united, in whom he may realise his own life, and in whom there is an inexhaustible fountain of life, we must go on sorrowing for ever, surrounded by a world which offers us continual hints of a blessing that can never be reached, hemmed in by death, which declares that all hopes of discovering it are gone for ever. But if the words of my text be true, this is not the state of man. There is one who had a right to say to the poor woman of Judea, "I am the resurrection and the life." There is one who shewed by raising a man out of the grave, that by his life men live. If our baptism be true, we are united to Him; if our creed be true, we may realise this union from day to day by trust in Him. If the Lord's supper be true, we may throw off our selfishness, and, as members of one body, be sustained by the Spirit which is in the one Lord and head of it. If our funeral service be true, we may believe that there is in this trust, and union, and love, that which death cannot interrupt or disturb; yea, that death changed its nature when it passed upon Christ, and became a new birth. Here, my brethren, is the rest which men have sought for and could not find. It is rest in the real love of a real Person, who has shewn that we are related to him, and that he cares for us, by taking our nature and bearing our death, and who has done this that we might be delivered from our death, and be made partakers of his true and heavenly life.

II. And here too, then, must lie the satisfaction of that other desire which men have thought to realise by the mere separation of the soul from the body. All the language which has been used upon this point, has indeed much force and truth in it, though I believe it has been perverted to a false end. It is true that the body does become the 'prison-house' of the spirit. It is true that the mind which muses upon many things is held down by the low and earthly appetites of the flesh. It is true that every exercise of the intellectual powers is a witness that such slavery was not intended for us. There must be an emancipation from it, and he who does not seek it, is content to part with the privileges of a man. But if what we have already said be reasonable, the soul has power to be its own tormentor, yea, is its own tormentor. In its thoughts, broodings, recollections, do its torments consist. If the body help to aggravate those torments, as assuredly it does,—if the sense of degradation to animal wants and the difficulty of satisfying them, and the satiety and sorrow which follow after they have been gratified, grieve and afflict it still more, as assuredly they do,— yet nothing of this would happen if the worm were not within—if there were not a secret bitterness which turns all that is tasted to gall. And, therefore, it is from this that we want emancipation. When man has been conscious that there is a spirit within him, he has always cried for something higher than himself to help him; when he thinks only of himself, his wings soon droop, he falls back into the very charnel-house which he had found so degrading and so loathsome. Whenever he has been conscious that he had spiritual powers, he has lifted up his voice to a higher spirit to raise him to himself; he has felt that all his misery came from the separation between him and some being whom he ought to trust in and obey; he has felt, at the same time, that he could not destroy the separation, that the being whom he had invoked must descend to him, or he could never rise. Unless some one has entered into our mortal condition who could say, "I am the resurrection and the life," this groan for deliverance has been poured out in vain. If such a being has come, we may rise up in Him to newness of life. Here on earth we may begin to claim this victory of the spirit over the body: here on earth we may look upon every power which there is in our minds as a God-like power, which He himself will give us strength to use, upon every end to which those powers are devoted, as a sacred end which He has ordained; here on earth we may fight and struggle with every temptation which checks us in the free and zealous exercise of these faculties, or in the full, zealous, and devoted application of ourselves to the duties, whatever they be, to which we have been called; here on earth we may feel that all these powers and duties are not given to separate us from the humblest of our brethren, but to unite us more closely with them, to make us more effectually their servants, to enable us to clear away hindrances which prevent them from enjoying that life which is as much intended for them, which they are as much capable of entering into, as the greatest sage. But, at the same time, we shall feel that this earth is but the first stage for the exercise of these powers. It will not be a difficult thing to us to believe that they are intended for a higher expansion and for nobler services; it will be hard, almost impossible, to think otherwise; for, believing that we are united to One who has himself shared our weakness and has himself entered into a state of perfection and glory, we must believe that everything in us which is in an imperfect seminal condition, is destined somewhere or other to attain its complete growth, to put forth its perfect fruits; we must believe that nothing is intended to die but that which chooseth death, by choosing separation from Him; we must believe, not only that this soul, with every function and faculty that it possesses, is intended for an immortal freedom and vigour; but that this body, though the husk of it may be the food of worms, shall, in all its essential properties and life, be made like unto his glorious body, by that power whereby he subdueth all things to himself.

III. And thus, I think, we shall be able to understand how that feeling of a requital for unjust treatment in this world, of a perfect reward for whatever has been right and true in our conduct here, of a righteous condemnation for what has been evil, may be separated from its selfish ingredients, and may be rightly connected with that belief in a resurrection of the just and of the unjust, which taken alone seemed to be incapable of exercising any healthful influence over the character. When we remember that the wish for selfish gratification has been the great torment of the world, nay, that it is the torment of each man's own individual heart, and becomes at last such an intolerable torment to him, that he would be glad to lose himself altogether; it does indeed seem a strange and monstrous notion that the consummation of all things, the final righting and restoration of the universe, should consist in the awarding to each man of a certain portion of separate felicity, as the compensation for his wrongs, or a prize of his virtue. And yet no man can divest himself of the conviction that there will be a consummation of all things, that all things from the beginning of creation have been moving towards it, that every human soul which has ever existed must have a personal share and interest in it. I say, no man can, let him labour as he will, throw off this conviction. If he rejects it in one form, it comes back to him in another; if he will not acknowledge it as a waking reality, it haunts him in his dreams. He may change the names by which he describes it, but the actual vision remains the same. The world, my brethren, is not too old for this faith; it clung, indeed, about its infancy; heathen fables recognised it; the Jewish seer saw the final judgment pictured in every precursive judgment by which his nation was visited; the apostle spoke of it as he stood upon Mars' Hill, to the cultivated Athenian; all the forms of society, as they have risen and perished to testify that there is an order which cannot be violated, and to shew that they themselves are subject to this order, have prophesied of it. As the world advances into its hoary age, when its sins become more multiplied, and it becomes harder to live a true life in the midst of it, and the different threads of its history are seen to be all interwoven together, and the crimes of one age are found to beget the miseries of the next, and the goodness and depravity of particular men are found to exercise the mightiest influence on the whole mass, the evidence becomes more irresistible, even though the faith in it may become weaker, that all things must be tending towards some great issue, and that only One who sees the past, the present, and the future, who knows the whole order of things, and knows each person in himself, with all the train of his thoughts, words, acts, and the influences which have affected him, and the use which he has made of them, can pronounce the final verdict upon our human life and destiny.

And this, my brethren, is the point to which the Scriptures always lead us when they speak of the final resurrection. They speak of it as a day of light and revelation, which shall discover Him who said to the Jewish woman, "I am the resurrection and the life," as the centre of the universe, as the source whence all its light and beauty have proceeded, as the being who has ordered all its movements, as the being in whom each man alone has lived, whose wisdom has alone enabled him to understand his place in the world and to fulfil it, in whose righteousness alone any creature has become righteous. In the clear sunlight of that day, everything will stand out exactly as it is in its own distinctness, yet in its relation to all other things, because in its relation to him who formed all things. In the brightness of that judgment, every person will understand his own responsibility for that which has been lent to him, and which must then be restored. Each one will feel and understand how every relation in which he stood upon earth was pointing the way to him, who is the common Lord and brother of man; how each duty was a call to ask for his strength, and an assurance that it would be granted. And, therefore, in that day, all self-seeking must be confounded, and shewn to be a vain thing, under whatever names or disguises it may have been concealed; and all who, under whatever clouds and confusions, have struggled after Him who is the one good and life of the world, must obtain what they seek, and find that infinite reward which eye hath not seen nor ear heard, nor it hath entered into the heart of man to conceive; which only love can give and only love can take in.

My brethren, if there is anything which can keep down the presumptuousness of human judgments, the uncharitableness and self-conceit of human thoughts, it is surely the belief and expectation, yea, the certainty that He will pronounce the decision who knows the truth, and that it will be according to truth. To Him, with perfect submission and confidence, we may commit the whole creation, and everything which he has made. But, oh! let us remember that the thought of this judgment, which is to make us humbly hopeful for every one whose heart's secrets we cannot read, is to make us watchful, earnest, suspicious, about the one creature, whom each of us does know, and for whose acts each one of us is answerable. Let us not look upon a judgment day as some notion of our childhood, which we need no longer when we have put on our manly dress, and have entered upon the business of the world. Be assured that we want it then most. Our childish notions respecting it may be put away, but only because they were not clear, distinct, awful enough. The words, "There is no peace, saith my God, to the wicked," were then but taken upon trust; now we know them to be true by the verdict of experience, and we know that they can never cease to be true, that death will not make them obsolete, but will ratify them. The words, "In me ye shall have peace," were then sweet and pleasant sounds; now our hearts demand them as the only possible deliverance from an eternal war. We want, then, the fullest, most continual, faith in the truth that Christ will judge the quick and dead, not to disturb us, but to calm us—not to make us restless, but to force us, amidst all the restlessness of the world, to seek our rest in Him who has said, "I am the resurrection and the life."

SERMON XXIII.

THE INVISIBLE GUIDE.

(*Preached at Guy's Hospital.—The Fourth Sunday after Trinity*, 1839.)

I will inform thee, and teach thee in the way wherein thou shalt go:
I will guide thee with mine eye.
Be ye not like to horse and mule, which have no understanding:
which must be held in with bit and bridle, lest they fall upon
thee.—PSALM xxxii. 9, 10.

I WILL bring the collect which you have already prayed twice, again to your minds, that you may see why I have chosen this text. "O God, the protector of all that trust in Thee, without whom nothing is strong, nothing is holy, increase and multiply upon us Thy mercy, that Thou being our ruler and guide, we may so pass through things temporal that we finally lose not the things eternal. Grant this O heavenly Father for Jesus Christ's sake our Lord." In this prayer you see we are taught to think of God as of a guide; we are taught to desire that we may trust in Him because we have no strength of our own in which we can trust; we are taught where the way lies through which he is leading us, viz. through things temporal, and we are taught what the danger of this road is, the danger of losing the things eternal. Now all these same thoughts are brought before us in the passage I have taken out of the 32nd psalm, only there they are in the form of a promise instead of a prayer; God is speaking to man, instead of man speaking to God. But He is speaking in answer to a prayer which a man had offered up, a prayer full of confession that he had not trusted and taken Him as his guide, that he had lost his way and had wanted courage to acknowledge it. When he did speak (he says) after long restraint and silence he found forgiveness and comfort. And this was the great security and witness for both, that God had promised to him and to all men, "I will inform thee and teach thee in the way wherein thou shalt go, I will guide thee with mine eye," provided only that they did not determine not to have his guidance, to be curbed like animals instead of being governed like men; to be like the horse and mule which have no understanding, but must be held in with bit and bridle.

First, then, you have asked to be ruled and guided, and you have an assurance in these words which were spoken to one man for the good of all, that you may have that which you desire. This is very wonderful, the prayer is wonderful, and the answer is wonderful. For what do they mean? Do you pray to be ruled as all things in heaven and earth are ruled, as the stars are ruled in their courses, as it is ruled what shall be seed-time and what harvest, when the trees shall put forth their leaves, and when they shall cast them off? You feel that there must be something more in it than this. 'There is something in me which there is not in them. I cannot be ruled and guided just as they are. I may be told just when I shall do such things or omit such other things, all may be set down for me most carefully and I may be enabled to understand what is meant by these orders, but when I receive them there will be something in me which says 'I will,' or 'I will not.' Some strange power I have of not obeying even the most powerful king or ruler in the universe. Yea, I know it well, I have a power of disobeying God's commands, I have a power of saying even to them, 'I will not.' It is most strange, but it is most true, and therefore that rule which is sufficient for trees and flowers, for sun and moon, is not sufficient for me. I, a poor worm of the earth, want a guidance which they do not want. If I needed only what they need, I should not ask at all, a prayer would mean nothing, I should simply move or be still as he bade me without thinking or feeling or wishing at all about either.' Or does it mean, 'Let me be guided and ruled in spite of this will of mine. Though I be ever so unwilling let me be forced on in a certain course, though I hate to move, compel me to move, though I hate to be still, compel me to be still.' This would be a strange contradictory kind of prayer. For prayer must mean a wish, and how can you wish that everything should go contrary to your wish? Besides it would be an unnecessary prayer. For in this way you will be guided and ruled if you do not pray at all. God's order is established in the world. If you and I do not like it yet it will go on, it does go on in spite of us, and we are compelled in some way or other to do homage to it, let us be as disobedient as we will. A murderer breaks God's law, but his murder is found out and he suffers, and God's law is shewn to prevail still. A proud powerful man goes on for years oppressing and trampling upon his fellow-creatures, saying, "I am, and there is none beside me;" but death comes and mocks at him, and the worms feed on him, and men curse his name from generation to generation, and all along he has had a worm within feeding upon him; so that the truth and love against which he was fighting were stronger than he. They forced him to do them homage in spite of himself, though he never wished or prayed that they might. So that it is not this we ask for. And you see from what I have just said, that it cannot mean this either: 'Guide me and rule me according to my own inclinations. Take the conduct of me, but let me say in what way I wish to be conducted. Let me do service to Thee, but in nothing let me be crossed.' That would be asking the thing which I just said could never be. It would be asking that God's order, which he has established for the whole universe, should be altered whenever I wish it, and altered whenever any other man wished it, and so that there might be no order at all, no guidance at all, all things moving at hazard and in confusion. Well, then, if it does not mean either of these three things, if it does not mean Guide us as the sun and stars are guided, if it does not mean Guide us contrary to our own wills, and if it does not mean Guide us just according to our own wills, what can it mean but this: 'Take the rule and guidance over our wills, fashion and direct them, mould them according to Thine, so that the things which please Thee may please us, that Thy will may be done in earth as quietly, obediently, joyfully, as it is in heaven.' Yes, this is the prayer, and to this the promise makes answer and says, 'I will inform thee and teach thee in the way wherein thou shalt go, I will guide thee with mine eye. I take the charge and government of thy will, I undertake to chasten it, soften it, subdue it, to enlighten and inform it respecting my will, to make it feel and know the blessedness of that will, the intense misery of self-will. You shall see what things you have to aim at. You shall understand what things hinder you in attaining these ends, and in what way you may reach them. You shall walk in the sense and knowledge that there is an eye over you which sees that which you cannot see yet, which sees every winding of the path between you and it, you shall feel your own eyesight becoming clearer day by day to distinguish little things from great, and good things from evil, and if you walk in trust and hope, what you do not know now, you shall know hereafter.'

But what proof have I, my brethren, that this promise is really intended for us when it only occurs in a psalm of King David's? I have an assurance of it which King David and all the kings and prophets of the old time had not. In some moment of confession and prayer the thought was mightily brought home to him: 'I am under a divine and spiritual guidance. Not merely all the course of my life, but all the strange passages of my thoughts, all the movements of the heart within me, are beheld and watched over by a loving friend. He will inform me and teach me in the way wherein I shall go. All my wanderings in conduct and in heart have been through forgetting that guardianship; I must commit therefore my memory, as everything else, to Him, that I may be kept from this forgetfulness and from all the consequences of it.' This confidence, I say, would take strong possession of them at certain times, and generally they acted under a feeling that in all their outward proceedings, in fighting with their enemies and in ruling their subjects, God would be with them to help them. But the assurance of a continual inward Presence was that which they looked and longed for, and had not yet received. Their first and highest desire was that He might come who was the bond between God and man, the great Reconciler. Their next was that God might dwell with them and in them, and make them his temples. Now, brethren, that promise of the Spirit which is to you and your children and to as many as the Lord our God shall call, is that which the great promise and gift of baptism and whereof baptism remains the perpetual pledge and assurance, is that which the holy man so earnestly hoped for, and of which he had a dim and faint intimation in his heart. This promise is, 'I will inform thee and teach thee in the way wherein thou shalt go, I will guide thee with mine eye.' It is the undoubted assurance that you shall have one with you who is able to govern your unruly wills and affections, who is able to direct, sanctify, and govern both your hearts and bodies in the ways of God's laws and in the works of his commandments. It is the witness that the most secret workings of our minds, our deepest purposes, the determinations over which we seem to have least control shall be all overseen and controlled by an invisible guide and friend with whom we may converse, whom we may ask to interpret whatever in ourselves or in the world about us puzzles and confounds us, by whose aid we may be able to separate thoughts and feelings and wishes and hopes that seem most strangely mingled together, who can explain to us the discipline of our own lives, and what we have to do with our fellow-creatures, who can show us the meaning and purposes of things, who can keep us quiet and alive to notice them, who can bring whatever is most rebellious within us under government, whatever is most entangled into order. This, and nothing less than this, is what we want, nothing less than this will satisfy our desire of a guide and a ruler. And nothing less than this did Christ promise to his disciples when he said they should have a comforter to be with them and to abide with them, to guide them into all truth, to bring all things to their remembrance, and to teach them of things to come. Nothing less than this does he promise to you through infancy and youth when he owns you as members of his body at baptism, nothing less does he promise you for the years of manhood when he ratifies and renews his words at confirmation, nothing less does he repeat to you when you come to claim the privilege of belonging to his body and to seek strength for your daily and hourly life in the holy supper.

Now, since this is so, my brethren, the great thing for us is to consider how we may keep ourselves in mind of this holy presence, and behave ourselves as if we really had such a guide ever nigh to us. That is what the Church teaches you to do when she puts into your mouth these words, "Without Thee nothing is strong, nothing is holy." It is the sense of this that brings us under the conduct of that guide, it is the want of that sense which makes us try to direct our own steps, which makes us live as if this were an easy world to walk in, and there were no skill wanted to pick our path through it. As long as a man feels that he can trust his own understanding, he will trust it; as long as he feels he can trust his own heart, he will trust it; as long as he finds his own will a safe will, he will obey it. Yes, and when he has given up this opinion for the best reason in the world, that it has betrayed him and cheated him, he will take to it again and again, and make one trial more of his powers to see whether they will not do to lean upon now, though they did not before, and feel his crutch break under him again, just as it has broken under him so many hundred times. And therefore you see that to have this thought pressed upon us and worked into us, to be reminding ourselves of it, and to have others reminding us of it, "Without Thee nothing is strong, nothing is holy," is most needful for us all. And this, I think, we feel needful too, that God himself should remind us of it, that he should make us understand by his providence what this strength we have got in us is worth, what this holiness we have in us is worth, that he should by all means break up this conceit of ours, and make us ashamed of it, and make us know that we are fools for entertaining it. Which lesson, however it comes to us, must needs, I think, be a good lesson. If we get it by being made sick when we were well, that is good. If we get it by being made poor when we are rich, that is good. If we get it by losing our wits on some great occasion when we thought they were very bright, that is good. If we get it by missing the praise of our fellow-creatures when we thought to win it, that is good. If we get it by finding out that we had something most base, and dark, and unholy within us when we thought all was clear and bright, that is good; because it is good to see things as they are. It cannot profit us to shut our eyes and fancy that things are otherwise. It must be best, anyhow, to have our eyes open and to have the light falling upon all things, and that the colours and the size of them should not mislead us. It must be best, for truth is better than falsehood, and it is not only disagreeable truth which we discover when our eyes are thus opened; we find out also the comfortablest of all truths, that we have a guide, though we did not know it, one who is ready to inform us and teach us in the way wherein we should go, and is only holding us in with a bit and bridle till we shall have learnt that we are human beings, and not brute beasts, and are meant to be under a better and nobler government than theirs.

And this will explain a third thing in our collect, why it speaks as if God's guidance and protection were only for those that trust in him. It does not mean that the unseen guide is not there. It does not mean that the promise of our Baptism has been broken, it does not mean that he is not going with us where we go, and staying with us where we stay, that he is not willing to rise with us in the morning, and scatter our enemies before us, that he is not willing to return to us at night, and give us the peace and rest which our spirits as well as our bodies are craving for.

If this were so, we should have no one to trust in, and it would be absurd to bid us trust. But what it means is that by this act of trust we put ourselves under his guardianship. We acknowledge that we cannot do without him, we give up that effort and violence of will which is striving against him. And so it comes to pass that you pray for his guidance, though you have him for your guide. You ask for the Spirit, though you have the Spirit. You would not ask if he were not with you, you feel the necessity of asking because he is with you. This may seem strange, but it is true, and you would find your whole lives far stranger and more contradictory if it were not true. If I have a friend I may very well ask for his help; if he is near me I may call him to me; if he is willing to give me advice, I may consult him. But if I have no notion that I have such a friend, or believe that he is far away, or doubt whether he will listen when I speak to him, the case is changed. I may make now and then a sudden effort when I am in great difficulty, to lay hold of a hand that I think must be somewhere, and which I feel is needed to help me; but for the most part I shall go on trying to work out my dark mazy path as well as I can, hopeless of any succour or guidance, not fancying it possible that there can be any one to inform me and guide me with his eye. And therefore, brethren, I beseech you, do not put away this thought of a presence near you and within you, of an almighty friend ready to direct your steps, as if it were something too dangerous and awful for you to think of; truly it is most awful, and that is the very reason I bring it before you: there will be no real awe and reverence in your mind till you entertain it. You may have some tremblings of fear, and then the rashest presumption following them, but you will not have that settled abiding fear which is no enemy to peace, which love doth not cast out, but with which love and peace delight to dwell, until you receive this belief into your hearts, and labour that it should govern all your acts.

And thus you will be able to understand the sense of the last words in the collect. "That Thou being our ruler and guide, we may so pass through things temporal, that we finally lose not the things eternal." You cannot think that all this wonderful and mysterious guidance is for nothing; you cannot think that the creature who requires it is made only to maintain a hard fight with a set of cruel enemies and then to perish. There must be things eternal, and we must be meant to share in them. But what are they, and where are they, and when may we hope to enter into possession of them? Mark the words. The prayer supposes that in some sense they are ours now; for it speaks of our losing them; it asks that they may not be taken from us. And this is the language of the New Testament. "He hath given unto us eternal life," saith St. John, "and this life is in his Son." Which words would be strange and unintelligible to us, if they were not explained by one greater than St. John. "This is life eternal, saith our Lord, that they may know Thee, the only true God, and Jesus Christ whom Thou hast sent." This mighty knowledge has been given to us; the Son of God has brought it near to us. In him we possess it. In him man is taken into the height, and depth, and length, and breadth of that love, which passeth knowledge. This love enfolds us at our baptism. The name of the Father, and the Son, and the Holy Ghost is the utterance of it. From this love the images and pictures of this world, the created, temporal things, are seeking to withdraw us. We cannot enjoy them without it; from it they borrow their lustre. Yet they would tempt us to forsake it for them; to dwell in them and not in it. The invisible guide of our hearts is drawing them by a thousand gracious acts and influences, and invitations, from the perishable to the eternal; from that which is the likeness of the thing they long for, to the thing itself; from that which loses its beauty when we can no longer give it beauty, to that first source of beauty from which we and they alike draw our life. We pray this week that his power might not be exerted in vain; we pray it for His sake who died that these eternal treasures might be ours, who lives that we may not be defeated of them through our own wilfulness and folly; for the sake of Jesus Christ our Lord.

SERMON XXIV.

THE FEAST OF PENTECOST.

(*Preached at Guy's Hospital.—Whit-Sunday Morning, June* 7, 1840.)

If ye love me, keep my commandments; and I will pray the Father, and he shall give you another Comforter, that he may abide with you for ever, even the Spirit of truth.—JOHN xiv. 15, 16.

You have heard in the first lesson for this morning's service how God appointed three feasts, which the Jews were to observe from generation to generation. One was the feast of the Passover, in which they remembered how their fathers were brought out of Egypt; one was the feast of the Tabernacles, in which they remembered how their fathers lived in tents in the wilderness; one was the feast of Pentecost, in which they remembered that it was God who gave them the fruits of the earth. These feasts held the Jewish people together; they came up from all quarters of the land to Jerusalem to celebrate them; and the very events themselves that they were remembering, taught them that they were connected with those who had lived hundreds of years before, as well as with those who were living then. We know, from the history of the Jews, that whenever they sunk into a low, selfish, divided state, these festivals were neglected, and whenever they were restored to a better state, they instantly began to care about these festivals again, and to keep them as if they were one people. The best thing that their best kings, Hezekiah and Josiah, did for them, was to bring them together to the Passover, after it had been disused for many years. It is as good as saying to them, 'You have been living together as if you had nothing to do with each other; but you have to do with each other; you are members of one nation, whether you like to own it or not; and if you will own it, and will come and act as if it was so, there will be a blessing upon you greater than you can understand.'

But why were the Jews to come up to these feasts? Was it because their kings invited them and commanded them to do it? That would have been a good reason for doing many things; but these kings had a reason for issuing such invitations or commands. They did not issue them because they thought it was a clever plan of bringing the people together, but because they believed God, who was their King, had appointed them. The difference between a righteous and an unrighteous king, a self-willed tyrant and a merciful ruler, was this: one believed that all rules and laws came from himself, the other believed that he was set up to execute the commands and ordinances of a Divine Being who had raised him to his office, and to whom he was answerable for his conduct in it. Therefore Hezekiah and Josiah exhorted the people to come to these feasts.

The king did not, therefore, say to them, 'This Passover, or this Pentecost, is a good time for bringing you up to Jerusalem, and making you acquainted with each other;'—he did not say, 'If you have a great many good and kindly feelings toward one another, or a great stock of gratitude to God, you may come and express yourselves in this way;' but he said, 'It has been a great sin and transgression of the commandments of God in you and me, and all of us, that we have not kept these feasts. It proved that we were ungrateful, that we were disunited; it proved that we had that sin which is the beginning of all ingratitude and all disunion—the sin of disobedience. Let us repent of this (he said), by keeping these feasts; then God may restore to us those happy feelings and that good-fellowship which we have lost by neglecting them.'

This was the way in which the good kings of the Jews had acted, and while they acted so God blessed them, and their people were happy. They kept God's commandments and ordinances in faith, nothing doubting that God was present in them, and that they should find the blessing of them. The prophets and holy men, it is true, warned the Jews that it was a great mockery to come to these ordinances, as his people came, and to sit as his people sat, when their hearts were far from him. But what did they mean by that? Did they mean that God was not present, of a truth, when they came to keep the feasts, and offer their sacrifices before him? No! they meant that he was there; that he was present in all these ordinances, and that, therefore, it was a sin and a mockery to act as if he were absent from them. So that these prophets were not contradicting the words of the kings, when they warned the people not to come with vain hearts to God's ordinances, but were confirming them.

Now when Jesus of Nazareth came into the world, he came as a poor and suffering man, yet for all that, he came as a king; he said that he was to set up a kingdom in the world, the kingdom for which all former kings and prophets had been preparing men. He went up into a mountain, and declared what this kingdom was. He said that he did not come to destroy God's former laws, but to fulfil them; he spoke, as the people testified, with authority, like one who had a right to command, and whom men ought to obey. All through his life, though he was exhibiting meekness in every act, he was also exhibiting power in every act; He made men feel that he was thus their master—the master of their bodies, the master of their spirits, the master of the whole universe—even while he was submitting to the greatest poverty and contempt. And now it wanted but one day of his crucifixion. He and his disciples were met at that feast of the Passover, which had been instituted 1,400 years before, to commemorate the deliverance of their countrymen; and after duly and faithfully observing all the rites belonging to this institution, and heartily giving thanks to God, he had instituted another ordinance; he had taken bread and broken it, and said, "Take, eat, this is my body," and poured out wine, saying, "This is my blood, this do in remembrance of me." Then, shortly after uttering these words, he began to discourse with his disciples respecting a mighty promise which was to be fulfilled to them after he should have left them; he told them that higher blessings should belong to them than any which they would enjoy while he was staying with them; that he was going to the Father; that he would prepare a place for them; that they should be with him more perfectly and completely than they had been while he was present to their eyes; that he would give them another Comforter, even the Spirit of truth, to abide with them.

It was evident to the disciples, when they heard these words, that their Lord was speaking of something too high for them to enter into at present. He told them so himself—he said the very gift which he promised was needful for them, in order that they might understand the words which they were hearing then, and those which they had heard from him before. What were they to do? How could they both benefit by what they heard, and yet acknowledge that it was above them? How could they be prepared to receive that Spirit, when it was He himself who must give them the preparation? Our Lord knew that they would be puzzled with these questions, and he himself answered them: "If ye love me," he said, "keep my commandments, and I will pray the Father, and he shall give you another comforter, that he may abide with you for ever."

I have told you he had already set them an example of the way in which God's commandments were kept. On this the last night that he was to be upon earth, he kept the commandment by eating the passover. He said he had longed to do so, he taught them that there was something very wonderful in this commandment, and that the full meaning and blessing of it would one day be known to them and to the world. He obeyed his Father's ordinance because he loved him, and could trust him to give all that he had promised in it. His apostles were to do the like. They were not to say, 'We love our Lord, and that is

what he requires, and everything else is indifferent.'
They were not to say, not even hereafter when he had
risen from the dead, 'Now we have all the blessings
which we can have, that which God had told us he
would bestow, he has bestowed; we want no more.'
They were not to say, 'Christ is above all ordinances,
and if we have him we may throw the ordinances
away.' They were not to prove their love to him in
any such way as this, for he had not proved his love
to the Father in any such way as this. But they were
first obediently to keep all the commandments which
God had given of old time, looking for the promise of
the Father in them. And then if there were any
deeper commandments, any new commandment which
contained the meaning of all these, they were to keep
that, believing that the blessing which had always
flowed from faithful obedience would come upon
them.

The last commandment which our Lord gave to his
disciples before he left them, was that they should
tarry in Jerusalem expecting the gift which he had
told them of the night before his crucifixion. Their
callings would have led them different ways; it was
safer for them to be anywhere than in Jerusalem; it
was less safe now than at any time, for the great feast
of Pentecost was at hand, and the Jews who had slain
the Master for the sake of hallowing the Passover,
might slay the disciples as a way of doing God service
at the Pentecost. And they might have thought with
themselves, 'What good can these feasts do, now that
this city is accursed, and all we can look for is that
our Master will save us out of the ruin?' But they
loved Christ, and therefore they kept his command-

ment without reasoning about it or considering what other course might seem wiser. They assembled in an upper room near the temple, they chose another apostle into the place of Judas, or rather submitted the choice to God by casting lots. They kept themselves in silent expectation of that power which Christ had said should be given them. They did not venture to speak of him to the people till they had received it. They prepared themselves for keeping the festival as their fathers had been wont to do.

At that festival their Lord's meaning was explained to them. The power of making him known to men was conferred upon them; and they felt that this power, wonderful as it was, was yet not the greatest wonder of that day. It was a mighty thing that Galileans should be able to speak with other tongues. It was a mightier thing to know who gave them utterance, a mightier thing to believe and understand that the Spirit of the Father, and the Son, he who first moved upon the face of the waters, and made everything capable of receiving light, had actually taken possession of their spirits and bodies. I do not say that they would yet fully enter into the meaning of this truth. Every day and hour of their lives was to shew them a little more of it. The very blessing they had gained was the certainty that they had a teacher who would make everything they saw and everything that happened to them, the means of imparting to them more knowledge and more life. The great effect of his presence was to make them more humble, and apt to learn, and sensible of the infinite things around them which they could not grasp. But they must have begun to perceive this very soon, that the feast which they were celebrating was connected with the gift which had been bestowed upon them. It was the feast of the wheat harvest, the feast which told that the life which there was in seeds and in the ground, was given by God, that he nurtured it, and caused the fruits of it in due time to appear. It was the feast which brought men together to rejoice that God had given them this common food to nourish them, and had given them powers in their bodies to receive it. Even so they felt, 'He is putting life into these spirits and understandings of ours, he is telling us that their power of bringing forth fruit, of uttering words which other men shall hear and profit by, is from him. Only this is his higher work. We have found the deepest sense of the feast. The life which comes from God works in all seeds and plants, and causes them to grow up and bring forth. But in these spirits of ours, it is He himself who works; he has made us to know him and hold converse with him, and to be his ministers in carrying on his work in the world; and as that feast is a common blessing, because the food of the earth is for all, so is this Spirit come upon us as the witness that the highest blessing is a common blessing, and meant for all. This Spirit must speak in us only that he may make us one with all in whom he shall dwell now and hereafter, only that we may be the instruments in building up a Universal Church, which he shall fill with his presence.' You see this was their meaning, for their words and their acts expressed it. St. Peter declared that this gift was to the Jews, whom he addressed, and to their children, and to as many as the Lord their God should call;

and in the faith of this promise he baptized three thousand men and women.

See what a blessing came to these apostles from their obedience. They kept their Lord's command, and he gave them another Comforter; he gave them all this wisdom and knowledge of the purposes for which he had sent them into the world. Do you suppose that if they had scorned God's feasts, this blessing would have come upon them? Or do you suppose that they forgot the lesson afterwards, and thought that because they had the Spirit, all such things were needless? It was, indeed, a wonderful change which took place in their condition, when the promise of the Father was fulfilled, and the mighty Teacher came. But what kind of change was it? They had received the Spirit of Peace, and they were afraid of being restless; they had received the Spirit of Humility, and they were afraid of choosing for themselves; they had received the Spirit of Order, and they dared not to sanction any confusion; they had received the Spirit of Unity and Love, and they dared not set up themselves as separate from their brethren; they had received the Spirit of Wisdom, and they could see a beauty and a harmony in that which other men thought was insignificant. Therefore it was not merely on this day that they showed their love to Christ by keeping his commandments; it was not on this day only that they received the comfort of his Spirit, when they recollected his ordinances: but every day they found that their light and wisdom grew in proportion to their obedience; that when they were heedless of that which had been appointed, the life and the power which the Spirit gave became feeble. They did not venture to forget the festivals of the Jews, though they knew that God was bringing the Jewish kingdom to an end, and though their Master had given them signs by which they might know that the end was near. What they were careful of was so to keep their Lord's new commandment — the commandment which he had given them on the night before his passion, that when the Jewish feasts could no longer be observed, all the meaning of them should still remain, and should be stored up in a feast for all mankind. When our Lord took the bread and blessed it, they knew that he had given them a new Passover. He had told them that they were delivered out of bondage, that the true Lamb had been slain for them, that they might feed upon it with the bitter herbs of repentance, and the thankfulness of faith. But that feast was also a Pentecost; it told them of a life continually coming down upon them from the Source of life, to renew their hearts, to enable them to offer up acceptable sacrifices unto God, to speak his words, to do his works. And it was a feast of Tabernacles, for there God promised that they should dwell in Him and He in them.

My brethren, this feast is preserved to you, and therefore all those other feasts of which I have been speaking to-day are preserved to you. At Easter, we think of the Lord's Supper chiefly in connection with the great offering for the sins of the world. To-day we think of it in connection with the gift of the Holy Spirit. At all times, equally, it is a feast of thanksgiving for the highest blessings which God gives to his church, as well as for all his lesser mercies.

At all times He himself is present in the feast, He himself is the great blessing of it. You say you cannot understand these things, and you say rightly; you do not understand Whitsuntide, nor do I, nor does any man: it would not be Whitsuntide if we did. We should not want a Spirit to guide us into all truth, if we could take in all truth; we should not have cared to give ourselves to One who is wiser and mightier than ourselves, if we had wisdom and might of our own. But I do give God thanks for Whitsuntide just because my understanding is so weak, and because yours is so weak, and because the teacher of whom it speaks is able to open our understandings, that we may receive all the wonders of God's love. If we love Christ with ever so feeble a love, let us keep his commandments, and the promise is still to us and to our children; He will give us a Comforter, and that Comforter will strengthen our love to Him by enabling us to drink of the river of God's love. If we love our brother with ever so feeble a love, let us keep Christ's commandments, and the promise shall be fulfilled—He will give us that Spirit who abides for ever with the Church his body, that we may feel ourselves members of that body, and may love the other members of it as we love ourselves.

SERMON XXV.

STRENGTH IN WEAKNESS.

(Preached at Guy's Hospital.—August, 1838.)

My strength is made perfect in weakness.—2 CORINTHIANS xii. 9.

AT a certain time in the life of the Apostle St. Paul, he was permitted to have a wonderful vision of the glory of God.

We, even you and I at this moment, are surrounded by this glory, we are in the midst of the heavenly kingdom, we are in the presence of Jesus Christ, and of God the judge of all. If it pleased God to take the veil from off our hearts, we might any of us behold these wonders with our inward eye, as clearly as we behold the pillars and walls of this chapel with our outward eyes. The vision of the Eternal God might open upon us; we might feel that he was looking upon us. It is nothing strange, then, that God should, at times, bless those servants who faithfully do his work, and long to know him better, with this new and amazing discovery. It is not meet that they should have it frequently: this world is a place of toil and tears; the belief that God is with us, the hope of seeing him as He is, the assurance that he loves us and is love, these are to be our supports here; perfect vision is reserved for those who have fallen asleep in Jesus. But it is a gracious and comfortable token of God's mercy that he does not permit the fallen bodies of those who truly love him, to keep them even here from some taste of that joy which is to be their portion for ever. And, surely, if we might suppose that any one would be thus honoured, it was that St. Paul, who for the love of God and of man counted nothing dear unto himself, cheerfully bore all sorrows of body and mind, yea, would have been willing to be accursed from Christ for his brethren's sake. Surely, to comfort such a man in that bitter anguish of body and soul which was his daily portion, one might expect that glimpses would be given him of the perfect beauty and loveliness of him in whom he believed, and of whom he was ready to testify even unto death.

And so it was. As the moon bursts forth sometimes from behind a cloud, and the traveller who has been walking in the dreary night, knowing it was there, and seeing the ground at his feet brighter for it, hails, and blesses its beams, so all at once the spirit of St. Paul, wearied with this body of death, was refreshed with a vision of his Lord. Whether he was in the body or out of the body he could not tell; God only knew; but this he could tell, that he beheld those real things of which all things that we see here upon earth are but faint shadows, and that he heard words which it would not be lawful, no, nor possible, for human tongue to utter. Like that vision to the three older disciples on the mount, when the countenance of their Lord became changed and his garment white as snow, and when they heard him talking with Moses and Elias, this, also, passed away; but the sense and the savour of it remained, and fourteen years after, the remembrance of it was fresh in the Apostle's heart, as if it had happened the day before.

But, perhaps, you may remember what a sight it was which Peter, and James, and John beheld when they came down with their Lord from the Mount of Transfiguration. A noisy crowd of people there were at the foot of that hill, a hum of confused turbulent voices, men quarrelling and murmuring, and in the midst of all a poor suffering boy, tossing about in a fit of epilepsy, which sometimes threw him into the fire, and sometimes into the water, and which no man had been able to cure. And, perhaps, you may remember what speech it was which our Lord had with his disciples as they were coming down from that glorious place into the midst of this tumult. He told them how he should be set at nought by elders, and chief priests, and scribes; how he should be scorned and spitted upon; how he should be crucified, and how the third day he should rise again from the dead. Now that tumult and confusion, and that boy in the epileptic fit, represent to us this world in which we are living, full of the strife of tongues, and sorrow, and misery in the midst of it all. And that prophecy which our Lord gave of what should happen to him, is a prophecy of something like what must happen to all his servants who are passing through this confused world. They, too, must be set at nought by the rulers, and great men, and wise men of the earth, they must be ready for scorn, and if not a violent death, yet death of some kind must end all this, and they, too, will rise again. St. Paul, when he had seen these wonderful sights, and heard these unspeakable words, came down again into this world of sin and misery, and he had to act in it, to witness for God in it, to bear its scorn, to love those who despised him, and at last to give up his body to death for his Master's sake, and for theirs. This was his appointed task. But though he was a brave man, one of God's bravest warriors, yet was he a weak sinful man, too. And pride, which was his great snare once, which had led him to close his eyes fast against the light of the Sun of Righteousness, till, by that sudden appearance, on the way to Damascus, Christ had opened them; this pride might rush in upon him again, and turn this new vision into a means of darkening him more than ever. For if God show a man a glorious thing, and he does not think of the thing that he has seen, but he thinks, 'What a great man am I, that it was shown to me,' then would it have been better for him that the blessing had never been imparted. St. Paul might have grown sick of his work, and have thought that he who had been in the third heaven, had no need to be travelling to the ends of the earth, preaching the good news of Christ's Kingdom to poor, ignorant, gainsaying men, who would not love him the more for his pains, but, perhaps, would count him their enemy because he told them the truth. St. Paul might have thought that his day of suffering was over, that it could not be meant he should go crying to his grave, when he had seen the joyful things that lie beyond it. He might, as he says himself, have been puffed up with the abundance of his revelations. The sight of God might have been the means of filling him with the spirit of the devil.

You may think it strange that I should speak these things of the great and chosen Apostle, or suppose that they could possibly happen to him. But, my brethren, we know from St. Paul himself, that they might have happened to him. We know, that every man here upon earth stands between two worlds; above him is the light, and love, and glory of God, this is the heaven of heavens; beneath him is pride, and ignorance, and despair, and atheism, this is the pit of hell. And as any man may ascend up and see that love, and glory of God, in the face of Jesus Christ, so any man may sink down into the pit, and God may be shrouded from his eyes, and he may be able to see nothing but himself, and sin, and death. It is no security to a man that he has done great things or beheld bright visions; these may be the very cause of his downfall. If he learn to think that he has some great strength within him to do, some bright eye within him that can always see, his great doings, and his glorious success will be the very means of separating him from the light and the life of God. He will feel that he can go on without God in the world, and God may leave him to try how far he can go. What security, then, has a man who, after all this glory, is yet in such peril? He may trust that the Lord in whom he has believed, who has shown him such marvellous things, will not suffer his foot to be moved. "He who keepeth him does not slumber or sleep." He knows when the enemy will take advantage of a man who is too high or too low, and he knows how to cross and defeat the designs of that enemy, how to bring down those that are exalted, lest they should fall, and how to raise up those that are bowed down, lest they should lose all heart and hope.

My brethren, if a man be a teacher of others, a commissioned servant of God, a proclaimer of his name and of his Kingdom, he is in the front rank of God's army. He has marks and signs by which he is known to all; if he fall there is a fright through all the troops. You may be sure, then, that the devil has a band of riflemen always aiming at him; to lead him into open sin, or secret pride, which will soon end in open sin, must be a great plot and purpose of his. Do you not think, then, that to strike at the heart of St. Paul, the most glorious of all these ministers, must have been his dearest wish? And how else do you suppose that the spirit of pride can ensnare any of us so completely, as by infusing into us some of his own venom, by making us conceited of some gift of God, be it a little or a great one, and so leading us to use that gift against God himself?

But now, by what means was St. Paul delivered from this terrible danger? The Lord sent him, he says, a thorn in the flesh. What this was, it is a waste of time to inquire. St. Paul would have told us if it had been needful for us to know. This much we may be sure of, that it was some very sore trial, which did not only affect his body, though that may have been the seat of it, but which disquieted and upset his whole mind, and made him understand that he was a poor, miserable, paltry creature after all. Whatever it was, it taught him that he was a man of flesh and blood, that the sufferings of his brethren were his sufferings, that their sins were his sins; it took him off the stilts, and brought him to feel that for all he was an Apostle, for all he had been in the third heaven, he must walk this common earth, and bear its burdens, his own and other men's. At first, when he felt this trial, it seemed to him that it was a mighty hindrance to the labours which God had set him. It weakened his influence over others; it gave him wretched feelings of shame, it confused all his thoughts of God's ways to himself, and to the world. It may have been in itself a little thing or a great thing; but a little thing will often prey upon a man's soul and eat the life of it more than a great one. Perhaps the degradation of being so hurt by a little thing made him feel more bitterly that he was a man whom God had wonderfully exalted, and then had utterly cast down. Hope and energy almost forsook him. One power, however, remained to him. His converse with the unseen world was over; he felt no longer as a citizen of heaven; he felt as the wretchedest worm of earth. But he had learnt that the wretchedest worm of earth can make his voice heard by Him before whom angels veil their faces. "I prayed," he says, "thrice, that it might depart from me." In vain, as it seemed; the thorn remained, the anguish of his heart was not less. But, my brethren, the man who, when all things without and within are fighting against him, has made an effort to pray, who has compelled himself to cry, 'Lord, have mercy upon me,' though ten thousand feelings of pride and anger are closing his lips, and saying, 'It is useless, thou shalt not do it,' the man who has sworn that he will pray though the words die in the effort to utter them, this man has won the greatest of all victories. To get into the third heaven is a light thing in comparison with this triumph over the powers of hell. He who does this has claimed the rights of a man. He has said, 'I know that there is a bond between me and the Omnipotent God. I know that I have a hold upon him who cannot change. I know that the agony and bloody sweat of Jesus have established an eternal union between the weakest of human beings and Him, who is, and who was, and who is to come.' It was hard to bring forth the prayer, the struggle rent his soul asunder; but it did come forth, and the answer came forth too. It was this, "My grace is sufficient for thee; my strength is made perfect in weakness." 'My grace is sufficient for thee.' 'In the time of thy darkest and dreadfullest necessity thou art not alone. Thou hast this miserable feeling of being alone; but it is not true. Down in the very depths of this being, where thy thoughts have never reached, is a fountain of life. He who cried, "Father, let this cup pass from me," and "My God, my God, why hast thou forsaken me," He, even He is there. The springs of life seem to be dried up within thee, but it is that thou mayest discover the source of life.'

All, and far more than this, was contained in these first words. For the Apostle's consolation at that moment they might have been enough. But though men are always craving for consolation, God has greater purposes with them than merely to give them consolation. He wishes to teach them of Himself—and to make them teachers about Himself to others. In the words which followed, "And my strength is made perfect in weakness," there was yet a deeper meaning for St. Paul and for you. Let us try to discover that meaning; and let us believe that Christ himself is feeding our spirits with it.

My brethren, it has pleased God that his own might and wisdom should be made known to us through beings of the same flesh and blood with ourselves. There is, indeed, might and wisdom throughout the universe in every star, and insect, and flower; but this might and wisdom would never be understood by us, if it were only shown us in this way. We must see *men* putting forth strength, and shewing skill, and exercising kindness before us, and on our behalf, or we shall never know what strength, and skill, and kindness are. But when we do see all this in our fellow-creatures, how shall we be taught that it did not dwell first in them, that there is an infinite strength, and skill, and kindness, from which theirs has come forth, and of which it is only the poor likeness? This can only be when we see by some clear token what these creatures are in themselves, what they would be if they were left naked and alone. Therefore, when God manifested himself perfectly to his creatures, in the Man Christ Jesus, in what wise did he declare himself? He brought the Man down into the lowest depth of humiliation and wretchedness, that it might be seen that all the strength, and wisdom, and love which were in him, did not belong to him because he had flesh and blood, because he had the soul of a man, but because "it pleased the Father, that in Him should all fulness dwell," because he was the Eternal Son of God. And as it was with the Master, so must it be with the disciple. The privilege of our being members of Christ's body consists in this, that we have the Spirit of God given us to dwell in us. And it must be seen and understood by all who behold that it is by this Spirit we act, and speak, and think, that whatever there is in us which is not helplessness, is his; whatever is not folly, is his; whatever is not malice, and hatred, and revenge is his. Therefore it is that God makes strong men helpless, that all may know what it was that enabled them to lift their arms and move swiftly over the ground; therefore does he make wise men babble like children, that it may be seen who enabled them to discern more than their neighbours; therefore does he let kind and gracious men, when they forsake his guidance, shew forth most godless and inhuman passions, that it may be seen who gave them any heart to be good. God's strength is made perfect in weakness. Because man is seen to be nothing, God is felt to be everything, and those things which make men most murmur against him, are the very means by which we are taught to know him, and adore him. My brethren, till we get this thought into our hearts, everything in this world is cloudy, and dark to us; when we receive it, everything begins to be bright. I do not say that we become merry when we know this. We are in God's schoolhouse, under God's rod, chastised by him often, and when we have escaped from one chastisement needing another. It is a world where men must be sad who know themselves, and love their brethren, and are zealous for God. But yet I say, that all things begin to be bright, and that we feel they will grow brighter unto the perfect day. That there should be poor men in this world sighing and crying for their daily bread, what a sad and oppressive thought it is; but when we know that this poverty, this want of the things that we see, and taste, and handle, has led men to lift up their hands and hearts to an unseen Father, and ask him to look into their lonely souls and cheer them; and when we believe they were made poor on purpose that they might raise up this cry, and become acquainted with their true friend, and that he hears them, and hastens to reveal Himself to them, and that there is joy among the angels of God, because they have found their Father's house; then we can bear to look upon poverty, and say, 'Verily, this too is God's gift, this is a token of God's love, his strength is made perfect in this weakness.' It is a trying thing to witness health and strength departing from those who seemed best able to use them for the glory of God and the good of man; but when we know that it is not strong and healthy men who have done most work upon this earth; that feeble men have been enabled to suffer and to act, when the stout have been oftentimes restless and idle; and when we find that sickness brings down the self-sufficiency of men, and makes them lean their tottering frames upon an Almighty Friend, we learn that this too is God's gift; herein is his strength made perfect. It is a sadder sight when men upon whom God has bestowed great gifts of wit and wisdom, turn them against him, and against their brethren, teaching them to worship themselves as gods, and yet tempting them so to indulge themselves that they become beasts. But when we consider that their sin is the greatest witness of the truth which they deny, that they prove God to be just, and loving, and true, by showing what they are when they renounce him; we may believe that, even in this way, God's strength may be made perfect in weakness, and that He will show both that he needs not the help of the cunning artificer and the eloquent orator, and that they cannot prevail against the humblest of those who put their trust in Him.

For this, brethren, is the lesson from the whole matter :—the lowly and contrite heart is that which God seeks to form in us; without this, all other good things turn to evil; with this we may turn even the things which seem most evil into good. Therefore, all methods which he takes to deliver men from their pride, are merciful and gracious; as such let us receive them, and then whether we are here on earth, or in the third heaven, all is well, for God has said that He will dwell with us.

SERMON XXVI.

THE MUSTARD TREE.

(Preached at St. Mary's Church, Warwick.—The Morning of the Fourteenth Sunday after Trinity, 1841, on behalf of the Society for the Propagation of the Gospel.)

Another parable put he forth unto them, saying, The kingdom of heaven is like unto a grain of mustard seed, which a man took and sowed in his field: which indeed is the least of all seeds; but when it is grown, it is the greatest among herbs, and becometh a tree, so that the birds of the air lodge in the branches of it.—MATTHEW xiii. 31, 32.

EVERY one who reads the chapter from which this text is taken, must be struck with the homeliness of the images which occur in it. There is not one which is drawn from the more magnificent objects in nature. A sower sowing the ground; a field containing wheat and tares; a merchantman seeking pearls; a woman leavening cakes; these are the types which our Lord uses to express truths that had been kept secret from the foundations of the world.

It has sometimes been supposed that the parable before us is an exception to this remark. The tree in whose branches the fowls of the air might lodge, seems to suggest a thought of something vast and noble. Hence it has been concluded, that while the parables of the sower and of the tares describe the commencement of our Lord's kingdom, and the hindrances to its progress, this one is intended to carry us onward to its full expansion and perfect glory. I cannot see that this opinion is borne out by the similitude to which our Lord resorts on this occasion. It is very true that the mustard plant in Palestine, and even in some parts of Western Europe, attains a height which to us would seem astonishing. In the words of the parable itself, it is the greatest among herbs, and it becometh a tree. But the Jews were familiar with the very noblest trees of the forest; the cedar of Lebanon was continually present to their imagination, if not to their eyes; it had served for the building of the Temple, and it had suggested innumerable comparisons to their holy men. Whatever other thoughts, then, the observation of a mustard tree may have awakened in an inhabitant of the East, certainly his first impression will not have been, that it was the likeness of anything very stately and majestical.

I think, then, that this parable is probably cast in the same mould with those which were spoken at the same time, and are recorded in the same narrative. In them our Lord was evidently not directing the thoughts of his hearers so much to great results as to the causes and processes which lead to them. He tells us, indeed, in the last verse of the parable of the Sower, that the good ground brought forth, some thirty, some sixty, some an hundred fold; he tells us at the end of the parable of the Tares of the field, that the corrupted and degenerate produce was at last burned, and the good gathered into the master's granary. But the main subject of the first is the quality of the different soils upon which the seed fell; the main subject of the other, the secret reason of those bad outward effects which the servants of the husbandman had observed. The mighty teacher is drawing away our minds from strange and startling phenomena, to those wonderful transactions which are going on unseen by the human eye, which are pregnant with the most amazing consequences, but which are too ordinary not to be passed over by the greater part of men as if they were utterly insignificant. Such are the mysteries of that life which is in seeds or plants; the mysteries of their birth, growth, and decay; the mysterious properties of the earth which receives them; the mysterious influence of human toil and cultivation. All these are surely mighty wonders, and instead of ceasing to be wonders, when we think steadily about them, and endeavour to enter into their meaning, they only become more unfathomable. For every sound explanation of them is but the discovery of a more deep and astonishing truth than any we knew before; and any attempt to get rid of the marvel, is only an attempt to substitute pompous and empty words for living realities.

The parables contained in the gospels would be the noblest instruction that men ever received, if they went no further than this; if they merely forced us earnestly to notice and solemnly to meditate the facts of our common life. And this effect they may have produced even upon those whose ears were dull of hearing, and whose eyes were so dim that they could see nothing beyond the shell of our Lord's discourses. Even these may have been awakened to observe a whole world of things of which they had taken no heed; they may have been inspired with some awe and wonder when they found themselves working in the midst of such unseen powers; they may have learnt, at the same time, that these powers were not to call forth a vague superstitious dread, as if they came forth from some capricious genius or blind fate; that they were all calmly moving in an order which had been fixed for them on the creation-day—all obeying one who cared for the meanest of his creatures.

But to those who had been prepared by previous discipline, to those who had what had been given them, and therefore could receive more, these words must have come with a much higher significance. The longings and anxieties they will have felt previously, will have been about that more wonderful world within them; about the meaning of their own thoughts and doubts and questionings; about the unseen Being of whom their Law and their Covenant spoke, and of whom their consciences witnessed; about the relation in which He stood to them; about the sins which separated him from them, and the means of approaching Him. They will have had, too, other feelings closely connected with these, and yet which they did not know how to reconcile with them; passionate desires for the freedom of their nation—for the coming of the Deliverer whom the law and the prophets spoke of—for the restoration of that kingdom of David of which it was said there should be no end. To men full of these anxieties, crying, 'Who will go up for us into heaven

—who will go down into the deep, to bring us the answer to them,' what could be so cheering, so satisfying as to be taught to see the image of what was passing within them in the world without, to be reminded of secret powers that were in operation in the faith of which they had been continually acting, and without which their commonest labours would have been ineffectual ; to be taught that as it was not in the fire and the whirlwind, but in the daily working of God's providence, they might behold his presence, so in like manner a power was at work in their spirits, implanting within them the seeds of a truer life, nourishing them by steady and orderly influences, causing them to bring forth fruit which should never wither or grow old, and that it is not in sudden bursts or momentary impulses, but in an operation as even and harmonious as that of nature, that they might expect this power would reveal itself, that they might hear the still small voice speaking to them.

How consolatory it must have been to them to find that there was a link between these truths and their hopes of a Kingdom which should be ruled by One who would not judge after the sight of his eyes, nor the hearing of his ears, but who in righteousness would rule the earth, and govern the people with his equity ; to find that by these secret processes in the hearts of men this mighty Sovereign was actually asserting his dominion; was bringing them into a society of which he would be the head, all the subordinate rulers of which would work with the powers he had committed to them, and the poorest member of which should be subjected to his mighty and invisible discipline.

Now the parable of the mustard seed, it seems to me, though it has a distinct purpose of its own, is yet like those which precede it in this, that it forces us to think more of the gradual growth of that which it describes, than of its ultimate greatness. The very words with which the parable is introduced, seem to prove this; the kingdom is said to be like, not to the tree, but to the seed. No one, indeed, who attends to our Lord's ordinary language, will suppose that by such words as these He means to restrict the comparison to one point; still we ought not to overlook the fact, that it is the starting-point. A man is said to take this seed and sow it in his field; he puts it in with the undoubting faith, that, utterly paltry as it looks—the proverbial type, for such it was among the Jews, of everything too tiny to be taken account of—it will assuredly not lie there in vain; that at its appointed season it will exhibit itself in a form altogether different from that which it had in his hand—so different, as to make it impossible, according to all mechanical calculations, that there should be any relation between them. At the time appointed it does appear. But it has within it that mysterious principle of growth. It becomes the greatest of herbs. And then, as from a seed it has risen into a herb, so from a herb it rises into a tree, and the birds of the air, which would scarcely have stooped to peck at it in its first estate, now lodge in the branches of it.

Perhaps this description of a gradual progress and development may have seemed to the apostles, when they first heard it, somewhat disappointing. They had dreamed, probably, that the palace of the great king would rise up at once, as by the wand of an enchanter, and that the Roman tyranny would sink into the earth at its appearance. "Wilt thou at this time," said they to our Lord immediately before his ascension, "restore again the kingdom to Israel?" as if a revolution in the national condition of the world were to be the immediate effect of his manifestation. But afterwards, when they became really the Ministers of his Cross, the Princes of his Kingdom, they will, I think, have found in this parable more instruction and consolation than they would have derived from the most brilliant picture of the glories of the Church, if it had been separated from the history of its mean commencement and silent progress. They could easily conjecture, nay, they had the mightiest assurances, that the new Jerusalem would eclipse all the splendours of the old. When they thought of the promise which had been made to Abraham, that in his seed all nations of the earth should be blessed, of the preservation of their nation through so many ages, of the wonderful promises contained in the writing of their prophets; above all, when they thought of him who had been exalted far above all principalities and powers, that he might fill all things, no vision which they could form of that kingdom which he came to establish upon earth, would seem to be too magnificent. The Gentiles were to come to the brightness of his rising, the isles were to wait for his law, the knowledge of the Lord was to cover the earth as the waters covered the sea. Such thoughts will have become brighter and deeper in their minds every day, as they meditated upon the love of God, upon the incarnation of the Son, and upon the descent of that Spirit who had broken down all the barriers which separated man from man, and had established a universal commonwealth. But when they descended from these lofty contemplations into their actual toil and business, when they saw how they were regarded by the world about them, when they thought of the mighty power and complicated machinery of that empire in which their own country formed but the section of a province, when they remembered that even of that little society they were some of the very humblest individuals, when they saw themselves contemned and scourged by the rulers of that Sanhedrim which was itself regarded with utter contempt by the Roman procurator and the Roman soldiery, and when the thought presented itself to them—'We, and we only, are the appointed proclaimers of this new kingdom. It is by us that the image whose top reaches to heaven is to be broken in pieces. It is by our agency that the stone which has been cut out of the mountain without hands, is to fill the whole earth'—they must have been at times utterly staggered, they must have laughed in their hearts as Sarah did, and have fancied that if a Church were indeed to be formed on earth, it must be by a sudden and new Divine intervention, and not through the instrumentality of Galilean fishermen. And we must remember that these thoughts will have easily connected themselves with many feelings which it was their duty and which they were most careful to cherish. The Christian saint did not, like the philosopher, console himself with his self-applauses at home, for the scoffs of the world. He retired to his closet to mourn over duties neglected and sins committed, to gather from each new day a lesson of greater abasement. And although his humiliations will all have been connected with an acknowledgment of the love and power of God, and will have made him only the more ready to toil and able to conceive that the divine strength might be made perfect in his weakness, yet when united to the manifold outward discouragements to which the apostles were subjected, they must sometimes, as St. Paul tells us they did in his case, have touched almost upon the borders of despair. In such states of mind these words of their Master will have seemed to them indeed words of life; for they will have said, 'That which seems to you the reason for despondency, is the very warrant of your hope. Do you wish to feel that the Church is really a Divine handiwork? Then look at the meanness of its origin. See how exactly that resembles the beginning of all the great works of God in the universe. Look at the outward appearances which it is now exhibiting. See how they resemble the first shooting forth of the seeds which are deposited in the earth. And then let the same quiet expectation which supports you in one case, support you in the other. Use your husbandry as the gardener uses his, knowing that it would be worth nothing if there was no living soil to work upon, no living plant to grow, no sun to ripen it, but knowing also that his work is just as much appointed, just as needful as soil, as rain, as sun; knowing that without it the promise may not be fulfilled, the reward secured.'

My brethren, I cannot think that the reflections which this parable must have awakened in those who first heard it when it was interpreted by their experience, can be needless for the Church in any age. We are all very prone to two errors against which it supplies a very remarkable warning. At one time we fancy that a human machinery is all we want to produce great moral results. At another time we conclude that if the work we are engaged in is a mysterious and spiritual one, we may enter upon it without the least care about the order and method of our procedure. Both these notions are undoubtedly very plausible. We look at the works of human industry, and we see how poor and paltry are the effects of mere manual labour if it be not artificially assisted. We look at the mighty transformation which has been sometimes wrought in the thoughts and feelings of a human being, nay, in the condition of the world, by a few words; and we say to ourselves, 'How pitiful in comparison with these is all that can be accomplished by the most systematic contrivances.' Both notions I say are plausible, because both are partially true; but the whole truth is contained in our Lord's parable. He teaches us, that the effect of spiritual operations is incomparably more astonishing than all which the most skilful combination of material instruments can produce. But He teaches us also that these operations, just because they are spiritual, are orderly; that though they cannot be likened to the movements of a machine, they have their exact counterpart in that which is far more even and regular, the growth of natural things.

I. The applications of this truth are so manifold, that I can but allude to one or two of them. The feeling with which we regard the ordinances of the Church must surely be regulated by this lesson of its Lord. If we listen to it, we dare not believe that we are merely brought into a system consisting of skilful contrivances, to assist our thoughts, and direct our devotion. We must believe that we are brought under a divine education and discipline, that He who has taken us into His kingdom is Himself preparing us to enter into the meaning of it, and to fill our places in it; that He Himself is present with us when we are seeking to hold communion with Him; that a divine power is at work on our behalf to mould our characters into conformity with His; that if we thankfully and reverently submit ourselves to that power, it will destroy that which is evil in us, and enable us to bring forth fruits unto life eternal.

II. This truth, again, should be constantly present to the minds of parents and teachers. The whole care and discipline of children must be a miserable work indeed, if it be not carried on in the conviction that there is a seed of a pure and heavenly life to be called forth in them; that it has been planted by Christ himself, that He will make it mightier than all the influences which oppose it; that it is not to start up at once into a precocious and treacherous maturity, but to exhibit itself at its appointed season, and in its appointed stages; that it will be nurtured by dews from heaven, and that all human care and diligence is to be applied to the soil, not in sudden starts, but in steady faith, in the assurance that it will not be in vain. Through family life and discipline, through an education grounded upon baptismal rights and baptismal obligations, the kingdom of God has spread itself in the world, and this is still the most direct means of its extension and purification.

III. But, my brethren, there is another consideration which grows out of these two, and is closely connected with the parable. We are not merely individual Christians, or members of a family; we belong to a nation. When we claim that great and honourable name, we say that we belong to the same society with those who lived on our soil a thousand years ago. We say that as we still preserve the tokens of their having lived and died among us, as the castles in which they dwelt still look down upon us, as we have their emblazonments and their pictures, as we are surrounded by their tombs, as we worship in the churches where they worshipped, we know they were meant to be bound to us by links which time cannot break. My brethren, how did this feeling come to us? or rather let me ask another question which practically is not very different, How did we become a nation at all? How is it that we are one now? How is it that our children may be members of one hereafter and may feel that the privilege is not a dream but a reality? We have selfish feelings which are continually tearing us one from the other. No such feelings, no calculations grounded upon them, can have given us this position, or can preserve it to us. Human wisdom has no doubt been at work to counteract these feelings, and to raise up something better in place of them, to maintain that which they would have destroyed. But there must have been something for this human wisdom to work upon, or it could have done nothing. There must have been something higher than itself to sustain it, or it would have defeated its own objects. This, brethren, is the secret of our national fellowship. Holy men came and told our fathers that One had been in the world who had given men power to be the children of God, and brethren one of another; that He had broken through the bonds of space and time; that He had died, and risen, and ascended on high. They believed his words, they were received into Christ's family; all other feelings and sympathies expanded themselves under the influence of this highest and most universal one, and therefore is it that we claim this glorious fellowship with men of other days, which raises us above the narrow thoughts and petty interests of our own, and therefore is it that we can look forward with hope to a posterity who shall live when the places we live in shall know us no more.

Our nation, then, like our family and like our own lives, has been established by an unseen hand, and lives and grows by a mysterious influence. When we forget this truth, and think that we can sustain its institutions, or extend its borders, on merely commercial principles, or for commercial ends, we set the lessons of history at nought, and the event will shew that we have deceived ourselves. On the other hand, it seems to me, brethren, that we forget the lesson which the parable of the mustard seed suggests when we attempt to spread Christ's Gospel without attending to the course of Providence, and observing what regions it points out as especially fields for us to labour in. If, as Englishmen, we continually remember that the nation cannot really establish itself in any land unless Christ's kingdom establish itself there also; if, as Churchmen, we constantly recollect that wheresoever our countrymen are by any motives tempted to settle themselves, there is a place marked out, by a divine signal, as one in which the holy ark may rest; we seem to be best following the instructions with which the wisdom of God has supplied us in the Bible and in our own experience.

Yet both these principles would have been utterly neglected if the Society on behalf of which I am to ask your help this morning, had not come forward to assert them. For nearly a century and a half it has maintained this doctrine, that we have no right to send forth a colony of Englishmen, and not send with it those principles and ordinances which connect the earthly life of man with his heavenly life, and so which make society something else than a collection of incoherent atoms, the existence of man something else than a feverish dream. Every year has made the doctrine more important; the last few years, nearly the most memorable in the history of English colonization, have made it a solemn obligation upon every one who feels its importance to assist in giving effect to it. It may be shewn, I think, also most satisfactorily, that while the Society has been labouring to discharge the consciences of Englishmen of a heavy responsibility, and has been providing for the safe diffusion of our English name, it has also been taking the most humble and simple course for enabling Christians to fulfil the commission of their Master; to go and preach the Gospel in all nations. I may shew you on another occasion, that recent circumstances will enable the Society more fully and consistently than it has ever yet done, to fulfil its office as a missionary body. At present I would rather fix your thoughts upon the benefits which it is conferring upon us as citizens of this soil. It is binding together those who have gone forth from among us to us who are left behind. It is making them feel that they and we have not ceased to be members of the same family, seeing that we need not cease to commune together at the same altar, and to worship the same Father. It is saving our sons from the heavy curse which must come upon them if they should spread darkness instead of light in the regions to which they go. It is saving us from the curse of neglecting those whom God has bound to us by the most holy ties, and of making the character of our nation odious to heathens and to Christians. It is acting as God's agent by taking care that the mustard seed which was planted so long ago in our own soil, shall not perish through our neglect in cultivating it, but shall grow, and become a tree in which the birds of the air may lodge.

SERMON XXVII.

THE PRINCIPLES AND METHOD OF CHRISTIAN CIVILIZATION.

(Preached at St. Mary's, Warwick.—The Evening of the Fourteenth Sunday after Trinity.)

Let every soul be subject to the higher powers; for there is no power but of God, and the powers that be are ordained of God.—ROMANS xiii. 1.

It has often been observed, and I think truly, that this precept derives much additional force from the position of the Church to which it was addressed. The Roman governors, in many provinces of the empire, preserved a respect for those principles of law and equity which had been the foundation of their nation's greatness. They frequently protected the Christians from the violence of Gentile mobs and Jewish incendiaries. But the government of the capital was becoming every day more reckless of all principles, more merely a government of self-will and brute force. It may not be certain that the Epistle to the Romans was written at one of the worst moments of this tyranny. It may, possibly, belong to that short interval of promise which preceded the full outburst of Nero's natural atrocity. But the character which the empire had assumed must have been perfectly well known to St. Paul. It could have been no surprise to him that within a few years the Christians whom he was addressing should be called to expiate the emperor's own crime by frightful tortures, or that he himself should be one of the victims. He wrote to prepare them for such events. And yet he says, "Let every soul be subject to the higher powers, for they are ordained of God. Let every soul be subject not only for wrath, but also for conscience' sake."

No doubt these considerations prove that the Apostle could contemplate no exception to his rule; no case in which a Christian might, on any personal grounds, refuse submission to the civil government of a country in which he was placed; no case in which he might plead that the powers he found himself subject to were not of God. But we lose, it seems to me, much of the Apostle's meaning, and pervert it to a purpose the most opposite to that which he contemplated, while at the same time we weaken the obligation which is laid upon us, if we do not perceive that these words contain the most strong and effectual protest ever made against that tyranny which they command Christian men patiently to endure. I do not mean merely that all meek sufferance of wrong is a mighty condemnation of wrong-doing, because it shews how utterly false and ridiculous the pretexts are by which the injury is justified; this is certainly true, and has been proved to be true by every record of martyrdom which the history of the world supplies. But this is not all. The very reason upon which St. Paul rests his exhortation to the Roman Christians is the reason which proves all such oppression as the Roman emperors were guilty of to be a false and a hateful thing, a contradiction so gross and monstrous, that it can last only for a short time. "There is no power but of God." As if he had said, 'Let this power be turned to what mischievous or abominable purposes it may; yet he who taught the evil use of it did not bestow it. The Evil Spirit may prompt a man to make the energies with which he has been entrusted curses to himself and to his fellows, but they have been entrusted to him by the Author of all Good, nevertheless. From a holy and righteous Being has every gift and faculty of man proceeded; for righteous and holy ends has it been given. Because tyrants deny this, see that you do not deny it; though they say the power is their own, take care that you do not yield to their wicked thoughts. Declare, by submitting to their government, that you understand it to be for the protection of them that do well, and for the scourge of evil-doers. So far as it is a government at all it is this, so far as it is not this it is an anarchy. Be sure that whoever else would make it an anarchy, you do not; declare that you believe it to be ordained of God—the God of all mercy, and truth, and equity—and that therefore you reverence it; that therefore you are subject to it.' Now, is it not obvious that no assertor of men's right to rebel ever bore such a witness as this against that arbitrary power which sets itself above all that is called God, which assumes the functions, if it do not, as the Roman emperors did, actually appropriate the name, of the Supreme Being? If the powers that be are ordained of men, they may be used according to the pleasure of men. It is merely a conflict between this form of self-will and that; between a despotism that exists and a despotism that is struggling to exist. If the powers that be are ordained of God, they must be designed to accomplish the good pleasure of God; all self-will must be at strife with a perfect will which is working continually for good. All efforts at absolute dominion must be a daring outrage upon Him who alone is absolute. And such struggles and such outrages, though they may be permitted a while for the fuller manifestation of that purpose which shall be accomplished in spite of them, have a lying root, and must at last come to nought.

My brethren, the words of the Apostle which occur in our lesson this evening seem to explain one of the objects for which the Church of God has been set up on this earth. The worship of visible power is the great disease of the world. It had reached an amazing height at the time when the Gospel was first preached. The feeling of anything unseen had gradually disappeared; the ruler of the Roman world was more and more regarded as the actual and only ruler of men. Just at this moment a society was seen rising up which seemed to treat outward strength with utter contempt, and yet which showed that it did possess a strength of some strange kind by the manner in which it diffused itself, as well as by the deeds which its members performed. What this strength was the rulers of the earth could not guess. They heard a Crucified Man declared to be the source and spring of it. They knew that certain ceremonies were performed by this people, all of a very simple character, but all importing that a communion had been established between the worshippers and the object of their worship; and that life and power were communicated to them from Him. They could not charge the Christians with any violent excitements, any maniac exhibitions, such as they were used to witness when their priests or priestesses supposed themselves to be under the Divine inspiration. The more solemn the service they were engaged in, the more quiet and calm they appeared. Yet it was evident that they attributed the greatest significance to these services. They affirmed that every child whom they baptized was taken under the Divine government. It is still more evident that they believed those who presided over them were appointed to the work which they fulfilled by their unseen Lord, and received their powers directly from Him. The ceremony which expressed this conviction was most simple; the language which was habitual among them certainly did not indicate that they regarded the powers of their teachers as any warrant for usurpation; their ordained men were called *Ministers*, the chief of all were said to be the servants of all. Nevertheless, they did affirm most distinctly that submission to this rite *was* necessary to every person who assumed the office of priest among them. No great acquirements without this, no quickness of wit, no holiness of life, were considered qualifications for the great task to which they were called. They must, by a distinct act of homage, testify whence it was that their power came, otherwise it was said the power would not be such a one as could enable them to further the objects of the body to which they belonged.

I entreat you, my brethren, to consider what an effect such a witness as this must have produced upon a heathen world; how wholly different an effect from any which could have been wrought by mere words. And we know that it did produce this effect. It was not because the Christians proclaimed a certain doctrine that they were the subjects of persecution in the early ages. The infidel historian is perfectly right in his opinion, that the Roman emperors were disposed to be most tolerant of all strange opinions. They would have been tolerant of Christianity if that had been only an opinion; but the Church they saw was a body, which was as much held together by certain bonds, as much ruled over by certain persons, as completely an organisation, as the empire itself. But it was an organisation which rested upon precisely the opposite principle to that empire. It declared that all power was ordained of God; that man could look up through the visible to the Invisible. If that principle were true, the opposite principle which substituted men for God must be false. One must prevail, and the other be confounded.

There can be no doubt, I think, that a great part of the feeling respecting the Church, which was imparted in this way to the heathens, arose from the marks which it bore of perpetuity. During all its three hundred years of struggle and persecution, and amidst continual declensions of faith and purity which, though chiefly observed by the members of the Church itself, must have been visible also to her adversaries, she had still retained the same institutions, the same witnesses of her fellowship with an unseen power. But what was more remarkable, the

Christians believed that their ministers who lived centuries after the Son of Man had left the earth as much received their commission from Him as those on whom He had himself breathed. For, they said that those who had first received the power had ordained others, and had committed it to them. This they said was the law of Christ's kingdom; by this means it was testified that He abides the same from generation to generation; that all who exercised powers were exercising them under Him; that whatever blessings were communicated through men were really communicated by the Lord of men.

But this perpetuity of the Church would not have seemed so marvellous to the heathens if the same facts had not borne witness of its universality. There were ministers of the Church who presided over distinct and particular congregations, but there were also those who exercised a large and general oversight over cities and neighbourhoods, and who, though responsible for such cities and neighbourhoods, were recognised as possessing a divinely-bestowed power among Christians at the greatest distance from their own locality. It was from this class of ministers that the rest derived their appointments. These were believed to represent the first chosen Apostles; these were the main instruments for spreading the Gospel from land to land; these gave the Church that formidable aspect in the eyes of the surrounding world, which provoked the bitterness of its persecutions. It was *their* position, more than that of all other ministers, which testified that the powers which be are ordained of God. If the time permitted it, my brethren, I could bring you abundant proofs from the records of the progress of Christianity in different lands that the Bishops were its great missionaries; that the more their function was regarded, the more the baptismal commission, "Go ye unto all nations," was felt to be addressed, not to the first Apostles merely, but to descend with all its obligations and powers upon each succeeding age. I could shew you, too, that the fact of these Bishops being ordained, of their acknowledging their powers as a direct gift from above, was the great means of infusing into the minds of those chieftains, who would else have felt themselves rulers by mere strength or will, the conviction that they too were ordained of God. I could shew you, too, that when these Bishops degenerated, when they abused their powers to personal aggrandizement, when they became wolves instead of shepherds, the sin might be traced in every case to their forgetfulness of the principle upon which they stood; to their taking advantage of the truth, that their powers were of God, while they practically denied that truth, and lived as if their powers were their own. But the illustrations of this truth are, unfortunately, in modern times to be obtained principally from the effects which have followed from our neglect of it.

Christian nations have doubted whether they did possess an order exercising the apostolic function. They have doubted whether ordination meant anything; they have taken it to be a mere insignificant form. Hence that feeling of the perpetuity of the Church, and of its universality, which I said was so vigorous in the first ages, has become weaker and weaker. The feeling that it is meant to diffuse itself into every corner of the world, necessarily disappeared along with this which was its great support; men became almost indifferent about the spread of the Gospel in other lands, and, as a judgment, it became less and less efficient in their own. God mercifully broke this slumber; we felt here in England that we had a truth committed to us, which was of mighty worth, and that we ought to tell it abroad. But our commission was not merely to tell a truth, it was to establish a kingdom; in fact, the truth was unintelligible when it stood alone. Those who heard it thought it was one theory, or notion, or opinion, out of a great many; and they were confirmed in their judgment when they saw different sects coming forth to declare what they said was the same truth in different, and sometimes contradictory, language. And worldly men said, not without some warrant for their assertion, that by proclaiming our opinions we were unsettling the faith of those among whom we went, often without giving them a substitute for it; that we were not really doing anything for the civilization of the nations by merely publishing our theological dogmas in the midst of them.

The Society, my brethren, for which I am asking your help to-night, has, as I have told you already, borne witness for many years, on behalf of the principle that the Church is really God's handiwork, and that we are to be his ministers in establishing it, wherever our nation sets up its own power. It has done, also, all that seemed possible to its members— all that I believe was possible—for the purpose of putting its missions upon a right foundation, and making the chief ministers of the Church the centres of them. From time to time it used the most earnest entreaties and arguments to induce the Governments of the day to send Bishops into our colonies; in a few instances it was successful. In many parts of the world it has been obliged to wait, feeling that it had no power of its own to do that which the English State was unwilling to do. It was fully conscious of the feebleness of the efforts which it could make to establish a church polity, where the main constituent of that polity was wanting; conscious, too, how imperfect all efforts for the dissemination of the Gospel must be so long as it was not what it is always described in Scripture as being— the Gospel of a kingdom. Still it was better to wait than to do anything rashly and prematurely; such waiting is never in vain. A new period has begun in the history of the Society; the Bishops of the Church have themselves come forward to say, that Bishops must go forth from the Church itself to our different colonies. The missionaries of the Society will go forth as the missionaries did of old, under the captains and leaders whom Christ himself has appointed to carry on his conquests in the world.

From what I have said it will be apparent to you, that the Society for the Propagation of the Gospel is not itself the organ of this movement; it could not, in conformity with its principles, have proposed such a measure on its own responsibility. Nevertheless, the measure is one which gives the Society a claim upon your support, far greater than it ever possessed before. I do not mean merely because it has contributed a large sum—very large indeed, in proportion to its income—to the fund for Colonial Bishoprics; I do not mean merely because while it has thus diminished its means for the sake of this object, the demands which will be made upon it for missionaries will be multiplied ten or twenty fold—I mean that when this scheme shall be carried into effect, this Society will possess, in the highest and truest sense of the word, facilities for evangelizing and civilizing the dependencies of the British Crown, which no state patronage, no amount of voluntary zeal could have conferred upon it. Let me at once prove my assertion, and connect what I am saying with the words of St. Paul, by referring to one or two of the colonies in which our missionaries are now labouring.

For some time past we have had bishops in the *West Indies;* there is a hope that the number will be considerably multiplied. Think only, I beseech you, of the condition of that part of the world, of what it was, of the new and grand experiment of freedom which is making in it, how immeasurably important it is to England and to humanity that the white and the black race should feel themselves to have a real and not a mere nominal bond of union, and then say whether the practical enforcement of the truth, "The powers that be are ordained of God," be not the one great hope for that region. We may send out just magistrates, kindly governors, good regulations, to raise one class of the inhabitants and protect the other. But if we would give effect to any of these blessings, we must have some officer who does not come forth merely or chiefly as the agent of the mother country, who carries in him another kind of authority, who is felt to be a witness that the Most High Himself careth for the children that he has made, and that he claims all, of every clime and colour, as his children. I am satisfied that this benefit has already proceeded from our episcopacy even during the short time that it has been established in these islands. It will be felt, I trust, yet more strongly as we become more conscious that we need it. Those who have held power under conditions which made it most perilous, often quite fatal to the possessor, it will teach in a silent, practical method, what the nature of power is, and what responsibilities attach to it; how it attains its greatest height when it is regarded as an instrument of doing good to the weak; to those who have been tempted to look upon all subjection as bondage, it will explain in a manner far more intelligible and level to their capacities than maxims and propositions can ever be, that the great privilege of a man is to be obedient; that the most perfect freedom is a service.

On the continent of *India* I need not tell you that we have had, for above twenty years, one bishop; and that within the last ten we have had three. Miserably insufficient as this provision is, I do believe that it is quite impossible to calculate the difference between our position, in reference to India, before and since it has been made. The Mahometan conquerors of the East traversed it as the soldiers of God, their triumphs and establishment were throughout connected with religion. English Christians subdued India, as merchant adventurers. What a contrast for the mind of a native to reflect upon! how impossible it must have been for him really to believe that the Christian faith was the more practical and operative faith! The religion of the Hindoos enters into every department of their lives; has organised their whole society. Our English religion was thrust into a corner of our time, if it claimed even that; it had, apparently, no influence on our institutions. What signified it that we sent out a man here and there to say, 'We profess a meek, gracious, humanizing religion; yours is one of blood.' In the building up of our existence it seemed as if our religion had no place at all; and one that is ever so little humanizing must be felt to carry stronger evidence with it, if its professors shew that they are earnest in its behalf, and that it determines their actions. Nothing then, I think, but some strong and resolute effort to prove that the cross has its soldiers and officers as well as the crescent; that the Incarnation is the ground of a real and universal Society, such as could never have been raised on the belief of mere natural gods or a mere mortal prophet; that all the justice and wisdom of our English rule has been indirectly derived from Christian principles; that all our injustice and crimes have been a rebellion against them—nothing but such demonstration as this, can really come home with power to the minds of the natives of India, or can induce them to substitute something better than mere unbelief for that which had been their faith hitherto.

A bishop is on the point of sailing to *New Zealand*; I will not indulge in the auguries which I hope it is lawful for an Englishman and a Christian in humble faith upon God's blessing, to draw from his mission. I will only entreat you to consider the deep and awful responsibility which is laid upon us, to establish that new world upon principles which our descendants will not be ashamed to acknowledge as our handiwork.

But if this is to be done, it must be done by a zealous and united effort on the part of the Church at home, to lay the foundations of it as deep as the foundations of God's church itself; to construct it according to the pattern which he himself has shewn us; to prove in the way which his word and the history of mankind shew to be the only efficient one, that all power is ordained of him. Surely, to have the least share in contributing to such a work, to be instrumental in adding one stone to the temple which we trust He himself is raising, to be able even to throw one mite even into His treasury, is an honour which when you look back and see things in those measures and proportions in which they present themselves to a man on his dying bed, you would be sorry to exchange for any gifts which the world can bestow.

SERMON XXVIII.

THE HINDRANCE TO CHRISTIAN MISSIONS.

(*Preached in the Parish Church at Leamington Priors.—The Seventeenth Sunday after Trinity, 1841. In compliance with the Queen's Letter directing a Collection on behalf of the Society for the Propagation of the Gospel.*)

There is one body and one Spirit, even as ye are called in one hope of your calling; one Lord, one faith, one baptism, one God and Father of all, who is above all, and through all, and in you all.—EPHESIANS iv. 4, 5, 6.

IF a person were enquiring what was the main cause of the opposition which the Gospel encountered in the first ages, I think the words in the Epistle of to-day would give him the answer. Imagine a Jew of Tarsus, a tentmaker, travelling through the different provinces of the Roman Empire. He finds everywhere similar forms of government, and the same power recognised as supreme. But he finds in different cities and different neighbourhoods different presiding divinities, different degrees of respect paid to this and to that, different forms of worship. He finds these tastes and predilections tolerated, and even encouraged, by the rulers of the world. Here and there they may have suppressed some inhuman superstition, but in general their policy, he will have seen, was to allow each people its own modes of thought and opinion, to incorporate them, when it was possible, into their own system, and only to require, that whatever other power their subjects might reverence, their chief and most practical homage should be rendered to Rome. Imagine a man, such as I have described, travelling through these different countries, not chiefly for the purpose of pursuing his trade, not for the purpose of ascertaining the superiority of his own national customs and religion by comparing them with a number of others, but for the purpose of making this proclamation, "There is one body, and one Spirit, one Lord, one faith, one baptism, one God and Father of all, who is above all, and through all, and in you all." Could there be any announcement so strange and startling as this? 'You are members of countries which are divided from each other by language, by race, by hatred; within each of these are neighbourhoods and families which are at war with each other. I say to you all, "There is one body." Your tastes and inclinations are the most unlike imaginable. I declare, "There is one Spirit," to inform you all. There is a particular divinity over each of your towns and neighbourhoods. I say, "There is one Lord." Even when you use the same words, you attach the most various conceptions to the beings you reverence. Your common people identify them with the images which represent them; your philosophers think all the vulgar notions respecting them delusions. I assert that "There is one faith," for rich and poor, for wise and ignorant. You have the most different methods for approaching your gods, and of attaining a knowledge of them. To each and all I proclaim, "There is one baptism." Some of you aim at this reward for some devotion, some at that. I say that there is one calling for us all, and that there is "one hope of our calling." The highest dream you have ever had of a power presiding over the destinies of the whole universe, is that which you get by remembering that there is an Emperor a long way off from you, to whom your destinies are subject. I tell you that there is one God and Father of all, who is above all, and through all, and in us all.'

This was the tentmaker's proclamation. He did not enter into long arguments to prove the truth of it. He said these things were so. He had no secret ally to assist him or encourage him; all the powers of the world were against him. He had no strong national prejudices to which he could make his appeal, and shew that he was maintaining them, though he was insulting all others: his own countrymen were his greatest adversaries. Can we wonder that his language should at first have been treated as ridiculous, and when it could be despised no longer because it gained a hearing, that all the resources of human power should have been put forth to suppress it and to punish those who uttered it?

But if we need not go further than these words to discover the cause of the opposition to the Gospel of Christ, they contain also, I believe, the charm with which it worked, and the secret of its success. We may remind ourselves that the early preachers of the Gospel were endowed with strange powers over the bodies of men, and even over the elements of nature. They were, and they did on certain occasions, though by no means habitually or constantly, exercise these powers. They took this method of proving to men that there was a connection between the unseen world and their own, and that a mighty spiritual influence was continually going forth on their behalf. But these miracles were not in themselves good for anything; they were good only on account of the words which accompanied them, and of the facts which they attested. And these words were, "There is one body, one Spirit, one Lord, one faith, one baptism, one God and Father of all." These facts were the life, death, and resurrection of Christ, which declared that there was one Lord in whom the one universal Body consisted, who had bestowed upon it the one Spirit, who was the object of the one Faith, who had established the one Baptism, who had revealed the one Father.

We may speak again of the purity of the Gospel morality, and the divine example which shewed that it was not merely a morality of words. Assuredly we cannot say too much on this point, unless we forget that the promise which made it possible that this morality should ever be practised by man is contained in the words, "There is one Spirit;" that the acknowledgment of Christ's example, as the standard of human morality, depends upon the truth, "There is one Lord;" that the attainment of the moral perfection which is set forth in Him, by men of different habits and dispositions, would be a dream unless there was "one hope of our calling;" that there would be no proof of men being called to strive together for the one hope, or that they were all to receive the one Spirit, unless there were one Baptism; that there could be no ground for an universal and absolute morality at all if there were not one God and Father of all. Deny the assertion of the text, and then try whether you can contrive to find a meaning in any precept of our Lord, or in any act of his life.

If, again, we dwell upon our Lord's passion and death as the great subject of the Apostolical message, and as constituting the distinction between it and every other that was ever heard in the world, we shall assert a great truth. This was the object on which their own thoughts were continually fixed, and to which they desired that the thoughts of their converts should be ever turning. But that very fact is the strongest confirmation of the point I am maintaining. It was this mighty difference between the "One Lord" and all who came before him, and all who shall come after him, that he laid down his life that he might take it again. This, as he said himself, was the mark by which he was signified to be the true Shepherd of the sheep. It is the cross which testified what that one Spirit was which he would bestow upon his disciples, the spirit of love and voluntary self-sacrifice. It was the cross which taught the disciples what was the one hope of their calling—what that joy of their Lord was into which they were to enter, and how it was to be reached. It was the cross which fulfilled the words, "He that hath seen me hath seen the Father;" in that it manifested forth the love, and power, and glory of God in the weakness and nothingness of man, to the intent that afterwards, by that same love and power, mankind might be redeemed and exalted. And surely this was not all;—surely our Lord's words, "I, if I be lifted up, will draw all men unto me," indicate most clearly that the cross was to be the centre of common attraction, and therefore of union, to men, that while they really rest upon it, and believe in it, they must claim fellowship with each other; they cannot tolerate the notion of warring sects and separate interests. Surely they must signify, 'As there is one Lord, one Spirit, one hope, one Father, so also is there one baptism, in which each may die to himself, and therefore rise up in union with the one body of his Lord.' Whatever influence then the miracles of the first Apostles may have exercised, in preparing men's minds for receiving the faith—whatever witness the pure and holy lives of those who held it may have borne to its reality—whatever deep mysteries were revealed in the preaching of the cross—we may be sure that all were drawing men to this point, all were declaring the one body, the one Spirit, the one Lord, the one faith, the one Father.

And this declaration was the one which men wanted to hear; no other could have been substituted for it. In all those forms of belief and worship of which I have spoken, there had been a whisper or prophecy of it. There was a longing in men's hearts for a universal fellowship, which neither their incapacity of realizing it, nor the disputatious hateful feelings which made them recoil from it, could quench. Separated as they were from each other by such innumerable varieties of circumstance and oppositions of feeling, God had not left them without witness that they were meant to be one. The same sky over their heads; the same sun shining from generation to generation on all kindreds and people; limbs and countenances of the same mould; the same craving for society. And since these were all in vain to give the blessing which they shewed that man had need of; since all nature said, 'It is not in me;' since the desire of sensual enjoyments only separated men further from each other, because all wanted that which only a few could obtain; since the fellowship in sensual delights, while it promised friendship, ended in strife; since laws, though they could curb the inclinations which separated men from each other, yet were unable to create any bond between them; the fragments of humanity lay scattered like the dry bones in the Prophet's vision, now moving towards each other, and trying to unite, now clashing violently against each other till some breath from above should quicken them, and some voice should bid them rise up, and become a great army. That voice was heard; it might come from Galilean fishermen, or from a tentmaker of Cilicia. But it was felt to be the voice of God, speaking through them. They had a commission to declare that there is one body, and one Spirit, one Lord, one faith, one hope, one baptism, one God and Father of all, who is above all, and through all, and in all. They had a commission to receive men, by that one baptism, into that one body, to make them partakers of that one Spirit, to deal with them as the members of that one Lord, as the children of that one Father.

My brethren, these words have helped us to account for two facts apparently of the most opposite character; the persecution which befell the first preachers of Christianity, and its success. There is another fact, far sadder than the first, as certain as the second, which still needs to be explained:—Why has not the Gospel spread itself more widely? Why have not the inhabitants of the world fallen before the Church? Why do her early achievements stand out in such dark contrast to her later days?

If the peculiar powers which were granted to the first servants of Christ could not be set down as the cause of their victories, the loss of those powers cannot be a sufficient reason for our feebleness. For consider whether we have a right to say that our powers are less than theirs were. We can appeal to the continued existence of a Christendom, which established itself in spite of all human opposition; they could not. Would any reasonable man exchange the evidence which this fact supplies, for the power of making a lame man walk? We have a continuous and complete record of God's revelations, and of the setting up of his kingdom. Is this no compensation for not having witnessed it in its embryo state, or in the struggles of its birth? And if we can say to every lame and sick man—'It is Jesus Christ who maketh thee whole, whether he works through the physician or without him,' why is our condition worse because in our day it rather pleases God to put honour upon his subordinate agents than to dispense with them?

Much we admitted of the demonstration which the Gospel carried with it was contained in the lives of those who professed it, and especially of those who preached it. The melancholy difference in ourselves we are bound with shame and contrition to confess. But the confession is a useless one, I suspect it is a dishonest one, unless we inquire further what is the cause of our hollowness and inconsistency, *why* we do not feel as the first Christians did, that the message from heaven is one in which we and all men are interested, which it is our highest glory to make known.

But the apostles gloried in the cross, and in the cross alone. Are we like them in this respect? If it be meant merely, 'Do we acknowledge the satisfaction of our Lord to be the one ground of individual salvation?' I think the majority of preachers and hearers in this day and this country might answer conscientiously, 'We do not reject this doctrine, we proclaim it and embrace it.' But if it be meant, 'Do we honour the cross as the centre of universal attraction, as the proclamation of a divine Head in whom all persons and things consist, in whose death we die to ourselves, by whose life we rise up to fellowship with God and with His Church universal,' then the question may be changed for another: 'Do we generally and habitually believe that there is one Body and one Spirit, one Lord, one Faith, one Baptism, one God and Father of all?'

The answers would be most various, but taken together they would be quite decisive. One would say, 'I acknowledge that one Spirit of love ought to fill all hearts, but I do not see why we may not call ourselves by different names, why we may not exist in different parties. I do not see why we should outwardly to the world exhibit any oneness.' In other words, he looks upon it as a harsh and cruel sentiment that there is one Body. Another, more consistently, feels that the real offence lies in the assertion there is one Spirit. He can submit very easily to mere badges and formalities, but the notion that the operations of our minds are to be controlled by a strange mysterious Ruler is intolerable. A third who has seen different countries and observed how their different customs and opinions divide the members of them, thinks it incredible and ridiculous that there should be one Faith which is meant to hold these unsociable elements together—faith, which is the very principle of discord! A fourth remarks that the world's history is full of conspicuous heroes. It is an insulting disparagement of them to affirm that there is one Lord. The desires and notions of happiness among men are infinite, saith a fifth; what arrogance and tyranny to merge them all in a one Hope. 'But even if these ideas are tolerable,' says a sixth, 'how can you associate with them a trifling ceremony performed on the most unconscious subjects? What is the meaning of a one Baptism?' There might still seem to be an agreement in the acknowledgment that there is 'one Father.' But this agreement is imaginary rather than real. It exists while you are content that the words should mean nothing, that they should be merely a figure of speech. Declare that they imply a real relation, declare that the Father has interfered on behalf of his children, has revealed Himself to them, and this doctrine awakens as much scepticism as the rest.

Now all these opinions, which are much more closely connected together, and pass much more easily into each other than we sometimes suppose, appear to those who hold them almost self-evident truths. We cannot be surprised that they should; we know that a divided worship and a divided heart have been natural to men in all ages. The wonder is, that a united worship, a united faith should ever have established itself in spite of these natural tendencies. The wonder is that the desires for union should exist so mightily, so unquenchably in the heart in the midst of them all.

The wonder is, that after the members of the Church had tried to substitute another unity for that in its immortal Head, unity in a dying man and in his decrees, and after this error had been discovered, and after in the rebound from it men had begun to think all unity unnecessary or impossible, the conviction that by some means or other it must be realised, that there is no life nor truth without it, should, in the most strange and various ways, be forcing itself upon us. But though these considerations dispel all astonishment at the return to those barbarous and dividing notions of the old world from which Christianity seemed to have rescued us, and though they hold out a sure promise that the purposes of God will not at last be defeated, but will be brought to pass through this very human opposition, they do not alter the fact or the consequences of it. Because the apostles believed that there was one body and one Spirit, one Lord, one Faith, one Baptism, because they believed that they had a commission to declare this truth, to put men in possession of its blessings, using all means which God had imparted, being content to want any which He did not vouchsafe, therefore their zeal for God and their love to men kept pace with each other, therefore they saw in the cross of Christ that power to which all human power and resistance must submit, therefore the results of their mission surpassed all their expectations from it. Because we do not believe this, far greater powers than they possessed are unavailing in our hands, the Cross seems to men but an unmeaning symbol, the Gospel is not spread, the Church does not enlarge her borders. What is the Gospel but the good news of a fellowship to all people and nations and languages?

What is the Church but that fellowship? If we do not believe there is such good news, is it strange that we are not instruments in carrying it to others? If we do not think there is such a fellowship, is it strange that we cannot persuade men to enter into it?

I. We have found, then, the causes of the Church's weakness in ourselves. We do not believe her to exist, therefore for us, in a great measure, she does not exist. But how can we recover the faith we have lost, and so restore that which has decayed through the want of it? St. Paul answers the question in the epistle to-day. "Walk worthy," he says, "of the vocation wherewith ye are called." You have this one hope, this one baptism, this one Lord. Act as if you have had them, and you will find that they are real. This is the secret of making our position a true one, to live as if we had it, to be that which we would wish to be, and which God wishes us to be. But to what height must we lift ourselves in order to become something so different from that which at present we seem to be? St. Paul answers again, 'To no height at all. You must sink instead of rising. What we want is "lowliness of mind."' Humility is the foundation of the Church; ceasing to think highly of ourselves is the beginning of being united to each other. By help of this grace we learn to forbear one another in love; without it, never. A man who thinks highly of himself, who values his own notions and opinions and the wit that has conceived them above all things, cannot be forbearing, let his professions be what they may. The man who loves truth above all things, and regards himself as nothing except the servant of it, must be forbearing; he is too anxious that his brother should find the truth to throw any hindrances in his way through his hastiness and vehemence; he must overlook his mistakes and misconstructions, for he knows how many he has been guilty of himself. And thus 'the endeavour to keep the unity of the Spirit in the bond of peace,' becomes a real, practical, honest endeavour which brings after it a sure reward. An endeavour it must be always, for it is no easy work to contend at once against other men's evil tendencies and our own. Those who feel how all important is the unity of the Church, are mightily tempted to advance it by means which are destructive of it; their zeal is called out in the defence of that which they know to be precious to all, and feel to be worth more to themselves than their lives; zeal passes into pride; they begin to defend not the Church of the living God, but their own opinions; not the one Lord, the one Faith, the one Baptism, but themselves and the words and phrases which they and those whom they associate with use; and so they find too late that they have been doing the work of the Evil Spirit, scattering where they looked to gather, destroying where they pretended to defend and restore. To resist such temptations is no light task; it requires all energy, all watchfulness, but the energy and watchfulness will be inspired by Him who asks them of us, and He too will recompense them. If we do earnestly and passionately strive, in whatever place or circumstances we may be living, to keep this unity of the Spirit in the bond of peace, we shall, in spite of innumerable errors and sins which we shall have to repent of, sometimes in dust and ashes, be enabled to keep it; and then the vision of a Church one and undivided, will become clearer and brighter to us because we shall see from our own experience and knowledge, that it is not a mere vision but the deepest of all realities.

II. This is one means to the restoration of Church unity, the other of which I am to speak to you this morning is different in form, but not in principle. Some may be tempted to say when they hear how the divisions of the Church have prevented its extension, 'For the present, then, let us forbear all efforts for its extension; when it is united there is a hope and promise that it may embrace all the corners of the earth; till then let us work at home in our own neighbourhoods, waiting and praying for a better day.' Such language as this may sound plausible, but it is very inconsistent with that which I have just quoted from St. Paul, and with the facts we have been considering.. We want the faith of a united Church for labours at home as well as labours abroad; if we may not act upon it there, we cannot labour here; the same necessity which compels us to suspend our missions, must compel us to cease from every other duty. We must wait for some miraculous change in our circumstances before we begin to walk worthy of the vocation wherewith we are called. Did the apostles wait till they saw proofs and tokens of unity in the world before they preached, "There is one Lord, one Faith, one Baptism"? On the contrary, they stood forth in the midst of facts which seemed to set their language at nought, to prove it utterly absurd. They declared that so it was, let men doubt it or disbelieve it as they might; they bound themselves in this fellowship, they baptized men into it, they produced the living evidences of their words; so the Church grew and became a great tree. This is our example. It matters not what men may be thinking or saying or doing. If we believe that there is one Lord, one Faith, one Baptism, that our bishops and priests have the same commission and power to proclaim them which the first teachers of the Church had, the same power to admit men into the fellowship of Christ; we can send forth this message with the clear undoubting confidence that it will be listened to because it is true, and because He who is truth will confirm the words which He Himself desires us to utter. Every such effort, be assured, will do more to establish unity at home, to prove that the Church has a foundation, that she is a reality, than ten thousand wailings over our condition or accusations of one another for having occasioned it. I believe it is the experience of our missionaries which has taught us of late to inquire so much more earnestly whether we can use the words of the apostle with an honest heart or no. We have wished to do something, and God has blessed the wish by shewing that we can do almost nothing till we submit to His methods, and seek to bless men, not by leaving them to their own divisions, but by bringing them into his family.

My brethren, upon this principle the Society has acted, which was recommended to your notice by a Royal Letter last week. It is this principle which has given our civil rulers an interest in its welfare. They find that the ordinary links which bind colonists to their mother country may be easily snapt asunder; they find that mere regulations, even if they were always wise, of mutual convenience, will never create sympathy; they crave our help to give the colonists some inward principle of concord which may make them our sons and our brothers indeed. The Sovereign, therefore, asks to-day that you will support this object for the sake of the nation; the Church asks you to support it for the honour of her Master, and for the good of our race; your own kinsfolk ask you to support it lest they should be left exiles in a foreign land, separated from you more in heart than by distance. May you feel besides all these obligations, the blessings of being yourselves members of the one Body, bound to the one Lord, taught by the one Spirit, and I know the appeal will not be made in vain.

SERMON XXIX.

DEATH AND LIFE.

(Preached in Lincoln's Inn Chapel.—March 25th, 1855.)

For if we believe that Jesus died and rose again, even so them also which sleep in Jesus will God bring with Him.

1 THESSALONIANS iv. 14.

THE Festival of the Annunciation is seldom separated by many days from Passion Week. That recollection may have given a tone to the Collect we have repeated to-day. But the principle of it depends upon no accidents of seasons. The mystery of the Cross and the mystery of the Resurrection are inseparably connected with the mystery of the Incarnation; when we try to view them apart from it, we fail utterly to enter into their meaning.

What was it that was announced by the messenger from the unseen world to the Virgin of Galilee? The Holy Thing to be born of her, the Child who was to be called Jesus, had, it was said, an elder parentage, another name. He was the Son of God. That He had been before the worlds were; that title He owed to no event which had taken place or was to take place upon earth. He was the brightness of His Father's glory; He was the express image of His person. In that image He had created men to be His sons. In the fulness of the time He would acknowledge them as His sons. Mary was to be the highly favoured among women—all generations were to call her blessed; because through her the purpose of the Eternal God was to be accomplished and revealed; because through her, He, who was one with the Father, was to make known the Father; He, who was the first-born of many brethren, was to make them aware of their condition, capable of claiming it. Through her, the real root of humanity, the real source of life and light to all the races which dwelt upon the earth, the real bond of their peace, was to come into contact with the actual conditions of men, with their death and darkness, with the strife that was tearing them from each other and from their Father in heaven.

When we say we believe that Jesus Christ, the only Son of God, was conceived by the Holy Ghost and born of the Virgin Mary, we say this:—we affirm Him to have verily become man in the fullest sense that we can give to that expression; not merely to be the type, and image, and root of humanity, which He always was, but to have entered into the stages of man's existence, into the innermost depths of man's experience.

And therefore when we say we believe that this Jesus Christ suffered under Pontius Pilate, was crucified, dead, and buried, we must mean that He—that Son of God, that root of humanity, that source of life and light to men, that Mediator between God and man, that Person in whom all races and orders of men were created and consisted—did actually enter into the conditions of *death,* into the experiences of *death,* into its most humiliating condition, into its most dreadful experiences. We mean this, and not merely that a certain man at a certain period underwent a painful death, not merely that He underwent it heroically or patiently, not merely that He underwent it as a witness for God and for truth. Each of these assertions we accept; but this is not what we intend when we preach a message of good-tidings to mankind; this is not the faith upon which a Christendom or a universe could stand. If this death was not the death of *the* man; if the heroism or the patience were not the revelation of the Divine Will and the Divine Mind, which the will and the mind of man are created to obey and to show forth; if the witness which He bore for God and for truth was not this —that God in His Son is reconciled to His creatures, and adopts them as His children; that He is true, and that they may be true in Him—there may be a new and noble fact added to the records of human history; but there is no explanation given of all the horrible confusions and contradictions of human history, of death the greatest of all; there is no foundation laid for a self-sacrifice, which not a few exceptional persons here and there, but all, may offer.

And therefore, when we say again, "We believe that on the third day He rose again from the dead," we do not and cannot mean, unless we have forgotten the part of the Creed which we have just before been uttering, that a certain man, by a strange and solitary departure from the law under which human creatures are formed, was permitted to break forth from the grave and revisit the world to which He had before belonged. We must mean that because He alone of all men had fulfilled the law of humanity, in Him alone of all men that law fulfilled itself; that He rose out of death, as St. Peter said, because it was not possible for Him to be holden of it; that He arose, because He Himself, and not Death, is man's Lord and King; that He ascended to His own proper home, that He might claim that kingship over this earth and over all generations of men, past, present, and to come; His death being not more emphatically an assertion of His relation with those who were heirs of mortality, than His resurrection was an assertion of their relation with Him as the inheritor of an eternal life, of His Father's glory.

I trust then I have shown you what ground there is for connecting, as our Collect does, the Incarnation of our Lord Jesus Christ with His Cross and Passion, and these with the glory of His Resurrection. But, in doing so, I have also vindicated the language of St. Paul in the text, in which at first sight there is something which surprises us. You expect him to say, "If we believe that Jesus died and rose again," then certain blessings will follow to us the believers, either as rewards bestowed upon our faith, or as the necessary consequences of it. But he does not say this. He does not say anything like this. He does not speak of us, the believers, at all; though what he does speak may concern us very intimately, may affect profoundly all our thoughts and hopes. He says, "Even so them also which sleep in Jesus will God bring with Him." Evidently he assumes the belief that Jesus died and rose again, to be the recognition of an everlasting truth which involves other truths, just as any mathematical proposition involves others, which must be assented to if that is. It is not what we shall gain by our belief that he is thinking about, or that he would have us chiefly think about. It is what follows from that in which we believe, what a principle and maxim lies in it, which must determine our conclusions about the questions that have interested us most and perplexed us most, those which most concern us individually, and in our relations with each other.

Even before you consider what the Apostle's inference from Christ's death and resurrection was, you must be struck with the change which his belief in them has caused in his mode of speech. Recollect the synonyms which we have adopted for the words—'That man is dead.' All point to some aspects of death; all are felt, at some point or other, to fail. We say, sometimes, "He sleeps in the grave,"—"After life's fitful fever he sleeps well!" There is something in such language which harmonizes with our feelings; there is something which jars with them. You remember the bodily pain, the restlessness of mind, you have seen in some one you have known well. The thought that he is in repose is the one you fly to most eagerly. But oh, that dreary, earthly repose! can it ever accord with the activity and energy which you knew were in him, which were expressed in his words, which you saw in his countenance? Was this all to end in a dull stagnation? You task yourself to discover some better form of thought than that:—"He has departed this life." There is a good sound in such words; somewhat of the same charm as in the other. "*This* life, with its weariness, is over; but there is a promise that *all* may not be over." You rest the emphasis upon *this*. Is that satisfactory? And was not *this* life, *this* very life, which he began here, that which you would wish to go on? Is it to be another? Is *he* to be another? No—we must seek again. "He has yielded to the inevitable destiny of man." Yes—there is a grandeur in that thought. He is one of a kind. He has but fallen as his fathers and the generations of old fell. It was ordered for him. He did not choose, but yielded. Grand—but still how cold! Destiny—inevitable destiny: how we shudder at the language —how we loathe it! "Lot of humanity;"—and is the winding-sheet the symbol and rightful vesture of the being whose first entrance into life was hailed with songs and rejoicings, who as he grew began to look before and after, who seemed to share the life of the ages that had been and that were to be? Is that what it means to be a man—that he is to die?

Now compare these expressions with St. Paul's; "He sleeps in Jesus." There is the rest which you were longing to claim for him, the termination of uneasy struggles, of doubts, of sufferings. But it is rest in Him from whom all his energies and activities were derived, in Him who was the secret spring of his soul's life and his body's life. It is the rest of one who has found what he has been looking for, who has reached his home after long wanderings; whom the Shepherd that had been seeking him and had been always secretly guiding him, has at last taken, rejoicing, to Himself. It is departure surely; something has been left behind, has been cast off. But it has not been *life*, not the true life which he has been leading upon earth, not the life which came forth in kind words and loving acts, not that which shone out in the countenance. From *this* he has not departed: the exercises of it are no longer apparent to us; so far as our consciousness goes, they are suspended. But if we believe that Jesus died and rose again, we must hold that they are not suspended in fact; that they have ascended into their inward and highest principle; that they have gone to be quickened and renovated with a diviner power. And all we can say that he has departed from —for of this our senses testify and have a right to testify—is the vesture of mortality, the case of death with which we saw him enveloped. Assuredly also this sleep in Jesus—if we accept St. Paul's statement of it— perfectly accords with the idea of a common humanity and of a fixed appointment, which I traced in another customary phrase respecting death. The Death and Resurrection of Jesus are taken as the facts which all men are invited to believe, because they interpret the law of man's being. They are taken as the facts which explain the destiny of man. But when we accept this interpretation, the law of man's being is not an inevitable lot; it is the law of voluntary union to a Divine Head, from whom we have tried to be separate; of obedience to a loving Master, who has redeemed us from slavery to a tyrant. Our destiny is not determined by a fate; it is the purpose of a Father who works in us to will and to do of His good pleasure. To sleep in Jesus, then, is to yield to the law to which He voluntarily submitted. It is to say, "Father, I come, for Thou who didst call Thy only-begotten Son to come to Thee through death and the grave, dost call me, Thy adopted child, to come to Thee by the same road. He who said to the thief by

His side on the cross, 'To-day thou shalt be with Me,' commands me, with as little right to His love, with as little virtue of my own to raise me to His presence, simply to trust myself to Him, simply to cast myself upon Him. Help me by Thy Spirit to do that; this is the rest that I desire."

Some of you may think that danger is lurking in this language; as if I supposed that all things would come alike to all, and that we might speak of the worst man no less than the best as falling asleep in Jesus. Let me explain to you why my statement is not open to that charge, yet why it is almost impossible not to incur it if one preaches that Gospel which St. Paul and our Lord Himself preached not to the righteous but to sinners. I have said already that we can only learn the law of humanity from Him who perfectly fulfilled it. Since His life, as a man upon earth, was a life of perfect union to His Father, and trust in Him, and submission to Him, since this was the law of His being which He never transgressed, so He has shown and proclaimed to us that a life of union with Him, of trust in Him, of submission to Him, is the law of our being as men. If we led that life, there would be no strife among us, no strife in our individual hearts. All strife comes from rebellion, from distrust. This we believe He is seeking by the whole of our discipline to overcome in us; to bring us to repent of our own self-seeking, self-willed ways; to bring us back to Himself.

There are some upon whom this discipline seems to have been spent in vain; some who are resolved that they will be their own masters—that they will not be under the yoke of love—that they will destroy themselves. What can we say of such, but that they are refusing the rights of men; that they are determined not to be what God hath made them to be? What can we say to them but this?—'If you sow the wind, you will reap the whirlwind; the wages of sin is death. You cannot be separated from goodness or truth in this world or any other, while the breath is in your body or when it leaves your body, without being miserable. There can be no tampering with that statement, no qualification of it. To be evil is to be damned; to be shut up in yourselves is to be given up to the devil. And because it is so, be assured that Christ is not, as you dream, afar from you; that you have not, as you fancy, succeeded in casting away His cords from you. You are a man, therefore He is with you; you are a man, therefore you are His subject, however you may reject His government. And if now, like that thief on the cross, you will confess His kingdom, you will ask Him to remember you for whom He died, He will speak to you as He spoke to him; that voice of yours will be the answer to all the thousand voices He has uttered in your ears; it will be that act of renunciation—that return to your true state—that confession of His rightful rule, to which His Spirit, through all the years of your pilgrimage, has been seeking to lead you. And therefore you shall be with Him; you shall rest in Him now, you shall rest in Him for ever.'

I wish you to see that we must speak of the principle as universal, that we must claim the language as universal, even that we may explain those frightful anomalies, the number of which makes no difference in their nature, that are so constantly forcing themselves upon us in our intercourse with other men, and in the experience of our own selves. I know well that when we see a fellow-creature plunging down deeper and deeper into the abyss,—when we think he has taken the final plunge, and when then, just then, the voice is heard, saying to him, " Thy soul shall be required of thee;"—and when, in our dimness and horror of mind, there seems no reason why we should not have been—why we may not be—like him—it appears for a moment as if the case for him and for us had been made more terrible by Christ's Death and Resurrection, because they tell us of a love slighted and resisted, which no other acts could tell us of. But when the waters have almost overwhelmed us, when we have come to the deep mire where no standing is, we discover, I believe, that we are blaspheming God by such thoughts; that, after all, the faith that Christ died and rose again gives us a hope for ourselves and for the universe, which, without this, we must soon lose altogether; that while we believe this, though we must be believing in the eternal union of sin and misery, we become absolutely unable to determine by our measures what victory may yet remain for love over sin; whether the rebellious spirit may not have been stopped in a career where all persons and circumstances were probably abetting its ruin, on purpose that it might be subjected to other methods of cure. We must, at least, in our ignorance and confusion, commit every creature, as well as our own souls and bodies, not to a blind fate, but to a most faithful and loving Creator.

But if even in these cases the text shows us a consolation coming out of the depths of despair, what a wonderful music lies in the words, " Sleep in Jesus," when we think of others whom we have seen and known, and whom we see no longer! I will not say, whom we know no longer, for oftentimes we know them better when we can contemplate the whole context of their life, than when it passed in broken and detached instants before us. If you have ever met with a soul which seemed always tending towards some invisible region, impatient of the earth as of a prison-house, yet ever discovering in the earth itself some new beauty, some token of its divine origin;—if you have thought with sorrow of its disappointments and perils from its aspirations after heaven and gravitation downwards—of its tears and repentances; or if you have seen with joy a growing gentleness and continued sympathy with the sufferings and pleasures of others —smiles coming out of a heart which was fed with love from some hidden source; if you have met ever with a spirit of this temper, even if there were no pain and anguish appointed for the body it dwelt in, to remind you that this corruptible must put on incorruption and this mortal must put on immortality, would there not be a blessed meaning in the words, " our friend Lazarus sleepeth," which would assure you that they must come from the same lips which spoke them once on the way to Bethany? Would you not feel that these words signified, in such a case, " The sleep is not a death sleep; it is a sleep in Me? It was I who was kindling its aspirations, giving that disappointment which humbles, but does not destroy hope, inspiring that sorrow which leads to repentance, by all outward influences and inward discipline bringing to Myself that which I had formed for My use and glory."

It would be quite inconsistent with the idea of this sleep in Jesus which I have endeavoured to set before you, if I had spoken of it as the termination of all the thoughts and expectations and studies in which we have been engaged here, whether these have been turned to the world of nature or of art, or of the laws which govern men individually and in society. If I looked upon death as heathens looked upon it, I should speak of it as they did. I should bid you always recollect that it was at hand to cut off all plans and projects, however noble, all the desires of men for knowledge, if those desires have been ever so much awakened in them by the Father of lights. But if we believe that Jesus died and rose again; if the sleep which we anticipate is not sleep in the grave, but in Him; if we account this life a glorious and mysterious seed-time for a harvest to come; if we do not dread the decrees of a capricious or malignant Fate, but await the summons of a Father; we cannot look upon a pursuit as finished when we close our eyes upon this world; we can only think that we have had certain glimpses of light which may grow brighter to the perfect day; that we have been permitted to work clumsily in certain tasks which hereafter we may see brought to perfection. On that night when Christ taught His disciples that He was the Way, the Truth, and the Life, and that no one came to the Father but by Him; on that night He said also, "In my Father's house are many mansions: if it were not so, I would have told you." 'If I had meant you, my poor friends, to shut yourselves out from all natural and human experiences, to stifle all the apprehensions and questionings concerning the world around you and within you, to dwell only on visions of the charnel-house and grave, I would not have left you to learn that meaning from others; I would have told you. But you know I have told you nothing of the kind. By every parable concerning the kingdom of Heaven which I have spoken to you, I have stirred up a multitude of strange musings concerning that which you see and that which you cannot see, where there had been a blank and vacancy before; I have opened to you depths that you had never visited, I have given you the first glimpses of light, the first promise of an order where all had been chaos and darkness. I have not been leading you to the grave; I have been leading you to my Father's house, to a region, not of dead bones, but of rich, various, holy life. I *have* told you indeed that the way thither is a narrow one, full of thorns and briars, and so you will find it the more closely you follow my steps. I have told you that the cross must be borne every day; that each hour, if you aspire to know what God would have you know, and be what God would have you be, you must ask Him to deliver you from yourselves, to give you self-sacrifice. But having walked in that path, having learned the secret of that surrender, you will be able to go in and out and find pasture; you will perceive everywhere ladders set upon earth and reaching to Heaven, upon which the angels of God are ascending and descending; you will learn that the key which opens the mystery of God's love, in the Word who has been made flesh and dwelt among you, opens a thousand locks which men have tried to force, admits to treasure-houses which they have dreamed of but never entered.' Believe, brethren, that it is the same still. Believe that if Christ had meant to shut up any avenue of thought or any kind of work from us, He would have told us. Believe that every careful and painful investigator of secrets which He has hidden that men may search them out, receives his impulse and vocation from Him,—an impulse and vocation to be obeyed, that some mansion in the Father's house which Christ has gone to prepare, may be opened for the blessing of those for whom He died and rose again. And the sleep in Him is, as I believe, not the shutting the eye to any of those visions which have been haunting it with occasional brightness here, but the shutting it to objects which have distracted it, the removal of the selfish films which have confused it, to the end that the things it has beheld through a glass darkly, it may see in their true nature and proper substance.

But I have dwelt too long upon the sleep. Christ, who said, "Our friend sleepeth," said also, "I go to awaken him out of sleep." St. Paul will not let us forget that the same who died for men, rose again for them, and that therefore, those who sleep in Him, God will bring with Him. What do the words *bring with Him* signify? Say, if you will, they are too high for us, we cannot attain to them,—and you speak truly. But do not cast them aside because they are too high for you. The sun which shows you all that is at your feet, is always too high for you to ascend to it, too bright for you to gaze upon it. These words may be full of illumination to us, in some of our dreariest and darkest hours, though they must be fulfilled to us, before the mists which rise from below to obscure them to us can be entirely scattered. St. Paul speaks elsewhere of a day when the sons of God shall be manifested; and he says, all creation is groaning and travailing for that day. The manifestation of the sons of God,—the full revelation of Him as the light of the world, as the centre of its order, the spring of all its movements, must come first, then the manifestation of all those who have received any rays of this light; that being now seen as true which the Gospel declared to be true, that all their life proceeded from His — that in Him only could they see light. When we reflect earnestly on this great announcement, it seems to me that the mystery of Death and of Life opens wonderfully upon us. And though it is very hard indeed to believe what we are told, because it sounds too good to be true, and all the discontent of the heart rises up to laugh at such tidings, as Sarah did when she heard of the child of joy who was to be born in her age; yet it comes to the reason with a mighty evidence, as if it were the carrying out to its highest accomplishment of a law which the unfolding of every bud and flower out of its root, the rise of every morning out of the night, the bursting of every spring out of winter, has been hinting and prophesying of. It is not science which raises a difficulty—it is much more the dry, hard contradiction of sense which science has to endure, and which makes all her greatest discoveries at first incredible. One doubt, perhaps the chief, which may confuse our thoughts about the gathering together and glorification of those who have dwelt in houses of clay, and whose dust has been committed to its kindred dust,

St. Paul himself has disposed of, calling all nature to witness to his solution of it: "How are the dead raised up, and with what body do they come?" The question, he tells us, must be repeated through every operation of the universe. How are the seeds of corn raised up, and with what body do they come? Is not the seed the same as the full ear? Is it not altogether different? Is not everything renovated and perfected, the same with that thing in its seminal condition? do you not know that it is, the more that you feel how it is changed? And so then it is not more reasonable to believe that the egg becomes the caterpillar, and the caterpillar the chrysalis, the chrysalis the butterfly; it is not more reasonable to confess any one of the most ordinary and recognized transformations of Nature, than it is to believe that every human creature formed in God's image, every one of those who have fallen asleep in Jesus, shall come forth with every beauty of soul and of form that was latent here renewed and regenerated in the likeness of Him from whom the beauty came; whose own face was marred more than any man's; who returned Himself to show the very hands and side which had been pierced; who ascended to the glory of His Father.

It is not wrong—there are times when it may be most right and healthful—to single out one and another of that company which no man can number, and to assure ourselves that Christ shall bring again that face, that form, with all the brightness we have ever seen in it, in all the fulness of its power, with all that dimmed it taken away. I say, such an exercise of hope may sometimes be very helpful and cheering, because it is not an exercise of fancy at all; it is an effort to remove the hindrances which our senses and fancy oppose to what in our hearts we confess as true. But I admit that the difficulty of such exercises will be great, and the profit comparatively little, if we do not join them with another; if we do not bid ourselves recollect that as the Son of man came not to be ministered unto, but to minister and to give His life a ransom for many, so all whom He has redeemed and renewed must cast away all selfish longings and ambitions, and must be occupied with that which is dearest to Him. Will that remembrance put them at a greater distance from us? Will it not bring them infinitely nearer to us? What was dearest to Him, but the recovery of this earth from its oppressors,—the assertion of it as His Father's possession? Because they have left the earth, have they ceased to care for it, seeing they are with Him who cares for it most, who has alone taught them to care for it? Whatever they cared for most, they must care for now, with a fuller sense of its worth, with an intenser zeal. Whatever sounds or sights they distinguished and delighted in, they must be able to perceive and interpret with a rarer and keener sense. Whatever evils they most mourned over, they must be seeking with a clearer intuition and deeper prayer to extirpate. And when God brings them with Him, it must be because the cry beneath the altar has been answered, and the long battle finished; because they can proclaim, in the completest sense of the words, that the kingdoms of this earth are indeed the kingdoms of our God and of His Christ, and that there is a new earth as well as a new heaven wherein dwelleth righteousness.

"Comfort one another," said St. Paul to his disciples at Thessalonica, "with these words." Strengthen one another to hard toils, to rough fights, with this assurance, that every toil has its issue, that Christ has overcome and has set down with His Father on His throne, and that He would have you overcome and sit with Him on His throne. But the one ground of comfort and strength are those words—"If we believe that Jesus died and rose again;" and they open a well of strength and comfort, deeper than there can be in any mere words. Christ's own death may be ours, we may feed upon it, and partake of it, and enter into it; Christ's own resurrection may be ours, we may confess it and aspire after it, if we have ever so little attained it. The feast that is provided for us at the altar is not for those who are rich and good, and have need of nothing. It is for the feeble, and the tempted, and the sinful. It is for those who feel they have no right to anything that is specially for them, but that they have need of a common Friend, of a universal Deliverer; of one who has stooped to all, that He might raise all to Himself. Let such draw nigh. Let them eat the Lord's Passover, the sure witness that He has delivered us from our enemy, that He has died and risen again. Let them eat it with their shoes on their feet and their staff in their hands, as pilgrims through a wilderness where there will be much drouth and lack of bread; as warriors who must suffer because they are to drive out enemies from a land that God has promised them. Let them eat it with the assurance that every one who has fallen asleep in Jesus is with them to partake of that which is the food of angels and of sinful men.

Let us ask that we may not by distrust of His free and full love cut ourselves off from communion with Him and with those whom He has taken to His rest, whom He will yet bring again to work for Him and with Him for ever.

THE END.

CHARLES DICKENS AND EVANS, CRYSTAL PALACE PRESS.

March 1892

A Catalogue

of

Theological Works

published by

Macmillan & Co.

Bedford Street, Strand, London

CONTENTS

	PAGE
THE BIBLE—	
History of the Bible	1
Biblical History	1
The Old Testament	1
The New Testament	3
HISTORY OF THE CHRISTIAN CHURCH	5
THE CHURCH OF ENGLAND	6
DEVOTIONAL BOOKS	7
THE FATHERS	8
HYMNOLOGY	9
SERMONS, LECTURES, ADDRESSES, AND THEOLOGICAL ESSAYS	9

March 1892.

MACMILLAN AND CO.'S THEOLOGICAL CATALOGUE

The Bible

HISTORY OF THE BIBLE

THE ENGLISH BIBLE: An External and Critical History of the various English Translations of Scripture. By Prof. JOHN EADIE. 2 vols. 8vo. 28s.

THE BIBLE IN THE CHURCH. By Right Rev. Bishop WESTCOTT. 10th Edition. 18mo. 4s. 6d.

BIBLICAL HISTORY

BIBLE LESSONS. By Rev. E. A. ABBOTT. Crown 8vo. 4s. 6d.

SIDE-LIGHTS ON BIBLE HISTORY. By Mrs. SYDNEY BUXTON. Illustrated. Crown 8vo. [*In the Press.*

STORIES FROM THE BIBLE. By Rev. A. J. CHURCH. Illustrated. Two Series. Crown 8vo. 3s. 6d. each.

BIBLE READINGS SELECTED FROM THE PENTATEUCH AND THE BOOK OF JOSHUA. By Rev. J. A. CROSS. 2nd Edition. Globe 8vo. 2s. 6d.

CHILDREN'S TREASURY OF BIBLE STORIES. By Mrs. H. GASKOIN. 18mo. 1s. each. Part I. Old Testament; II. New Testament; III. Three Apostles.

A CLASS-BOOK OF OLD TESTAMENT HISTORY. By Rev. Canon MACLEAR. With Four Maps. 18mo. 4s. 6d.

A CLASS-BOOK OF NEW TESTAMENT HISTORY. Including the connection of the Old and New Testament. By the same. 18mo. 5s. 6d.

A SHILLING BOOK OF OLD TESTAMENT HISTORY. By the same. 18mo. 1s.

A SHILLING BOOK OF NEW TESTAMENT HISTORY. By the same. 18mo. 1s.

THE OLD TESTAMENT

SCRIPTURE READINGS FOR SCHOOLS AND FAMILIES. By C. M. YONGE. Globe 8vo. 1s. 6d. each; also with comments, 3s. 6d. each.—First Series: GENESIS TO DEUTERONOMY.—Second Series: JOSHUA TO SOLOMON.—Third Series: KINGS AND THE PROPHETS.—Fourth Series: THE GOSPEL TIMES.—Fifth Series: APOSTOLIC TIMES.

The Old Testament—*continued.*

THE PATRIARCHS AND LAWGIVERS OF THE OLD TESTAMENT. By FREDERICK DENISON MAURICE. 7th Edition. Crown 8vo. 4s. 6d.

THE PROPHETS AND KINGS OF THE OLD TESTAMENT. By the same. 5th Edition. Crown 8vo. 6s.

THE CANON OF THE OLD TESTAMENT. An Essay on the Growth and Formation of the Hebrew Canon of Scripture. By Rev. Prof. H. E. RYLE. Crown 8vo. *[In the Press.*

The Pentateuch—

AN HISTORICO-CRITICAL INQUIRY INTO THE ORIGIN AND COMPOSITION OF THE HEXATEUCH (PENTATEUCH AND BOOK OF JOSHUA). By Prof. A. KUENEN. Translated by PHILIP H. WICKSTEED, M.A. 8vo. 14s.

The Psalms—

THE PSALMS CHRONOLOGICALLY ARRANGED. An Amended Version, with Historical Introductions and Explanatory Notes. By Four Friends. New Edition. Crown 8vo. 5s. net.

GOLDEN TREASURY PSALTER. The Student's Edition. Being an Edition with briefer Notes of "The Psalms Chronologically Arranged by Four Friends." 18mo. 3s. 6d.

THE PSALMS. With Introductions and Critical Notes. By A. C. JENNINGS, M.A., and W. H. LOWE, M.A. In 2 vols. 2nd Edition. Crown 8vo. 10s. 6d. each.

INTRODUCTION TO THE STUDY AND USE OF THE PSALMS. By Rev. J. F. THRUPP. 2nd Edition. 2 vols. 8vo. 21s.

Isaiah—

ISAIAH XL.—LXVI. With the Shorter Prophecies allied to it. By MATTHEW ARNOLD. With Notes. Crown 8vo. 5s.

ISAIAH OF JERUSALEM. In the Authorised English Version, with Introduction, Corrections, and Notes. By the same. Cr. 8vo. 4s. 6d.

A BIBLE-READING FOR SCHOOLS. The Great Prophecy of Israel's Restoration (Isaiah xl.-lxvi.) Arranged and Edited for Young Learners. By the same. 4th Edition. 18mo. 1s.

COMMENTARY ON THE BOOK OF ISAIAH, Critical, Historical, and Prophetical; including a Revised English Translation. By T. R. BIRKS. 2nd Edition. 8vo. 12s. 6d.

THE BOOK OF ISAIAH CHRONOLOGICALLY ARRANGED. By T. K. CHEYNE. Crown 8vo. 7s. 6d.

Zechariah—

THE HEBREW STUDENT'S COMMENTARY ON ZECHARIAH, Hebrew and LXX. By W. H. LOWE, M.A. 8vo. 10s. 6d.

THE NEW TESTAMENT

THE NEW TESTAMENT. Essay on the Right Estimation of MS. Evidence in the Text of the New Testament. By T. R. BIRKS. Crown 8vo. 3s. 6d.

THE MESSAGES OF THE BOOKS. Being Discourses and Notes on the Books of the New Testament. By Ven. Archdeacon FARRAR. 8vo. 14s.

THE CLASSICAL ELEMENT IN THE NEW TESTAMENT. Considered as a Proof of its Genuineness, with an Appendix on the Oldest Authorities used in the Formation of the Canon. By C. H. HOOLE. 8vo. 10s. 6d.

ON A FRESH REVISION OF THE ENGLISH NEW TESTAMENT. With an Appendix on the last Petition of the Lord's Prayer. By Bishop LIGHTFOOT. Crown 8vo. 7s. 6d.

THE UNITY OF THE NEW TESTAMENT. By F. D. MAURICE. 2nd Edition. 2 vols. Crown 8vo. 12s.

A COMPANION TO THE GREEK TESTAMENT AND THE ENGLISH VERSION. By PHILIP SCHAFF, D.D. Cr. 8vo. 12s.

A GENERAL SURVEY OF THE HISTORY OF THE CANON OF THE NEW TESTAMENT DURING THE FIRST FOUR CENTURIES. By Right Rev. Bishop WESTCOTT. 6th Edition. Crown 8vo. 10s. 6d.

THE NEW TESTAMENT IN THE ORIGINAL GREEK. The Text revised by Bishop WESTCOTT, D.D., and Prof. F. J. A. HORT, D.D. 2 vols. Crown 8vo. 10s. 6d. each.—Vol. I. Text ; II. Introduction and Appendix.

THE NEW TESTAMENT IN THE ORIGINAL GREEK, for Schools. The Text revised by Bishop WESTCOTT, D.D., and F. J. A. HORT, D.D. 12mo, cloth, 4s. 6d. ; 18mo, roan, red edges, 5s. 6d. ; morocco, gilt edges, 6s. 6d.

THE GOSPELS—

THE COMMON TRADITION OF THE SYNOPTIC GOSPELS, in the Text of the Revised Version. By Rev. E. A. ABBOTT and W. G. RUSHBROOKE. Crown 8vo. 3s. 6d.

SYNOPTICON: An Exposition of the Common Matter of the Synoptic Gospels. By W. G. RUSHBROOKE. Printed in Colours. In Six Parts, and Appendix. 4to.—Part I, 3s. 6d. Parts II and III, 7s. Parts IV, V, and VI, with Indices, 10s. 6d. Appendices, 10s. 6d. Complete in 1 vol., 35s. Indispensable to a Theological Student.

INTRODUCTION TO THE STUDY OF THE FOUR GOSPELS. By Right Rev. Bishop WESTCOTT. 7th Ed. Cr. 8vo. 10s. 6d.

THE COMPOSITION OF THE FOUR GOSPELS. By Rev. ARTHUR WRIGHT. Crown 8vo. 5s.

Gospel of St. Matthew—

THE GOSPEL ACCORDING TO ST. MATTHEW. Greek Text as Revised by Bishop WESTCOTT and Dr. HORT. With Introduction and Notes by Rev. A. SLOMAN, M.A. Fcap. 8vo. 2s. 6d.

CHOICE NOTES ON ST. MATTHEW, drawn from Old and New Sources. Crown 8vo. 4s. 6d. (St. Matthew and St. Mark in 1 vol. 9s.)

Gospel of St. Mark—
SCHOOL READINGS IN THE GREEK TESTAMENT. Being the Outlines of the Life of our Lord as given by St. Mark, with additions from the Text of the other Evangelists. Edited, with Notes and Vocabulary, by Rev. A. CALVERT, M.A. Fcap. 8vo. 2s. 6d.
CHOICE NOTES ON ST. MARK, drawn from Old and New Sources. Cr. 8vo. 4s. 6d. (St. Matthew and St. Mark in 1 vol. 9s.)

Gospel of St. Luke—
THE GOSPEL ACCORDING TO ST. LUKE. The Greek Text as Revised by Bishop WESTCOTT and Dr. HORT. With Introduction and Notes by Rev. J. BOND, M.A. Fcap. 8vo. 2s. 6d.
CHOICE NOTES ON ST. LUKE, drawn from Old and New Sources. Crown 8vo. 4s. 6d.
THE GOSPEL OF THE KINGDOM OF HEAVEN. A Course of Lectures on the Gospel of St. Luke. By F. D. MAURICE. 3rd Edition. Crown 8vo. 6s.

Gospel of St. John—
THE GOSPEL OF ST. JOHN. By F. D. MAURICE. 8th Ed. Cr. 8vo. 6s.
CHOICE NOTES ON ST. JOHN, drawn from Old and New Sources. Crown 8vo. 4s. 6d.

THE ACTS OF THE APOSTLES—
THE ACTS OF THE APOSTLES. Being the Greek Text as Revised by Bishop WESTCOTT and Dr. HORT. With Explanatory Notes by T. E. PAGE, M.A. Fcap. 8vo. 3s. 6d.
THE CHURCH OF THE FIRST DAYS. THE CHURCH OF JERUSALEM. THE CHURCH OF THE GENTILES. THE CHURCH OF THE WORLD. Lectures on the Acts of the Apostles. By Very Rev. C. J. VAUGHAN. Crown 8vo. 10s. 6d.

THE EPISTLES of St. Paul—
ST. PAUL'S EPISTLE TO THE ROMANS. The Greek Text, with English Notes. By Very Rev. C. J. VAUGHAN. 7th Edition. Crown 8vo. 7s. 6d.
A COMMENTARY ON ST. PAUL'S TWO EPISTLES TO THE CORINTHIANS. Greek Text, with Commentary. By Rev. W. KAY. 8vo. 9s.
ST. PAUL'S EPISTLE TO THE GALATIANS. A Revised Text, with Introduction, Notes, and Dissertations. By Bishop LIGHTFOOT. 10th Edition. 8vo. 12s.
ST. PAUL'S EPISTLE TO THE PHILIPPIANS. A Revised Text, with Introduction, Notes, and Dissertations. By the same. 9th Edition. 8vo. 12s.
ST. PAUL'S EPISTLE TO THE PHILIPPIANS. With translation, Paraphrase, and Notes for English Readers. By Very Rev. C. J. VAUGHAN. Crown 8vo. 5s.
ST. PAUL'S EPISTLES TO THE COLOSSIANS AND TO PHILEMON. A Revised Text, with Introductions, etc. By Bishop LIGHTFOOT. 9th Edition. 8vo. 12s.

Of St. Paul—*continued.*
  THE EPISTLES OF ST. PAUL TO THE EPHESIANS, THE COLOSSIANS, AND PHILEMON. With Introductions and Notes. By Rev. J. LL. DAVIES. 2nd Edition. 8vo. 7s. 6d.
  THE EPISTLES OF ST. PAUL. For English Readers. Part I, containing the First Epistle to the Thessalonians. By Very Rev. C. J. VAUGHAN. 2nd Edition. 8vo. Sewed. 1s. 6d.
  ST. PAUL'S EPISTLES TO THE THESSALONIANS, COMMENTARY ON THE GREEK TEXT. By Prof. JOHN EADIE. 8vo. 12s.

The Epistle of St. James—
  ST. JAMES' EPISTLE. The Greek Text, with Introduction and Notes. By Rev. JOSEPH MAYOR, M.A. 8vo. [*In the Press.*

The Epistles of St. John—
  THE EPISTLES OF ST. JOHN. By F. D. MAURICE. 4th Edition. Crown 8vo. 6s.
  THE EPISTLES OF ST. JOHN. The Greek Text, with Notes. By Right Rev. Bishop WESTCOTT. 2nd Edition. 8vo. 12s. 6d.

The Epistle to the Hebrews—
  THE EPISTLE TO THE HEBREWS IN GREEK AND ENGLISH. With Notes. By Rev. FREDERIC RENDALL. Crown 8vo. 6s.
  THE EPISTLE TO THE HEBREWS. English Text, with Commentary. By the same. Crown 8vo. 7s. 6d.
  THE EPISTLE TO THE HEBREWS. With Notes. By Very Rev. C. J. VAUGHAN. Crown 8vo. 7s. 6d.
  THE EPISTLE TO THE HEBREWS. The Greek Text, with Notes and Essays. By Right Rev. Bishop WESTCOTT. 8vo. 14s.

REVELATION—
  LECTURES ON THE APOCALYPSE. By F. D. MAURICE. 2nd Edition. Crown 8vo. 6s.
  THE REVELATION OF ST. JOHN. By Rev. Prof. W. MILLIGAN. 2nd Edition. Crown 8vo. 7s. 6d.
  LECTURES ON THE REVELATION OF ST. JOHN. By Very Rev. C. J. VAUGHAN. 5th Edition. Crown 8vo. 10s. 6d.

  THE BIBLE WORD-BOOK. By W. ALDIS WRIGHT. 2nd Edition. Crown 8vo. 7s. 6d.

Christian Church, History of the

Church (Dean).—THE OXFORD MOVEMENT. Twelve Years, 1833-45. Globe 8vo. 5s.
Cunningham (Rev. John).—THE GROWTH OF THE CHURCH IN ITS ORGANISATION AND INSTITUTIONS. 8vo. 9s.
Dale (A. W. W.)—THE SYNOD OF ELVIRA, AND CHRISTIAN LIFE IN THE FOURTH CENTURY. Cr. 8vo. 10s. 6d.

Hardwick (Archdeacon).—A HISTORY OF THE CHRISTIAN CHURCH. Middle Age. Ed. by Bishop STUBBS. Cr. 8vo. 10s. 6d.
A HISTORY OF THE CHRISTIAN CHURCH DURING THE REFORMATION. Revised by Bishop STUBBS. Cr. 8vo. 10s. 6d.

Hort (Dr. F. J. A.)—TWO DISSERTATIONS. I. On ΜΟΝΟΓΕΝΗΣ ΘΕΟΣ in Scripture and Tradition. II. On the "Constantinopolitan" Creed and other Eastern Creeds of the Fourth Century. 8vo. 7s. 6d.

Killen (W. D.)—ECCLESIASTICAL HISTORY OF IRELAND, FROM THE EARLIEST DATE TO THE PRESENT TIME. 2 vols. 8vo. 25s.

Simpson (W.)—AN EPITOME OF THE HISTORY OF THE CHRISTIAN CHURCH. Fcap. 8vo. 3s. 6d.

Vaughan (Very Rev. C. J., Dean of Llandaff).—THE CHURCH OF THE FIRST DAYS. THE CHURCH OF JERUSALEM. THE CHURCH OF THE GENTILES. THE CHURCH OF THE WORLD. Crown 8vo. 10s. 6d.

Ward (W.)—WILLIAM GEORGE WARD AND THE OXFORD MOVEMENT. Portrait. 8vo. 14s.

The Church of England

Catechism of—
A CLASS-BOOK OF THE CATECHISM OF THE CHURCH OF ENGLAND. By Rev. Canon MACLEAR. 18mo. 1s. 6d.
A FIRST CLASS-BOOK OF THE CATECHISM OF THE CHURCH OF ENGLAND, with Scripture Proofs for Junior Classes and Schools. By the same. 18mo. 6d.
THE ORDER OF CONFIRMATION, with Prayers and Devotions. By the Rev. Canon MACLEAR. 32mo. 6d.

Collects—
COLLECTS OF THE CHURCH OF ENGLAND. With a Coloured Floral Design to each Collect. Crown 8vo. 12s.

Disestablishment—
DISESTABLISHMENT AND DISENDOWMENT. What are they? By Prof. E. A. FREEMAN. 4th Edition. Crown 8vo. 1s.
DISESTABLISHMENT: or, A Defence of the Principle of a National Church. By GEORGE HARWOOD. 8vo. 12s.
A DEFENCE OF THE CHURCH OF ENGLAND AGAINST DISESTABLISHMENT. By ROUNDELL, EARL OF SELBORNE. Crown 8vo. 2s. 6d.
ANCIENT FACTS & FICTIONS CONCERNING CHURCHES AND TITHES. By the same. 2nd Edition. Crown 8vo. 7s. 6d.

Dissent in its Relation to—
DISSENT IN ITS RELATION TO THE CHURCH OF ENGLAND. By Rev. G. H. CURTEIS. Bampton Lectures for 1871. Crown 8vo. 7s. 6d.

Holy Communion—
THE COMMUNION SERVICE FROM THE BOOK OF COMMON PRAYER, with Select Readings from the Writings of the Rev. F. D. MAURICE. Edited by Bishop COLENSO. 6th Edition. 16mo. 2s. 6d.

BEFORE THE TABLE: An Inquiry, Historical and Theological, into the Meaning of the Consecration Rubric in the Communion Service of the Church of England. By Very Rev. J. S. HOWSON. 8vo. 7s. 6d.

FIRST COMMUNION, with Prayers and Devotions for the newly Confirmed. By Rev. Canon MACLEAR. 32mo. 6d.

A MANUAL OF INSTRUCTION FOR CONFIRMATION AND FIRST COMMUNION, with Prayers and Devotions. By the same. 32mo. 2s.

Liturgy—
A COMPANION TO THE LECTIONARY. By Rev. W. BENHAM, B.D. Crown 8vo. 4s. 6d.

AN INTRODUCTION TO THE CREEDS. By Rev. Canon MACLEAR. 18mo. 3s. 6d.

AN INTRODUCTION TO THE THIRTY-NINE ARTICLES. By the same. 18mo. [*In the Press.*

A HISTORY OF THE BOOK OF COMMON PRAYER. By Rev. F. PROCTER. 18th Edition. Crown 8vo. 10s. 6d.

AN ELEMENTARY INTRODUCTION TO THE BOOK OF COMMON PRAYER. By Rev. F. PROCTER and Rev. Canon MACLEAR. 18mo. 2s. 6d.

TWELVE DISCOURSES ON SUBJECTS CONNECTED WITH THE LITURGY AND WORSHIP OF THE CHURCH OF ENGLAND. By Very Rev. C. J. VAUGHAN. 4th Edition. Fcap. 8vo. 6s.

Devotional Books.

Brooke (S. A.)—FORM OF MORNING AND EVENING PRAYER, and for the Administration of the Lord's Supper, together with the Baptismal and Marriage Services, Bedford Chapel, Bloomsbury. Fcap. 8vo. 1s. net.

Eastlake (Lady).—FELLOWSHIP: LETTERS ADDRESSED TO MY SISTER-MOURNERS. Crown 8vo. 2s. 6d.

IMITATIO CHRISTI, LIBRI IV. Printed in Borders after Holbein, Dürer, and other old Masters, containing Dances of Death, Acts of Mercy, Emblems, etc. Crown 8vo. 7s. 6d.

Kingsley (Charles).—OUT OF THE DEEP: WORDS FOR THE SORROWFUL. From the writings of CHARLES KINGSLEY. Extra fcap. 8vo. 3s. 6d.

DAILY THOUGHTS. Selected from the Writings of CHARLES KINGSLEY. By his Wife. Crown 8vo. 6s.

FROM DEATH TO LIFE. Fragments of Teaching to a Village Congregation. With Letters on the "Life after Death." Edited by his Wife. Fcap. 8vo. 2s. 6d.

Maclear (Rev. Canon).—A MANUAL OF INSTRUCTION FOR CONFIRMATION AND FIRST COMMUNION, WITH PRAYERS AND DEVOTIONS. 32mo. 2s.

THE HOUR OF SORROW; OR, THE OFFICE FOR THE BURIAL OF THE DEAD. 32mo. 2s.

Maurice (Frederick Denison).—LESSONS OF HOPE. Readings from the Works of F. D. MAURICE. Selected by Rev. J. LL. DAVIES, M.A. Crown 8vo. 5s.

RAYS OF SUNLIGHT FOR DARK DAYS. With a Preface by Very Rev. C. J. VAUGHAN, D.D. New Edition. 18mo. 3s. 6d.

Service (Rev. John).—PRAYERS FOR PUBLIC WORSHIP. Crown 8vo. 4s. 6d.

THE WORSHIP OF GOD, AND FELLOWSHIP AMONG MEN. By FREDERICK DENISON MAURICE and others. Fcap. 8vo. 3s. 6d.

Welby-Gregory (The Hon. Lady).—LINKS AND CLUES. 2nd Edition. Crown 8vo. 6s.

Westcott (Rt. Rev. B. F., Bishop of Durham).—THOUGHTS ON REVELATION AND LIFE. Selections from the Writings of Bishop WESTCOTT. Edited by Rev. S. PHILLIPS. Crown 8vo. 6s.

Wilbraham (Frances M.)—IN THE SERE AND YELLOW LEAF: THOUGHTS AND RECOLLECTIONS FOR OLD AND YOUNG. Globe 8vo. 3s. 6d.

The Fathers

Cunningham (Rev. W.)—THE EPISTLE OF ST. BARNABAS. A Dissertation, including a Discussion of its Date and Authorship. Together with the Greek Text, the Latin Version, and a New English Translation and Commentary. Crown 8vo. 7s. 6d.

Donaldson (Prof. James).—THE APOSTOLICAL FATHERS. A Critical Account of their Genuine Writings, and of their Doctrines. 2nd Edition. Crown 8vo. 7s. 6d.

Lightfoot (Bishop).—THE APOSTOLIC FATHERS. Part I. ST. CLEMENT OF ROME. Revised Texts, with Introductions, Notes, Dissertations, and Translations. 2 vols. 8vo. 32s.

THE APOSTOLIC FATHERS. Part II. ST. IGNATIUS to ST. POLYCARP. Revised Texts, with Introductions, Notes, Dissertations, and Translations. 3 vols. 2nd Edition. Demy 8vo. 48s.

THE APOSTOLIC FATHERS. Abridged Edition. With Short Introductions, Greek Text, and English Translation. 8vo. 16s.

Hymnology

Brooke (S. A.)—CHRISTIAN HYMNS. Edited and arranged. Fcap. 8vo. 2s. net.
This may also be had bound up with the Form of Service at Bedford Chapel, Bloomsbury. Price complete, 3s. net.

Palgrave (Prof. F. T.)—ORIGINAL HYMNS. 18mo. 1s. 6d.

Selborne (Roundell, Earl of)—
THE BOOK OF PRAISE. From the best English Hymn Writers. 18mo. 2s. 6d. net.
A HYMNAL. Chiefly from *The Book of Praise*. In various sizes.—A. Royal 32mo. 6d.—B. Small 18mo, larger type. 1s.—C. Same Edition, fine paper. 1s. 6d.—An Edition with Music, Selected, Harmonised, and Composed by JOHN HULLAH. Square 18mo. 3s. 6d.

Woods (M. A.)— HYMNS FOR SCHOOL WORSHIP. Compiled by M. A. WOODS. 18mo. 1s. 6d.

Sermons, Lectures, Addresses, and Theological Essays

(*See also* 'Bible,' 'Church of England,' 'Fathers.')

Abbot (Francis)—
SCIENTIFIC THEISM. Crown 8vo. 7s. 6d.
THE WAY OUT OF AGNOSTICISM: or, The Philosophy of Free Religion. Crown 8vo. 4s. 6d.

Abbott (Rev. E. A.)—
CAMBRIDGE SERMONS. 8vo. 6s.
OXFORD SERMONS. 8vo. 7s. 6d.
PHILOMYTHUS. An Antidote against Credulity. A discussion of Cardinal Newman's Essay on Ecclesiastical Miracles. 2nd Edition. Crown 8vo. 3s. 6d.
NEWMANIANISM. A Reply. Crown 8vo. Sewed, 1s. net.

Ainger (Rev. Alfred, Canon of Bristol).—SERMONS PREACHED IN THE TEMPLE CHURCH. Extra fcap. 8vo. 6s.

Alexander (W., Bishop of Derry and Raphoe).—THE LEADING IDEAS OF THE GOSPELS. New Edition, Revised and Enlarged. Crown 8vo. 6s.

Baines (Rev. Edward).—SERMONS. With a Preface and Memoir, by A. BARRY, D.D., late Bishop of Sydney. Crown 8vo. 6s.

Barry (A.)—FIRST WORDS IN AUSTRALIA: Sermons. Crown 8vo. 5s.

Bather (Archdeacon).—ON SOME MINISTERIAL DUTIES, CATECHISING, PREACHING, ETC. Edited, with a Preface, by Very Rev. C. J. VAUGHAN, D.D. Fcap. 8vo. 4s. 6d.

Bernard (Canon T. D.)—THE CENTRAL TEACHING OF CHRIST. Being a Study and Exposition of St. John, Chapters XIII. to XVII. inclusive. Crown 8vo. [*In the Press.*

Binnie (Rev. William).—SERMONS. Crown 8vo. 6s.

Birks (Thomas Rawson)—
 THE DIFFICULTIES OF BELIEF IN CONNECTION WITH THE CREATION AND THE FALL, REDEMPTION, AND JUDGMENT. 2nd Edition. Crown 8vo. 5s.
 JUSTIFICATION AND IMPUTED RIGHTEOUSNESS. Being a Review of Ten Sermons on the Nature and Effects of Faith, by JAMES THOMAS O'BRIEN, D.D., late Bishop of Ossory, Ferns, and Leighlin. Crown 8vo. 6s.
 SUPERNATURAL REVELATION : or, First Principles of Moral Theology. 8vo. 8s.

Brooke (Rev. Stopford A.)—SHORT SERMONS. Cr. 8vo. 6s.

Brooks (Phillips, Bishop of Massachusetts)—
 THE CANDLE OF THE LORD, and other Sermons. Crown 8vo. 6s.
 SERMONS PREACHED IN ENGLISH CHURCHES. Crown 8vo. 6s.
 TWENTY SERMONS. Crown 8vo. 6s.
 TOLERANCE. Crown 8vo. 2s. 6d.
 THE LIGHT OF THE WORLD. Crown 8vo. 3s. 6d.

Brunton (T. Lauder).—THE BIBLE AND SCIENCE. With Illustrations. Crown 8vo. 10s. 6d.

Butler (Rev. George).—SERMONS PREACHED IN CHELTENHAM COLLEGE CHAPEL. 8vo. 7s. 6d.

Butler (W. Archer)—
 SERMONS, DOCTRINAL AND PRACTICAL. 11th Edition. 8vo. 8s.
 SECOND SERIES OF SERMONS. 8vo. 7s.

Calderwood (Rev. Prof.)—
 THE RELATIONS OF SCIENCE AND RELIGION. Crown 8vo. 5s.
 THE PARABLES OF OUR LORD. Crown 8vo. 6s.

Campbell (Dr. John M'Leod)—
 THE NATURE OF THE ATONEMENT. 6th Ed. Cr. 8vo. 6s.
 REMINISCENCES AND REFLECTIONS. Edited with an Introductory Narrative, by his Son, DONALD CAMPBELL, M.A. Crown 8vo. 7s. 6d.
 THOUGHTS ON REVELATION. 2nd Edition. Crown 8vo. 5s.
 RESPONSIBILITY FOR THE GIFT OF ETERNAL LIFE. Compiled from Sermons preached at Row, in the years 1829-31. Crown 8vo. 5s.

Canterbury (Edward White, Archbishop of)—
    BOY-LIFE: its Trial, its Strength, its Fulness. Sundays in Wellington College, 1859-73. 4th Edition. Crown 8vo. 6s.
    THE SEVEN GIFTS. Addressed to the Diocese of Canterbury in his Primary Visitation. 2nd Edition. Crown 8vo. 6s.
    CHRIST AND HIS TIMES. Addressed to the Diocese of Canterbury in his Second Visitation. Crown 8vo. 6s.
    A PASTORAL LETTER TO THE DIOCESE OF CANTERBURY. Written at the request of the Archdeacons and Rural Deans. Dec. 1890. 8vo, sewed. 1d.

Carpenter (W. Boyd, Bishop of Ripon)—
    TRUTH IN TALE. Addresses, chiefly to Children. Crown 8vo. 4s. 6d.
    THE PERMANENT ELEMENTS OF RELIGION: Bampton Lectures, 1887. 2nd Edition. Crown 8vo. 6s.

Cazenove (J. Gibson).—CONCERNING THE BEING AND ATTRIBUTES OF GOD. 8vo. 5s.

Church (Dean)—
    THE OXFORD MOVEMENT. Twelve Years, 1833-45. Globe 8vo. 5s.
    HUMAN LIFE AND ITS CONDITIONS. Crown 8vo. 6s.
    THE GIFTS OF CIVILISATION, and other Sermons and Lectures. 2nd Edition. Crown 8vo. 7s. 6d.
    DISCIPLINE OF THE CHRISTIAN CHARACTER, and other Sermons. Crown 8vo. 4s. 6d.
    ADVENT SERMONS. 1885. Crown 8vo. 4s. 6d.
    VILLAGE SERMONS. Crown 8vo. 6s.
    CLERGYMAN'S SELF-EXAMINATION CONCERNING THE APOSTLES' CREED. Extra fcap. 8vo. 1s. 6d.

Congreve (Rev. John).—HIGH HOPES AND PLEADINGS FOR A REASONABLE FAITH, NOBLER THOUGHTS, LARGER CHARITY. Crown 8vo. 5s.

Cooke (Josiah P., Jun.)—RELIGION AND CHEMISTRY. Crown 8vo. 7s. 6d.

Cotton (Bishop).—SERMONS PREACHED TO ENGLISH CONGREGATIONS IN INDIA. Crown 8vo. 7s. 6d.

Cunningham (Rev. W.)—CHRISTIAN CIVILISATION, WITH SPECIAL REFERENCE TO INDIA. Cr. 8vo. 5s.

Curteis (Rev. G. H.)—THE SCIENTIFIC OBSTACLES TO CHRISTIAN BELIEF. The Boyle Lectures, 1884. Cr. 8vo. 6s.

Davies (Rev. J. Llewelyn)—
    THE GOSPEL AND MODERN LIFE. 2nd Edition, to which is added Morality according to the Sacrament of the Lord's Supper. Extra fcap. 8vo. 6s.
    SOCIAL QUESTIONS FROM THE POINT OF VIEW OF CHRISTIAN THEOLOGY. 2nd Edition. Crown 8vo. 6s.

Davies (Rev. J. Llewelyn)—*continued.*
    WARNINGS AGAINST SUPERSTITION. Extra fcap. 8vo. 2s. 6d.
    THE CHRISTIAN CALLING. Extra fcap. 8vo. 6s.
    ORDER AND GROWTH AS INVOLVED IN THE SPIRITUAL CONSTITUTION OF HUMAN SOCIETY. Crown 8vo. 3s. 6d.
    BAPTISM, CONFIRMATION, AND THE LORD'S SUPPER, as interpreted by their Outward Signs. Three Addresses. New Edition. 18mo. 1s.

Diggle (Rev. J. W.)—GODLINESS AND MANLINESS. A Miscellany of Brief Papers touching the Relation of Religion to Life. Crown 8vo. 6s.

Drummond (Prof. James).—INTRODUCTION TO THE STUDY OF THEOLOGY. Crown 8vo. 5s.

ECCE HOMO. A Survey of the Life and Work of Jesus Christ. 20th Edition. Globe 8vo. 6s.

Ellerton (Rev. John).—THE HOLIEST MANHOOD, AND ITS LESSONS FOR BUSY LIVES. Crown 8vo. 6s.

FAITH AND CONDUCT: An Essay on Verifiable Religion. Crown 8vo. 7s. 6d.

Farrar (Ven. F. W., Archdeacon of Westminster)—
    MERCY AND JUDGMENT. A few last words on Christian Eschatology. 2nd Edition. Crown 8vo. 10s. 6d.
    THE SILENCE AND VOICES OF GOD. University and other Sermons. 7th Edition. Crown 8vo. 6s.
    IN THE DAYS OF THY YOUTH. Sermons on Practical Subjects, preached at Marlborough College. 9th Edition. Crown 8vo. 9s.
    EPHPHATHA: or, The Amelioration of the World. Sermons preached at Westminster Abbey. Crown 8vo. 6s.
    SERMONS AND ADDRESSES delivered in America. Crown 8vo. 7s. 6d.
    THE WITNESS OF HISTORY TO CHRIST. Being the Hulsean Lectures for 1870. 7th Edition. Crown 8vo. 5s.
    SAINTLY WORKERS. Five Lenten Lectures. 3rd Edition. Crown 8vo. 6s.
    THE HISTORY OF INTERPRETATION. Being the Bampton Lectures, 1885. 8vo. 16s.

    New and Collected Edition of the Sermons, etc. Crown 8vo. 3s. 6d. each. Monthly volumes from *December* 1891.
SEEKERS AFTER GOD.
ETERNAL HOPE. Sermons Preached in Westminster Abbey.
THE FALL OF MAN, and other Sermons.
THE WITNESS OF HISTORY TO CHRIST. Hulsean Lectures.
THE SILENCE AND VOICES OF GOD.
IN THE DAYS OF THY YOUTH. Sermons on Practical Subjects.
SAINTLY WORKERS. Five Lenten Lectures.
EPHPHATHA: or, The Amelioration of the World.

Farrar (Ven. F. W., Archdeacon of Westminster).—*continued.*
  MERCY AND JUDGMENT. A few last words on Christian Eschatology.
  SERMONS AND ADDRESSES delivered in America.
Fiske (John).—MAN'S DESTINY VIEWED IN THE LIGHT OF HIS ORIGIN. Crown 8vo. 3s. 6d.
Forbes (Rev. Granville).—THE VOICE OF GOD IN THE PSALMS. Crown 8vo. 6s. 6d.
Fowle (Rev. T. W.)—A NEW ANALOGY BETWEEN REVEALED RELIGION AND THE COURSE AND CONSTITUTION OF NATURE. Crown 8vo. 6s.
Fraser (Bishop).—SERMONS. Edited by Rev. JOHN W. DIGGLE. 2 vols. Crown 8vo. 6s. each.
Hamilton (John)—
  ON TRUTH AND ERROR. Crown 8vo. 5s.
  ARTHUR'S SEAT: or, The Church of the Banned. Crown 8vo. 6s.
  ABOVE AND AROUND: Thoughts on God and Man. 12mo. 2s. 6d.
Hardwick (Archdeacon).—CHRIST AND OTHER MASTERS. 6th Edition. Crown 8vo. 10s. 6d.
Hare (Julius Charles)—
  THE MISSION OF THE COMFORTER. New Edition. Edited by Dean PLUMPTRE. Crown 8vo. 7s. 6d.
  THE VICTORY OF FAITH. Edited by Dean PLUMPTRE, with Introductory Notices by Prof. MAURICE and Dean STANLEY. Crown 8vo. 6s. 6d.
Harper (Father Thomas, S.J.)—THE METAPHYSICS OF THE SCHOOL. In 5 vols. Vols. I. and II. 8vo. 18s. each. Vol. III. Part I. 12s.
Harris (Rev. G. C.)—SERMONS. With a Memoir by CHARLOTTE M. YONGE, and Portrait. Extra fcap. 8vo. 6s.
Hutton (R. H.)—
  ESSAYS ON SOME OF THE MODERN GUIDES OF ENGLISH THOUGHT IN MATTERS OF FAITH. Globe 8vo. 6s.
  THEOLOGICAL ESSAYS. Globe 8vo. 6s.
Illingworth (Rev. J. R.)—SERMONS PREACHED IN A COLLEGE CHAPEL. Crown 8vo. 5s.
Jacob (Rev. J. A.)—BUILDING IN SILENCE, and other Sermons. Extra fcap. 8vo. 6s.
James (Rev. Herbert).—THE COUNTRY CLERGYMAN AND HIS WORK. Crown 8vo. 6s.
Jeans (Rev. G. E.)—HAILEYBURY CHAPEL, and other Sermons. Fcap. 8vo. 3s. 6d.
Jellett (Rev. Dr.)—
  THE ELDER SON, and other Sermons. Crown 8vo. 6s.
  THE EFFICACY OF PRAYER. 3rd Edition. Crown 8vo. 5s.

Kellogg (Rev. S. H.)—THE LIGHT OF ASIA AND THE LIGHT OF THE WORLD. Crown 8vo. 7s. 6d.

Kingsley (Charles)—
VILLAGE AND TOWN AND COUNTRY SERMONS. Crown 8vo. 3s. 6d.
THE WATER OF LIFE, and other Sermons. Crown 8vo. 3s. 6d.
SERMONS ON NATIONAL SUBJECTS, AND THE KING OF THE EARTH. Crown 8vo. 3s. 6d.
SERMONS FOR THE TIMES. Crown 8vo. 3s. 6d.
GOOD NEWS OF GOD. Crown 8vo. 3s. 6d.
THE GOSPEL OF THE PENTATEUCH, AND DAVID. Crown 8vo. 3s. 6d.
DISCIPLINE, and other Sermons. Crown 8vo. 3s. 6d.
WESTMINSTER SERMONS. Crown 8vo. 3s. 6d.
ALL SAINTS' DAY, and other Sermons. Crown 8vo. 3s. 6d.

Kirkpatrick (Prof. A. F.)—THE DIVINE LIBRARY OF THE OLD TESTAMENT. Its Origin, Preservation, Inspiration, and Permanent Value. Crown 8vo. 3s. net.

Kynaston (Rev. Herbert, D.D.)—SERMONS PREACHED IN THE COLLEGE CHAPEL, CHELTENHAM. Crown 8vo. 6s.

Lightfoot (Bishop)—
LEADERS IN THE NORTHERN CHURCH: Sermons Preached in the Diocese of Durham. 2nd Edition. Crown 8vo. 6s.
ORDINATION ADDRESSES AND COUNSELS TO CLERGY. Crown 8vo. 6s.
CAMBRIDGE SERMONS. Crown 8vo. 6s.
SERMONS PREACHED IN ST. PAUL'S CATHEDRAL. Crown 8vo. 6s.
SERMONS PREACHED ON SPECIAL OCCASIONS. Crown 8vo. 6s.
A CHARGE DELIVERED TO THE CLERGY OF THE DIOCESE OF DURHAM, 25th Nov. 1886. Demy 8vo. 2s.
ESSAYS ON THE WORK ENTITLED "Supernatural Religion." 8vo. 10s. 6d.
ESSAYS. In Two Vols. (1) Dissertations on the Apostolic Age. (2) Miscellaneous. 8vo. [*In the Press.*

Maclaren (Rev. Alexander)—
SERMONS PREACHED AT MANCHESTER. 11th Edition. Fcap. 8vo. 4s. 6d.
A SECOND SERIES OF SERMONS. 7th Ed. Fcap. 8vo. 4s. 6d.
A THIRD SERIES. 6th Edition. Fcap. 8vo. 4s. 6d.
WEEK-DAY EVENING ADDRESSES. 4th Ed. Fcap. 8vo. 2s. 6d.
THE SECRET OF POWER, AND OTHER SERMONS. Fcap. 8vo. 4s. 6d.

Macmillan (Rev. Hugh)—
BIBLE TEACHINGS IN NATURE. 15th Ed. Globe 8vo. 6s.
THE TRUE VINE; OR, THE ANALOGIES OF OUR LORD'S ALLEGORY. 5th Edition. Globe 8vo. 6s.
THE MINISTRY OF NATURE. 8th Edition. Globe 8vo. 6s.

Macmillan (Rev. Hugh)—*continued.*
    THE SABBATH OF THE FIELDS. 6th Edition. Globe 8vo. 6s.
    THE MARRIAGE IN CANA. Globe 8vo. 6s.
    TWO WORLDS ARE OURS. 3rd Edition. Globe 8vo. 6s.
    THE OLIVE LEAF. Globe 8vo. 6s.
    THE GATE BEAUTIFUL AND OTHER BIBLE TEACHINGS FOR THE YOUNG. Crown 8vo. 3s. 6d.

Mahaffy (Rev. Prof.)—THE DECAY OF MODERN PREACHING: AN ESSAY. Crown 8vo. 3s. 6d.

Maturin (Rev. W.)—THE BLESSEDNESS OF THE DEAD IN CHRIST. Crown 8vo. 7s. 6d.

Maurice (Frederick Denison)—
    THE KINGDOM OF CHRIST. 3rd. Ed. 2 Vols. Cr. 8vo. 12s.
    EXPOSITORY SERMONS ON THE PRAYER-BOOK; AND ON THE LORD'S PRAYER. New Edition. Crown 8vo. 6s.
    SERMONS PREACHED IN COUNTRY CHURCHES. 2nd Edition. Crown 8vo. 6s.
    THE CONSCIENCE. Lectures on Casuistry. 3rd Ed. Cr. 8vo. 4s. 6d.
    DIALOGUES ON FAMILY WORSHIP. Crown 8vo. 4s. 6d.
    THE DOCTRINE OF SACRIFICE DEDUCED FROM THE SCRIPTURES. 2nd Edition. Crown 8vo. 6s.
    THE RELIGIONS OF THE WORLD. 6th Edition. Cr. 8vo. 4s. 6d.
    ON THE SABBATH DAY; THE CHARACTER OF THE WARRIOR; AND ON THE INTERPRETATION OF HISTORY. Fcap. 8vo. 2s. 6d.
    LEARNING AND WORKING. Crown 8vo. 4s. 6d.
    THE LORD'S PRAYER, THE CREED, AND THE COMMANDMENTS. 18mo. 1s.
    THEOLOGICAL ESSAYS. 4th Edition. Crown 8vo. 6s.
    SERMONS PREACHED IN LINCOLN'S INN CHAPEL. In Six Volumes. Crown 8vo. 3s. 6d. each. Monthly from October 1891.

Milligan (Rev. Prof. W.)—THE RESURRECTION OF OUR LORD. Fourth Thousand. Crown 8vo. 5s.
    THE ASCENSION AND HEAVENLY PRIESTHOOD OF OUR LORD. *Baird Lectures*, 1891. Crown 8vo. 7s. 6d.
    LECTURES ON THE APOCALYPSE. Cr. 8vo. 5s.

Moorhouse (J., Bishop of Manchester)—
    JACOB: Three Sermons. Extra fcap. 8vo. 3s. 6d.
    THE TEACHING OF CHRIST. Its Conditions, Secret, and Results. Crown 8vo. 3s. net.

Mylne (L. G., Bishop of Bombay).—SERMONS PREACHED IN ST. THOMAS'S CATHEDRAL, BOMBAY. Crown 8vo. 6s.
NATURAL RELIGION. By the author of "Ecce Homo." 3rd Edition. Globe 8vo. 6s.

Pattison (Mark).—SERMONS. Crown 8vo. 6s.
PAUL OF TARSUS. 8vo. 10s. 6d.
PHILOCHRISTUS. Memoirs of a Disciple of the Lord. 3rd Ed. 8vo. 12s.

Plumptre (Dean). — MOVEMENTS IN RELIGIOUS THOUGHT. Fcap. 8vo. 3s. 6d.

Potter (R.)—THE RELATION OF ETHICS TO RELIGION. Crown 8vo. 2s. 6d.

REASONABLE FAITH: A Short Religious Essay for the Times. By "Three Friends." Crown 8vo. 1s.

Reichel (C. P., Bishop of Meath)—
 THE LORD'S PRAYER, and other Sermons. Crown 8vo. 7s. 6d.
 CATHEDRAL AND UNIVERSITY SERMONS. Crown 8vo. 6s.

Rendall (Rev. F.)—THE THEOLOGY OF THE HEBREW CHRISTIANS. Crown 8vo. 5s.

Reynolds (H. R.)—NOTES OF THE CHRISTIAN LIFE. Crown 8vo. 7s. 6d.

Robinson (Prebendary H. G.)—MAN IN THE IMAGE OF GOD, and other Sermons. Crown 8vo. 7s. 6d.

Russell (Dean).—THE LIGHT THAT LIGHTETH EVERY MAN: Sermons. With an introduction by Dean PLUMPTRE, D.D. Crown 8vo. 6s.

Salmon (Rev. Prof. George)—
 NON-MIRACULOUS CHRISTIANITY, and other Sermons. 2nd Edition. Crown 8vo. 6s.
 GNOSTICISM AND AGNOSTICISM, and other Sermons. Crown 8vo. 7s. 6d.

SCOTCH SERMONS, 1880. By Principal CAIRD and others. 3rd Edition. 8vo. 10s. 6d.

Service (Rev. John).—SERMONS. With Portrait. Crown 8vo. 6s.

Shirley (W. N.)—ELIJAH: Four University Sermons. Fcap. 8vo. 2s. 6d.

Smith (Rev. Travers).—MAN'S KNOWLEDGE OF MAN AND OF GOD. Crown 8vo. 6s.

Smith (W. Saumarez).—THE BLOOD OF THE NEW COVENANT: A Theological Essay. Crown 8vo. 2s. 6d.

Stanley (Dean)—
 THE NATIONAL THANKSGIVING. Sermons preached in Westminster Abbey. 2nd Edition. Crown 8vo. 2s. 6d.
 ADDRESSES AND SERMONS delivered during a visit to the United States and Canada in 1878. Crown 8vo. 6s.
 THE ATHANASIAN CREED. Crown 8vo. 2s.

Stewart (Prof. Balfour) and **Tait** (Prof. P. G.)—THE UNSEEN UNIVERSE; OR, PHYSICAL SPECULATIONS ON A FUTURE STATE. 15th Edition. Crown 8vo. 6s.
 PARADOXICAL PHILOSOPHY: A Sequel to "The Unseen Universe." Crown 8vo. 7s. 6d.

Stubbs (Rev. C. W.)—FOR CHRIST AND CITY. Sermons and Addresses. Crown 8vo. 6s.

Tait (Archbishop)—
  THE PRESENT POSITION OF THE CHURCH OF ENGLAND. Being the Charge delivered at his Primary Visitation. 8vo. 3s. 6d.
  DUTIES OF THE CHURCH OF ENGLAND. Being seven Addresses delivered at his Second Visitation. 8vo. 4s. 6d.
  THE CHURCH OF THE FUTURE. Charges delivered at his Third Quadrennial Visitation. 2nd Edition. Crown 8vo. 3s. 6d.

Taylor (Isaac).—THE RESTORATION OF BELIEF. Crown 8vo. 8s. 6d.

Temple (Frederick, Bishop of London)—
  SERMONS PREACHED IN THE CHAPEL OF RUGBY SCHOOL. 3rd and Cheaper Edition. Extra fcap. 8vo. 4s. 6d.
  SECOND SERIES. 3rd Edition. Extra fcap. 8vo. 6s.
  THIRD SERIES. 4th Edition. Extra fcap. 8vo. 6s.
  THE RELATIONS BETWEEN RELIGION AND SCIENCE. Bampton Lectures, 1884. 7th and Cheaper Ed. Cr. 8vo. 6s.

Trench (Archbishop).—HULSEAN LECTURES. 8vo. 7s. 6d.

Tulloch (Principal).—THE CHRIST OF THE GOSPELS AND THE CHRIST OF MODERN CRITICISM. Extra fcap. 8vo. 4s. 6d.

Vaughan (C. J., Dean of Llandaff)—
  MEMORIALS OF HARROW SUNDAYS. 5th Edition. Crown 8vo. 10s. 6d.
  EPIPHANY, LENT, AND EASTER. 3rd Ed. Cr. 8vo. 10s. 6d.
  HEROES OF FAITH. 2nd Edition. Crown 8vo. 6s.
  LIFE'S WORK AND GOD'S DISCIPLINE. 3rd Edition. Extra fcap. 8vo. 2s. 6d.
  THE WHOLESOME WORDS OF JESUS CHRIST. 2nd Edition. Fcap. 8vo. 3s. 6d.
  FOES OF FAITH. 2nd Edition. Fcap. 8vo. 3s. 6d.
  CHRIST SATISFYING THE INSTINCTS OF HUMANITY. 2nd Edition. Extra fcap. 8vo. 3s. 6d.
  COUNSELS FOR YOUNG STUDENTS. Fcap. 8vo. 2s. 6d.
  THE TWO GREAT TEMPTATIONS. 2nd Ed. Fcap. 8vo. 3s. 6d.
  ADDRESSES FOR YOUNG CLERGYMEN. Extra fcap. 8vo. 4s. 6d.
  "MY SON, GIVE ME THINE HEART." Extra fcap. 8vo. 5s.
  REST AWHILE. Addresses to Toilers in the Ministry. Extra fcap. 8vo. 5s.
  TEMPLE SERMONS. Crown 8vo. 10s. 6d.
  AUTHORISED OR REVISED? Sermons on some of the Texts in which the Revised Version differs from the Authorised. Crown 8vo. 7s. 6d.
  LESSONS OF THE CROSS AND PASSION. WORDS FROM THE CROSS. THE REIGN OF SIN. THE LORD'S PRAYER. Four Courses of Lent Lectures. Crown 8vo. 10s. 6d.

Vaughan (C. J., Dean of Llandaff)—*continued.*
UNIVERSITY SERMONS. NEW AND OLD. Cr. 8vo. 10s. 6d.
NOTES FOR LECTURES ON CONFIRMATION. Fcap. 8vo. 1s. 6d.
THE PRAYERS OF JESUS CHRIST: a closing volume of Lent Lectures delivered in the Temple Church. Globe 8vo. 3s. 6d.
DONCASTER SERMONS. Lessons of Life and Godliness, and Words from the Gospels. Cr. 8vo. 10s. 6d.

Vaughan (Rev. D. J.)—THE PRESENT TRIAL OF FAITH. Crown 8vo. 9s.

Vaughan (Rev. E. T.)—SOME REASONS OF OUR CHRISTIAN HOPE. Hulsean Lectures for 1875. Crown 8vo. 6s. 6d.

Vaughan (Rev. Robert).—STONES FROM THE QUARRY. Sermons. Crown 8vo. 5s.

Venn (Rev. John).—ON SOME CHARACTERISTICS OF BELIEF, SCIENTIFIC AND RELIGIOUS. 8vo. 6s. 6d.

Warington (G.)—THE WEEK OF CREATION. Cr. 8vo. 4s. 6d.

Welldon (Rev. J. E. C.)—THE SPIRITUAL LIFE, and other Sermons. Crown 8vo. 6s.

Westcott (B. F., Bishop of Durham)—
ON THE RELIGIOUS OFFICE OF THE UNIVERSITIES. Sermons. Crown 8vo. 4s. 6d.
GIFTS FOR MINISTRY. Addresses to Candidates for Ordination. Crown 8vo. 1s. 6d.
THE VICTORY OF THE CROSS. Sermons preached during Holy Week, 1888, in Hereford Cathedral. Crown 8vo. 3s. 6d.
FROM STRENGTH TO STRENGTH. Three Sermons (In Memoriam J. B. D.) Crown 8vo. 2s.
THE REVELATION OF THE RISEN LORD. Cr. 8vo. 6s.
THE HISTORIC FAITH. 3rd Edition. Crown 8vo. 6s.
THE GOSPEL OF THE RESURRECTION. 6th Ed. Cr. 8vo. 6s.
THE REVELATION OF THE FATHER. Crown 8vo. 6s.
CHRISTUS CONSUMMATOR. 2nd Edition. Crown 8vo. 6s.
SOME THOUGHTS FROM THE ORDINAL. Cr. 8vo. 1s. 6d.
SOCIAL ASPECTS OF CHRISTIANITY. Crown 8vo. 6s.
ESSAYS IN THE HISTORY OF RELIGIOUS THOUGHT IN THE WEST. Globe 8vo. 6s.
LECTURES ON GOSPEL LIFE. Cr. 8vo. [*In the Press.*

Wickham (Rev. E. C.)—WELLINGTON COLLEGE SERMONS. Crown 8vo. 6s.

Wilkins (Prof. A. S.)—THE LIGHT OF THE WORLD: an Essay. 2nd Edition. Crown 8vo. 3s. 6d.

Wilson (J. M., Archdeacon of Manchester)—
SERMONS PREACHED IN CLIFTON COLLEGE CHAPEL. Second Series. 1888-90. Crown 8vo. 6s.
ESSAYS AND ADDRESSES. Crown 8vo. 4s. 6d.
SOME CONTRIBUTIONS TO THE RELIGIOUS THOUGHT OF OUR TIME. Crown 8vo. 6s.

www.ingramcontent.com/pod-product-compliance
Lightning Source LLC
Chambersburg PA
CBHW022141300426
44115CB00006B/285